Emerging Evangelicals

*Faith, Modernity, and the
Desire for Authenticity*

James S. Bielo

NEW YORK UNIVERSITY PRESS
New York and London

NEW YORK UNIVERSITY PRESS
New York and London
www.nyupress.org

References to Internet websites (URLs) were accurate at the time of writing.
Neither the author nor New York University Press is responsible for URLs
that may have expired or changed since the manuscript was prepared.

Library of Congress Cataloging-in-Publication Data
Bielo, James S.
Emerging evangelicals : faith, modernity, and the desire for
authenticity / James S. Bielo.
p. cm.
Includes bibliographical references and index.
ISBN 978-0-8147-8954-4 (cl : alk. paper) — ISBN 978-0-8147-8955-1
(pb : alk. paper) — ISBN 978-0-8147-8956-8 (inst. ebook) —
ISBN 978-0-8147-3918-1 (con. ebook)
1. Evangelicalism—United States. 2. Emerging church movement—
United States. I. Title.
BR1642.U5B53   2011
277.3'083—dc22   2011015755

New York University Press books are printed on acid-free paper,
and their binding materials are chosen for strength and durability.
We strive to use environmentally responsible suppliers and materials
to the greatest extent possible in publishing our books.

Manufactured in the United States of America

c   10 9 8 7 6 5 4 3 2 1
p   10 9 8 7 6 5 4 3 2 1

For Judith S. Bielo, my mother

Contents

Figures and Tables

Acknowledgments

An extremely deep debt of gratitude goes to the individuals and communities who gave so freely of their time, and graciously entertained my endless questions. Without them, this book would simply not exist.

The Department of Anthropology at Miami University provided countless forms of support for this project. In particular, I would like to thank Linda Marchant, Leighton Peterson, Mark Allen Peterson, John Cinnamon, M. Cameron Hay, Neringa Klumbyte, Susan Paulson, and Kathy Erbaugh for their insight and encouragement. At New York University Press, Jennifer Hammer's editorial advice and enthusiasm have been irreplaceable. Two anonymous reviewers offered extremely helpful comments. I am grateful also to have many valuable scholarly interlocutors. I would like to offer a special thanks to Jon Bialecki, Omri Elisha, Susan Harding, Joel Robbins, Brian Howell, Naomi Haynes, Gerardo Marti, Michael Jennings, Amy Fisher, and Ted Troxell for feedback at various stages of this project. My students in undergraduate classes at Miami University have been kind enough to endure some of my external processing about research and writing. In particular, I want to recognize students in the spring 2010 ATH185: Cultural Diversity in the United States courses, for thoughtful comments on a manuscript draft of chapter 8. Portions of chapter 8 were originally published in "Purity, Danger, and Redemption: Notes on Urban Missional Evangelicals," *American Ethnologist* 38, no. 2.

This book was written largely under the hospitality of one institution: the local coffee shop. As for anyone who writes, finding times, places, and rhythms where "things click" is something of an obsession. In no particular order, coffee shops in Lansing, Grand Rapids, Ann Arbor, Phoenix, Austin, Reno, Minneapolis, Tulsa, Boulder, Burlington, Newport, Memphis, Cincinnati, Columbus, Toronto, Lexington, Naples, Atlanta, Chapel Hill, and Boone provided reliable sanctuary. Most of all, my home coffee shop in Oxford, Ohio—Kofenya—has been a home away from home; many thanks to Liz and the Kofenya staff!

I count myself especially, irrationally, fortunate to have so many wonderful people in my life. In the years that this project consumed me, I offer many thanks and many apologies to those who helped keep me sane: my very dear friend Rita, my brother JD, my sister Mary, my mother Judith, my uncle Ed, my cousin Clay, Carri, Rowenn, Aaron, Dillon, Tim, Kaley, Christian, Michael, Freddy, Andrea, natalie, Emily, Maria, DJ, Keri, Bennie, Chris (and the comforts of Main Street Gourmet), Heidi, and Brandon (and the comforts of The Quarter Barrel). And, treasuring her as I do, an especially gigantic thank you to Lydia.

Above all, I thank the Lord, my God. Help me to do justice, love mercy, and walk humbly with You.

Introduction

Conceptualizing Emerging Evangelicalism

"This is the way it's supposed to be," Larry averred from the top of the stairs. I turned to offer an appreciative nod. His face was beaming, framed by a neatly kept white beard.

It was 4:30 p.m., mid-June 2009, and I had just finished a three-hour interview, preceded by two hours of talk, food, and coffee. The day had started with no anticipation of anything unexpected. I was to interview Aaron, a campus pastor in his late thirties. We had arranged to meet for lunch in Newport, Kentucky, just across the state line from Cincinnati. Aaron suggested a change of plan via email late the previous day, which I received the next morning:

> James,
>
> Not to throw a wrench in our plans, but I got to thinking about our topic of conversation and thought it might be a good idea to meet at a place that embodies what I think we might be discussing more than a restaurant. Can we meet in Norwood instead of Newport? There's a great place [called] 1801 Mills . . .

Along with the change of venue, he added that others might join us. And so it was: instead of interviewing one individual about the Emerging Church movement, I interviewed four. The typical two-hour event became five.

1801 Mills is in Norwood, Ohio—a Cincinnati neighborhood that is both struggling and lively. It is struggling because the local economy still suffers from the 1987 closing of a General Motors automotive factory. The outward aesthetic bares this impress. Houses are run down: crooked and broken fences, chipping paint, cracked windows, few attempts at outward beautification. Streets are uninviting: trash scattered along curbs, rusty and bent road signs, potholes, and eroding asphalt. Cars are categorically tattered, modest, and older; nothing glitzy or ostentatious. It is lively because Norwood is a lived-in place. Children play on sidewalks when days are not dampened by rain. Mothers push strollers. Older men and women sit in expired lawn chairs, idling or observing. Men congregate on corner pub stoops to smoke and talk.

Norwood is home to St. Elizabeth's cathedral, property of Vineyard Central since 1995. "VC" is a congregation of house churches and they use "St. E" as a multipurpose venue. Built in 1880, the former Catholic church has its own problems: leaking roof, outdated wiring, crumbling plaster, decaying wood, and plumbing that emits high-pitched screeches in between clanging jolts. Yet it is lovely. Its towering steeples make the surrounding buildings appear slight. The stone exterior is prominent and handsome. The broad entry stairs are backed by intricately engraved columns. If you harbor even the meekest curiosity for what occurs inside, it beckons. Directly across the narrow neighborhood street from St. E is 1801 Mills.

"1801" is Larry's creation. He completed renovations on the battered structure and opened it for use in 2007. He calls the nonprofit venture a "Third Place," somewhere to gather and be in community that is not home or office. It has hosted numerous groups: VC house church meetings, neighborhood film showings, and exhibits by local artists. Group and event facilitators are furnished with keys and security codes, encouraging a come-and-go-as-you-please attitude.

I arrived at 11:40 that June morning. It was a gorgeously sunny day. I had been to 1801 once before, and knew the way through the back metal gate, up the red wooden stairs, inside, and up the steep, narrow staircase to the third floor. Four floors in all, 1801 is a thin, deep rectangular building with ample windows. It is not particularly attractive from the outside, an assessment amplified by the neighboring St. E.

When I arrived Larry was concluding a casual chat with a middle-aged woman. He was expecting me. Several hours earlier he had accepted Aaron's invitation to join our interview. D.G. and Becky, he informed me, would also join us. Larry looked delightfully disheveled. His hair, also a thick white and gray, was slightly sloppy with stray curls. Smaller, tightly curled white locks snuck out the top of his navy summer linen shirt, which stayed half-tucked into baggy khakis, an arrangement to which he seemed gleefully oblivious.

The third floor is corridor-like, with four rooms separated by open door frames. The walls are painted with light pastels, each room a different hue. Candles are scattered generously along window frames. There are couches and chairs, most sumptuously comfortable. It is all a cluttered neatness—full, inhabited, a touch chaotic, organized, and functional.

The décor ranges in seriousness. There are medieval-style portraits, framed prayers by Patristic saints, and a painted etching that reads:

> . . . True Evangelical faith
> It clothes the naked
> It feeds the hungry
> It comforts the sorrowful
> It shelters the destitute
> It serves those that harm it
> It binds up that which is wounded
> It has become all things to all men
> —*Menno Simons, 1539*

These pious, earnest moments are interspersed with stuffed animals, a flat screen TV, and a collection of hopefully witty paraphernalia. A coffee mug reads:

> Jesus Loves You
> But everyone else thinks you're stupid!

A bumper sticker suggests:

> God Must Love Stupid People. . .
> Look How Many He Created!

And there is a veritable library of books. They are engulfing, and make a definitive claim on the space. A take-away, glossy pamphlet boasts that there are "over 10,000" available books at 1801. They range in subject from Christian theology to comparative religion, sociology of religion, church history, devotionals, Bibles, Bible commentaries, Christian biographies, Christian memoirs, poems, and novels.

Larry began by giving me a full tour of 1801. When we returned upstairs D.G. was plating his lunch. He and Larry shared a large, crunching hug, and I introduced myself. D.G. is a United Methodist church planter, then in his mid-thirties. Standing about 5' 9", he was large, not overweight, but rotund and stocky. A tattoo of a shamrock embedded in a Celtic cross dominated his right inside forearm. A silver Celtic cross with the Greek letters for alpha and omega hung midway down his chest. His hair was trimmed near to bald, and he wore a half-shaven beard with a long, narrow goatee that curled under his chin. A West Texas accent marked his speech.

As I introduced myself to D.G. the echo-y stairwell let on that we had company. I rose from my chair, prepared to meet Aaron, but in walked a woman in her mid-thirties. Becky's loud, carrying, voice greeted Larry and D.G., followed by a round of vigorous hugs. They were the kind of hugs that mock sadness, defer worry, and advertise hope. Becky was a flurry of energy and peppered me with interested questions. The day before, she had driven nearly twelve hundred miles from Denver and was moving into 1801's fourth-floor apartment. She is a church consultant and was in Cincinnati for the sole purpose of organizing a conference for the coming November. "Navigate," a follow up to 2008's "The Emerging Church for the Existing Church," was intended to educate Mainline Protestant church leaders about the Emerging movement.

We talked with little purpose for several minutes when the stairs returned to announcing, this time in a more kabooming fashion. Aaron seemed to barely fit through the door frame. His big, thick hand dwarfed mine and he smiled at me with a large face and dark goatee. His demeanor softened an easily intimidating physicality: he spoke with agonizingly intentional, nearly breathy, and stuttering thoughtfulness.

I began the interview in the same way as those I had done previously, with an explanation of my fieldwork. I concluded by voicing an off-the-cuff, hopeless wish for a tape-recorder. Handwritten notes would be difficult to manage with four people. No problem. A self-proclaimed technophile, D.G. immediately retrieved a digital recorder from his backpack, placed it at the center of the table, and hit "Record." No questions asked. There are times when I feel like a very competent ethnographer; this was not one of them.

The next three hours moved from each individual introducing themselves to my asking questions and their responding in turn and collaboratively. There were numerous, quick back-and-forth exchanges, as well as lengthy individual explanations laced with a constant use of illustrative story. They overflowed with talk and eagerness; I was only able to ask five questions in three hours. They were funny, candid, and clearly familiar with one another. Larry was frequently on the move, in and out of the adjoining kitchen with food and drink: coffee, homemade biscotti, unsalted cashews, black cherries, grapes, water. They made frequent use of the enveloping books: locating texts being referenced in conversation, pulling them off the shelf, and passing them around. It was a dizzying experience.

At the time, and still today, my afternoon at 1801 seemed like a very "Emerging" event. After all, for Larry and others: "This is the way it's supposed to be."

• • •

This book is about American Evangelicals. More precisely, it explores how some Evangelicals are consuming and enacting knowledge produced as part of the Emerging Church movement. Even more precisely, it is an ethnographic analysis of identities fashioned, practices performed, discourses articulated, histories claimed, institutions created, and ideas interrogated in this cultural field. Emerging Evangelicalism, we will come to see, is a movement organized by cultural critique, a desire for change, and grounded in the conditions of both modernity and late modernity.

The fieldwork encounter recounted above occurred twenty months into my research and captures numerous themes we pursue in the following chapters: sense of place, urbanism, dialogue, improvisation, irony, embodiment, narrative, textuality, community, ecclesiology, spiritual biography, church planting, social memory, denominationalism, and everyday religious subjectivity. As we traverse these themes a religious movement will be revealed, from the inner spiritual lives of adherents to their outer practices and institutions, and their relationship to American social conditions. My examination of Emerging Evangelicalism seeks to integrate multiple theoretical vantages: a *Verstehen* view of religious identity; the coupling of religious life to social structures; the mediating roles of language, text, body, materiality, memory, place, and the senses in religious experience; and the fostering of mental and bodily dispositions through participation in shared institutions.

To prepare the ground, we focus on three questions in this introductory chapter: What is Emerging Evangelicalism? Why is "authenticity" our organizing theme? And, as an ethnography, what kinds of fieldwork produced *Emerging Evangelicals*?

Emerging Evangelicalism: Context, Genealogy, Dialogue

"The Emerging Church" is a label, created by movement insiders, to mark a dual assumption: that contemporary Evangelicalism is undergoing profound change, and that the Christian Church always has and always will be changing. The label itself is increasingly of little interest to adherents as a meaningful self-identifier, but the movement it was intended to capture continues to thrive. Emerging Evangelicalism is, fundamentally, a movement of cultural critique. It materialized in the mid-1990s, with initial voicings from white, male, middle-class, well-educated, urban, Gen-X pastors, church planters, church consultants, and concerned laity. Their binding commitment was a severe disenchantment with America's conservative Christian subculture. Frustrations varied from Evangelicalism's image in the public sphere to the religious subjectivity being encouraged and the kinds of institutions being fostered. Emerging Evangelicalism is a diverse cultural field, but the cultural conditions that Emerging Evangelicals respond to are much the same. To be an Emerging Evangelical is to be someone taking the cultural critique of conservative Evangelicalism seriously, and attempting to live a response.

The Emerging Church is undoubtedly a transnational movement in the Anglophone world (Drane 2006). However, our ethnographic interest here is devoted only to its North American incarnations. Some ten years after its appearance, social scientists have begun piecing together empirically informed interpretations of the Emerging movement. Sociologists Poloma and Hood (2008) document a single inner-city Atlanta church that self-consciously affiliates as Emerging. While offering a detailed ethnography of everyday life in this congregation, Poloma and Hood misconstrue the movement writ large (for example, they uncritically adopt movement claims to "postmodernity" and reduce the Emerging Church to an iteration of Pentecostalism). Lee and Sinitiere (2009), a sociologist and a historian respectively, include the Emerging Church as one among several popular examples of religious innovation in the contemporary Christian marketplace. They focus on one widely cited author, Brian McLaren, who was an early outspoken voice on behalf of the movement. Apart from the difficulties of treating one author as representative, and the difficulty of equating knowledge produced with knowledge consumed, Lee and Sinitiere do not unpack, decode, or analytically translate the language and cultural categories used by Emerging Evangelicals. Anthropologist Susan Harding (2009, 2010) reckons the Emerging Church as a "revoicing" of traditional American Evangelicalism. Harding's theoretical vantage is spot on, but she marshals only a small sample of empirical evidence. Sociologist Gerardo Marti (2005) provides a well-researched ethnography of a single congregation in southern California whose pastor, like McLaren, was an early, nationally prominent voice on behalf of the Emerging Church. Marti emphasizes the relationship between religious and social change, focusing on how the church maintains a multiethnic identity. *Emerging Evangelicals* begins where this existing work leaves off: by providing a multisite, multimodal ethnographic analysis of how Evangelicals have consumed and enacted the kinds of knowledge produced under the moniker of the Emerging Church.

An Evangelical Primer

To understand the appearance of the Emerging Church on the American religious landscape we must address the historic development of Evangelicalism. Since the late 1970s many shelves of many libraries have been filled with accounts of the histories and varieties of Evangelical culture (Warner 1979). Noll (2003) dates the birth of American Evangelicalism to the early-eighteenth-century spirit of revivalism among Methodists, Baptists, and other homegrown denominations. The congealing of American Evangelicalism in the nineteenth century was fueled by a congeries of cultural forces: for example, biblical hermeneutic differences between "liberal" and "conservative" Protestants that ensued from the German Enlightenment (Engelke 2007: 22–24); debates over the Revised Bible translation (Theusen 1999); and materialist interpretations of human history sparked by interest in Darwinian evolutionary theory (Menand 2001: 121).

Conservative Protestant identity thrice-diverged between the early and mid-twentieth century. Fundamentalists sought to distinguish themselves from Pentecostals, and the label "Evangelical" entered popular use in the 1940s as an attempt to separate from the cultural separatism of Fundamentalists (Harding 2000). Neo-charismatics emerged in the late 1960s and early 1970s, drawing theological and cultural influence from all three of these precursors (Miller 1997). In the late 1970s and early 1980s conservative Christians from across theological and denominational spectrums mobilized politically and culturally as born-agains: "avowedly not militant and not separatist . . . committed to a more nuanced understanding of biblical truth" (Harding 2000: 17). Even in this overly cursory history a crucial dynamic of Christian cultural formation is evident: it is a history defined by cultural critique leading to schisms and the creation of distinct Evangelical identities. Emerging Evangelicals continue this dialogic tradition (cf. Garriott and O'Neill 2008).

What was happening in the Evangelical mainstream at the end of the twentieth century? Between 1995 and 1999 the first six novels of the massively popular *Left Behind* series were published, igniting Evangelicals' apocalyptic fervor. Rick Warren, who would later give the invocation at Barack Obama's presidential inauguration, entered Evangelical celebrity in 1995 with his first book. The iconic megachurch, Willow Creek Community Church located in Chicago's south suburbs, hosted its first Leadership Summit in 1995 (an event that would later headline everyone from Colin Powell to Bono). The creation-evolution controversy waged in public schools and courts. Christian Right and Christian Coalition politicians seated a majority in the U.S. Congress, previewing the two-term presidential election of George W. Bush. The Promise Keepers, an Evangelical parachurch for men, held their largest gathering on the Washington Mall in October 1997. Joel Osteen, who would popularize Prosperity Theology anew and whose Houston megachurch would later record the largest congregational membership in the United States, was nationally televised for the first time in 1999. At least in the public sphere, Evangelicals were born-again, culturally savvy, politically conservative, suburban, corporate-friendly, megachurch-attending, unapologetic proselytizers.)

An Emerging History

As highly visible incarnations like the Promise Keepers consumed widespread attention, a popular institution for Evangelical leaders, Leadership Network, launched a project in 1995 called Young Leaders Network (YLN). Many of my consultants, as well as movement chroniclers (Gibbs and Bolger 2005), consider 1995 to be a turning point year. YLN—consisting of demographically similar pastors, youth ministers, church planters, and church consultants—organized around three convictions. First, they voiced an adamant critique of conservative Evangelicalism, evincing frustration with politics, theology, worship, evangelism, ecclesiology, and capitalist-consumer impulses. Second, they diagnosed what they considered a detrimental problem facing the future of American Christianity: a cultural dissonance between Gen-Xers and Millennials and the organization, style, priorities, and assumptions of twentieth-century Evangelicals. Third, they were convinced that American society had shifted from being "modern" to "postmodern." They defined postmodernism largely in epistemological terms, asserting that America's youngest generations doubt the human ability to know absolute truth with absolute certainty. In 2000 a small number of YLN members branched off to create Terra Nova, which became Emergent Village a year later: an "online generative friendship" that functions as a resource sharing network and is known among movement advocates and critics for its ecumenical, boundary-pushing theology. In 2002 the first international Emerging Church conference was held in San Diego in conjunction with the National Pastors Conference (one of Evangelicalism's most widely attended annual meetings).

We can also use Evangelical book publishing to situate the movement's appearance. Anyone paying attention will affirm that books are important in Evangelical culture (though some stress the role of texts in the formation of religious subjectivity, while others stress the industry's political economy) (Bielo 2009; Fisher 2003). The first self-consciously "Emerging" books appeared slowly between 1997 and 2000. My consultants often named two as early, influential texts: *The Church on the Other Side* (McLaren 1998) and *SoulTsunami* (Sweet 1999). Since 2001—in a trend that shows no signs of slowing down—books advocating and criticizing the movement have flooded the market. Five of the most commonly cited by my consultants appeared in 2003: *The Post-Evangelical* (Tomlinson), *The Story We Find Ourselves In* (McLaren), *Blue Like Jazz* (Miller), *The Shaping of Things to Come* (Frost and Hirsch), and *The Emerging Church* (Kimball). As a clear sign of institutionalization, book series were established with major Evangelical publishers: Zondervan's "Emergent Youth Specialties" in 2000, Baker's "Emersion" in 2005, and Baker Academic's "Church and Postmodern Culture" in 2005.

Another barometer of Emerging Evangelicalism's arrival is its coverage in the mainstream media. The *New York Times* grazed the movement with "Hip New Churches Sway to a Different Drummer" in February 2004. Brian McLaren, controversial for his theological and political standpoints, appeared on *Time*'s February 2005 list of "The 25 Most Influential Evangelicals in America." *PBS* ran a two-part series in July 2005 on "The Emerging Church," interviewing prominent movement advocates and critics. In February 2006 the *Los Angeles Times* and the *Wall Street Journal* featured the movement in similar articles: "Plugged In" and "Getting Hip to Religion." Rob Bell, a Michigan pastor whose celebrity and controversy rivals McLaren's, was featured by *Time* in December 2007. That month also saw a cover story from *U.S. News and World Report* that reported on several Emerging churches: "A Return to Ritual: Why Many Modern Worshipers, including Catholics, Jews, and Evangelicals, Are Embracing Tradition." And in March 2009, *Time* included "The New Calvinism" on its list of "10 Ideas Changing the World Right Now." Mark Driscoll, a Seattle pastor and popular figure among New Calvinists (Hansen 2008), was featured three months earlier by the *New York Times Magazine* in an article entitled "Who Would Jesus Smack Down?" riffing on Driscoll's sardonic, hypermasculine style.

In short, between 1995 and 2005 a new, viable, amorphous form of Evangelical identity appeared. This timeline matches the religious biographies of my consultants, all of whom encountered the movement during this ten year period. Of course, Emerging Evangelicalism did not spontaneously generate. There were numerous twentieth-century precursors that made the movement possible.

Emerging Genealogies

⟨The appearance of Emerging Evangelicalism can be traced to five intersecting points of dialogue, a division that shapes the contours of the movement: theology, missiology, ecclesiology, liturgy, and politics.⟩

(1) The theological lineage of the Emerging movement is grounded in an epistemological critique. Their organizing claim is that conservative Protestant theology developed within the cultural context of philosophical modernism. As a result, conservative beliefs and methods are said to carry deeply rooted, questionable assumptions about formulating doctrine, interpreting the Bible, obtaining knowledge of God, and communicating that knowledge.

The premier example cited by Emerging Evangelicals is the hermeneutic method of systematic theology. In 1872 Charles Hodge, a Princeton Seminary theologian, published his seminal work, *Systematic Theology*. His idea of what constituted proper theology was explicit: "Nothing but the facts and truths of the Bible arranged in their natural order and exhibited in their natural relations" (quoted in Turner 2003: 47). Hodge accepted the tenets of Scottish Common Sense Philosophy: reality is objective and immanently knowable; the human mind successfully discerns that reality; and the faculty of language dutifully conveys that reality via factual propositions (Keane 2007: 63). Systematic theology, like the natural sciences, is said to be made of rational argument, certainty, proof, and logical apologetics.

Projects like systematic theology function as a conceptual and rhetorical foil for theologians who are critical of modernism. I asked all my consultants to discuss the theologians who had the greatest influence on their thought and practice. Their answers never became completely predictable, but a typical list would include: Walter Brueggeman (*The Prophetic Imagination* 1978); George Lindbeck (*The Nature of Doctrine: Religion and Theology in a Postliberal Age* 1984); Thomas Oden (*After Modernity...What? Agenda for Theology* 1990); MiroslavVolf (*Exclusion and Embrace. A Theological Exploration of Identity, Otherness, and Reconciliation* 1996); Nancey Murphy (*Beyond Liberalism and Fundamentalism: How Modern and Postmodern Philosophy Set the Theological Agenda* 1996); Dallas Willard (*The Divine Conspiracy: Rediscovering Our Hidden Life in God* 1998); Stanley Grenz and John Franke (*Beyond*

Foundationalism: Shaping Theology in a Postmodern Context 2001); and N. T. Wright (*Surprised by Hope: Rethinking Heaven, the Resurrection, and the Mission of the Church* 2008).

In some ways, this list is diverse. Denominationally, it includes Lutherans (Lindbeck), Southern Baptists (Willard), and Anglicans (Wright). Their objections to modernist thought vary, from the negative influence of Descartes (Grenze) to the neglect of linguistic performativity (Lindbeck) and the disinterest in power and colonialism (Volf). In other ways, they are quite similar. All but one are male. All but one are white Westerners. All wrote in the latter half of the twentieth century (and circulated their writings through established publishing houses). Most are thoroughly academic in nature. But what binds them, what makes them attractive to Emerging Evangelicals, is their attempt to theologize against the grain of modernist principles. This will be evident in numerous ways throughout this book: the aversion to dogmatic certainty in chapter 1; the suspicion of epistemological clarity in chapter 2, and the dethroning of doctrinal belief as the key signifier of Christian identity in chapter 4.

(2) The missiological foundation of the Emerging Church is much more direct than its theological lineage. It is defined by the idea of being a missionary in one's own society. Even after three years of fieldwork it is still remarkable that, in spite of difference at so many other turns, my consultants uniformly affirmed the desire to be "missional."

More than any other source, Emerging Evangelicals trace the origins of "missional" to Lesslie Newbigin (1909–1998), a British Anglican priest who spent most of his life as a missionary in India. In the early 1980s he began speaking and writing on the challenges of evangelizing in the West. Newbigin attributed this difficulty to the epistemological suspicions about religion produced by the Enlightenment's colonizing scientific worldview. He concluded that all Christians are missionaries and that successful mission work in the West meant learning the language and culture of the local mission field, wherever that might be and however familiar it might seem. He first articulated this missiology in two treatises: *The Other Side of 1984* (1983) and *Foolishness to the Greeks* (1986), the latter being more influential in the United States (Goheen 2000). He describes "modern Western culture" against a Weberian grain: "The result is not, as we once imagined, a secular society. It is a pagan society, and its paganism, having been born out of the rejection of Christianity, is far more resistant to the gospel than the pre-Christian paganism with which cross-cultural missions have been familiar" (1986: 20). Newbigin's organizing logic is that Christianity is no longer the default worldview among Westerners. Quite the opposite, it is widely considered to be anachronistic, irrelevant, destructive, or worse.

Emerging Evangelicals have applied Newbigin's missiology as a methodological critique of conservative Christian evangelism. They decry a wide range of common witnessing practices: street preaching, handing out Bible tracts, delivering finely tuned conversion speeches, using hyperlogical apologetics, and using weekly congregational events as the entrée to church. For those self-consciously striving to be missional, these methods suffer from several problems: a failure to understand the shift in American public consciousness from modernity to postmodernity; an inability to effectively use the mediums and idioms attractive to a postmodern audience; and the lack of meaningful, lasting personal commitments. Being missional means seriously cultivating relationships—not before or after conversion attempts, but in place of them. To accomplish this goal, they advocate mimicking the acculturating foreign missionary: settling into a locale and becoming intimately familiar with a place and its people. Chapters 5 and 6 explore how "being missional" has been internalized, and the kinds of institutions it inspires.

(3) Ecclessiology—or, the structure and organization of local church life—is also part of Emerging Evangelicals' history. This part of their genealogical story has encouraged the adoption of two main congregational forms: church planting and house churches.

When Evangelicals talk about "planting churches," they mean the process of starting a new congregational ministry. This is not about schism, where aggravated, dissatisfied, or otherwise hurt individuals leave one church to start another. This is about a small collection of people (in my fieldwork, anywhere between six and twenty individuals) starting their own church because they share a common sense of purpose and identity. Church plants are often, but not always, sponsored by an existing congregation, and the founding members typically come from that "home church." Churches are often, but not always, planted near the home church—for example, in a different neighborhood of the same city. The "vision" of many church planters is to create a "network" of "satellite" churches throughout a city. Church plants are often, but not always, sponsored by a denomination. Many denominations have created institutions devoted solely to church planting—for example, the Southern Baptist Convention's Nehemiah Project (1998) and the Presbyterian Church of America's Mission to North America (1973). There are paradenominational organizations designed to be resource networks for like-minded church planters—for example, the ecumenical Gospel and Our Culture Network (1987) and the strict Reformed theology of Acts 29 (2000).

There is nothing new about church planting for Evangelicals or for Christendom at large. Almost every church planter I interviewed reads the New Testament's "Acts of the Apostles" as the best model for planting new churches. The Vineyard Fellowship—a neo-charismatic denomination officially founded in 1982 (Bialecki 2009)—has always described itself as a "church planting movement." What is new about church planting among Emerging Evangelicals is the degree to which it has become institutionally organized—a phenomenon to be mastered through books, podcasts, blogs, conferences, and other resources of knowledge production—and how being a "church planter" has become an organizing identity. Chapters 7 and 8 explore the effects of church planting for religious subjectivity and institutional formation.

Emerging Evangelicals, far more than the born-again Christians who flourished in the late twentieth century, favor house churches. When they talk about house churches they mean a congregation that performs nearly all of collective religious life in members' homes. The house church communities I observed were diverse in many respects (though they all recognized one individual as the lead pastor). Some were affiliated with a denomination, others were not. Some had two or three groups that met weekly, some had eight or nine. Some weekly groups had five members, some had twenty. Some weekly groups were shifting and fluid, others were stable. Some house churches met monthly for a collective worship gathering, some never did. Some owned a church building, using it for regular events and/or renting it out to a community organization as a missional act. Others owned no building and spoke vehemently against the practice of churches owning buildings (for example, because the money used to maintain a building could be better used for mission work).

The Emerging Evangelical attraction to church planting and house churches follows from their cultural critique of the conservative Evangelical church growth and megachurch movements (Sargeant 2000). My consultants articulated no shortage of objections to the megachurch, describing it as:

- Tenuous. The money and resources needed to keep megachurches running is massive. They require distractingly constant maintenance and financial support from congregants.
- Exaggerated. Size matters. The bigness and expansiveness of megachurches falls prey to the same logic of overkill that produced Wal-Mart and civilian Hummers.

- Commodified. Megachurches are yet another example of conspicuous consumption. They fail to reject a pervasive social ill: the never-ending impulse to brand, package, mass produce, and generally plot everything in terms of buying and selling.
- Isolating. Intentionally set in suburbia, adherents are removed from urban conditions of social unrest. This removal is tantamount to racial and class confinement, and a gradual disappearance of non-mainstream experiences from everyday consciousness.
- Impersonal. The size and easy anonymity of the megachurch is at odds with a hallmark of Evangelicalism: the desire to cultivate spiritual intimacy (Bielo 2009:73–92).
- Spectacle. The epicenter of megachurch life, the weekly worship event, is a mass-produced production for the masses. It is a show, in the worst sense of the word. It plays into America's cult of fame by turning singers, musicians, and pastors into celebrities.

These ecclesiological critiques provide a binding thread for other issues of identity and practice. As my consultants continually reminded me, their objections to mainstream Evangelicalism always come back to matters of "community," and ecclesiology is the structural expression of how community is understood.

(4) The liturgical branch of the Emerging genealogy focuses on a desire to meaningfully connect with church history. This desire has been captured by the trope "ancient-future." As with theology and missiology, Emerging Evangelicals suggest an unfortunate entanglement with recent Western history. Here, the unwelcome modern influence appears as a regrettable disposition toward worshiping God: too much disconnection with past Christianities; too much emphasis on the power of the spoken sermon to convince and convert; too little emphasis on the power of nonverbal senses; and no integration of embodiment with mental comprehension.

Ancient-future was introduced by Robert Webber (1933–2007): an Episcopalian and a former professor of theology at Wheaton College (Evangelicalism's flagship university). He spoke in ancient-future terms as early as 1976 when he helped author a public confession: "The Chicago Call: An Appeal to Evangelicals." The document emphasized two major themes about Evangelical worship: ahistoricism ("We believe that today evangelicals are hindered from achieving full maturity by a reduction of the historic faith") and sacramentalism ("The historic church has affirmed that God's activity is manifested in a material way"). Webber's formulation of ancient-future casts worship as a communicative event between the religious subject and God. This communication should occur bodily, with all senses, not solely through the limited cognitive assent to meaningful words.

In his later work (1999), Webber connected the need to be ancient-future with America's generational shift. This was partly a matter of technology and communication, the shift "from a print-oriented society to an audiovisual society" (96). Webber argued, in concert with some scholars of American ethnopsychology (Luhrmann 2004), that the everyday flood of images and sounds resulting from late-twentieth-century media saturation has altered Americans' perceptual and cognitive sensibilities. We have shorter attention spans. We are more inclined to learn from sensory experience than exegetical reasoning. Our Internet/MTV/iPod-infused lives have created an unprecedented experience of intra- and intersubjectivity. Webber extends this dynamic to religious life. Different forms of worship are required from those that satisfied previous generations.

Ancient-future also carries an implicit critique of linguistic clarity. The modern Protestant language ideology, the same that buttresses Systematic Theology, has been described at length by the anthropologist Webb Keane (2007): words are trustworthy vehicles of interior states of knowledge and emotion; speakers use this relatively transparent relationship to pursue ideals of honesty, truth, and sincerity; and listeners focus on the referential qualities of language to properly interpret propositional content. These assumptions helped elevate the oratorical sermon as central to the Protestant worship experience. Ancient-future advocates insist that part of America's generational shift entails a rethinking of this posture toward language and the kinds of worship it encourages.

Chapters 3 and 4 explore how Emerging Evangelicals perform being ancient-future. This ideal of staying connected to church history takes a variety of forms: closer attention to the annual church calendar than conservative Evangelicals have required; designing multisensory worship experiences; performing monastic disciplines; integrating pre-Reformation theologians into public and private reading rituals; and rethinking the role of materiality in worship events. These chapters conceptualize ancient-future in terms of mediation, lived religion, and social memory.

(5) Lastly, Emerging Evangelicals continue the conservative Christian tradition of mobilizing in support of political causes. This genealogy begins in the early 1970s with the formation of Progressive Evangelicalism (C. Hall 1997; cf. Bialecki 2009). Like their conservative counterparts, Progressive Evangelicals are convinced that part of being Christian is being actively

involved with the political process in an effort to see policy reflect their interpretation of biblical tradition and scripture. Institutionally, Progressive Evangelicalism was born with the start of Sojourners in 1971 and November 1973's "The Chicago Declaration of Evangelical Concern." The latter was the effort of forty Evangelical leaders who signed and publicly released a brief confessional that addressed social justice, consumerism, and "a national pathology of war and violence." Since its origins in the early 1970s three individuals have been recognized as most outspoken on behalf of Progressive Evangelicalism: Jim Wallis (e.g., *The Soul of Politics: Beyond "Religious Right" and Secular Left"* 1994), Tony Campolo (e.g., *20 Hot Potatoes Christians Are Afraid to Touch* 1988), and Ron Sider (e.g., *Good News and Good Works: A Theology for the Whole Gospel* 1993).

Progressive Evangelicalism has transpired largely in dialogue with the political motions of conservative Evangelicals. Beginning in the same period, and arriving in force with the Moral Majority in 1979, conservative Evangelical leaders like Jerry Falwell, James Dobson, Pat Robertson, and Tim LaHaye managed to sustain a more vocal presence in America's public sphere. The overt difference between these Evangelical blocs is the Religious Right's emphasis on a small range of issues (for example—abortion, homosexuality) and left-leaning Evangelicals' wider set of concerns (for example—health care, welfare, environment, trade, foreign policy, war, housing). With very few exceptions, the individuals and communities that comprise this ethnography affiliate as Progressive Evangelicals.

At the risk of taking brevity too seriously, we might say that Emerging Evangelicals are those who have internalized and seek to enact most or all of these genealogies. Words like "missional" and "ancient-future" are not currently part of our lexicon—the way, say, "conversion" and "born-again" are. But given their significance in contemporary Evangelical debates about proper religious subjectivity, they need to be.

Authenticity: Modernity, Late Modernity, Christianity

During three years of fieldwork with Emerging Evangelicals, when I asked them to talk about their existing and desired religious lives, they repeatedly returned to one word: authentic. They spoke earnestly about wanting to have authentic lives, faith, community, relationships, experience, worship, tradition, and spirituality. This is not just about discursive circulation. Authenticity is an organizing trope for Emerging Evangelicals. At first glance, there is absolutely nothing astonishing about a Christian movement prizing authenticity. As the historian Paul Conkin (1997) observed: "In some sense, almost all new Christian movements have advertised their return to an early or pure New Testament church" (1). But, taking a second glance, there is very good reason to think more deeply about Emerging Evangelicalism's attraction to authenticity.

A central argument that carries throughout this book is that Emerging Evangelicals are religious subjects reflecting and responding to the cultural conditions of modernity and late modernity. While Emerging Church discourses are rife with references to "modern" and "postmodern," the emic dimensions of these terms are not our primary interest. A more fruitful orientation follows the lead of scholars who argue that the eras of modernity and late modernity instill action-generating dispositions. Authenticity provides an entry into that analysis.

The anthropologist Charles Lindholm (2008) observed that authenticity has become "taken for granted as an absolute value in contemporary life" (1). His book, *Culture and Authenticity*, is an ethnological survey that invites readers to question what might unite an unlikely group of phenomena: country music, national cuisines, the tango, skydiving, mountain climbing, bungee jumping, slow food, tourism, and art, to name a few. His answer is authenticity, that which is "original, real, and pure" (ibid.: 2). But why do we value authenticity so intensely? Is it a by-product of being human?

Lindholm does not think so. He suggests that authenticity's rise to prominence owed to the nature of urban industrialism, namely, the effects of alienation and estrangement: "[the] irreversible plunge into modernity, which can be succinctly defined as the condition of living among strangers" (ibid.: 3). He highlights a variety of developments that fueled our obsession with all things authentic: the discourse of sincerity among Protestants, the scientific revolution, and European encounters with "the primitive" in the age of exploration. His argument is not that modernity invented authenticity, only that authenticity became invested with unprecedented importance.

The anthropologist Steven Parish (2009), in an extremely favorable review of Lindholm's book, challenges urban industrialism as authenticity's root cause. He suggests an alternative: "Modernity is more than the condition of living among strangers; it is also a particular way of living among symbols" (143). The problem is one of semiotic mediation: "The plunge into modernity involves seeing symbols as subject to rational and instrumental manipulation, as having an arbitrary basis and no inherent connection to self" (ibid.). Parish argues that we value authenticity because our symbolic acts leave us wondering what is "really real" (ibid.), and not simply a product of arbitrary social convention.

Lindholm and Parish both agree and disagree. They disagree on the historical origins of authenticity, but agree that finding authenticity extremely attractive is a very modern disposition. A quick tour through contemporary ethnography affirms their agreement. Graham (2002), an anthropologist of indigenous Amazonia, demonstrates how judgments of authenticity confront Native Americans as they make motions in the global public sphere. Semiotic codes of language, dress, and bodily adornment become the Western litmus test for "real" Indians and strategic resources for natives. Katherine Frank (2002), in let us just say a somewhat different setting, illustrates how strip club regulars manage the tensions posed by tourism, commodification, and voyeurism to find an experience that is not just pleasurable, but "real." Ethnographers of global Hip Hop insist that authenticity is a dilemma faced by all nonurban African American rappers (Condry 2006). In the same spirit as these other authenticity seekers, Emerging Evangelicals bear the impress of modernity by a deep-seeded desire to be authentic.

Grounding authenticity in modernity recalls what Webb Keane (2007) calls the primary moral narrative of the modern era: "a story of human liberation from a host of false beliefs and fetishisms that undermine freedom" (5). But modernity is not simply a moral project, it "is a dynamic relationship between economy, polity, society, and culture" (Madsen et al. 2002: xiv). Modern dispositions trace to the urban industrial revolution, the spread of depersonalized bureaucratic structures, and the philosophical devotion to reason. As a result, there are multiple ways to be modern and multiple modernities in which to live. Along with the constant of authenticity, we will see numerous ways that Emerging Evangelicals reproduce modern cultural conditions.

Much like modernity, the origins of the late modern era are diverse. Philosophically, we could point to the critique of epistemological objectivity bobbing in the wake of Thomas Kuhn's theory of scientific paradigms (Lee and Sinitiere 2009), or the influence of poststructural theory on American intellectual life (Cusset 2008). Economically, late modernity was signaled by the shift to postindustrialism, in particular the post-Fordist foci of service-oriented labor, new information technologies, and mass consumption (Harvey 1989). Writing about the relationship between religion and late modernity, Lee and Ackerman (2002) characterize this cultural era as "a world marked by political upheavals, ethnic conflicts, economic uncertainties, ecological and gender crises" (vii). For many scholarly interpreters, the cultural conditions of late modernity are just this: political economies defined by fragmentation, rapid movement, and expendable labor forces, and emotional psychologies defined by anxiety, alienation, and dislocation (Allison 2006). *The Insecure American* (Gusterman and Besteman, eds. 2010) is a collection of essays that applies this view of late modernity to contemporary life in the United States. This volume plots gated communities, war making, mass incarceration, deindustrialization, commercialism, immigration, health care, homelessness, and religion as acts in the same drama. That drama is the prevailing mood of America's social climate: insecure, anxious, discontent, suspicious, and generally a psychological-emotional-physiological-economic-moral-social mess.

Emerging Evangelicalism needs to be understood vis-a-vis modern and late modern cultural conditions. Each of the chapters in this book addresses this dynamic: for example, chapters 1's analysis of the deconversion narrative and its ties to modern authenticity (Barbour 1994), and chapter 8's analysis of sense of place as a response to the late modern crisis of "de-territorialization" (Appadurai 1996). By situating Emerging Evangelicalism as a religious movement alive within and across these two cultural eras I join a thriving tradition among anthropologists of Christianity.

The anthropology of Christianity is a relatively recent invention, if by this we mean "a community of scholarship in which those who study Christian societies formulate common problems, read each other's works, and recognize themselves as contributors to a coherent body of research" (Robbins 2007: 5). Since early calls by Robbins (2003) and Cannell (2005), a productive and fast-growing comparative enterprise has materialized. One of the "common problems" ethnographers have posed concerns the relationship between Christianity and modernity. As Cannell (2006) observed, "The history of modernity is inextricably bound up with the history of Christianity" (38), and I would add the continuation of late modernity. This entanglement has a long history if we consider Weber's famous interrogation of Calvinism's influence on the rise of capitalism. (Although Cannell and many others have rejected Weber's secularization thesis of modern disenchantment, arguing instead that the unfolding of modernity has led, if anything, to a widespread spiritual-religious reenchantment.) Precursors to an established anthropology of Christianity also took up this question. Most notably, in her historical-ethnographic analysis of American Fundamentalists, Harding (2000) argued that born-again Christians achieved a "cultural alchemy," combining conservative Protestant theology with multiple discourses of secular modernity: for example—counseling, journalism, and youth cosmopolitanism. Bialecki, Haynes, and Robbins (2008) have given the most complete review of how anthropologists of Christianity have figured the intersection of Christian and modern subjectivities. With respect to the value of individualism, they observe: "[A] hierarchical relationship with a transcendent other foregrounds the dependent and contingent nature of the individual in relation to that authority. This latter, equally Christian formulation, stands in sharp contrast with the self-identical heroic subject valued in many streams of modernity" (1152). They ultimately conclude that "Christianity can serve at once as a vector for modernity and as counter-narrative to modernity" (1151). While they intend this as a cross-cultural observation about the heterogeneity of Christianity "as an anthropological object" (ibid.), it resonates loudly in my ethnographic work with Emerging Evangelicals. The following chapters will show that this dual relation to modernity is not only possible across Christianities, but that it occurs within the same movement, same community, and same individual life.

Why call such explicit attention to Emerging Evangelicals' status as modern and late modern religious subjects? First, the anthropology of Christianity has followed a broader social science trend of bifurcating modernity and late modernity. While distinct, these two cultural eras are not discrete and they work together to shape everyday life in societies across the globe. In turn, the interpretation of Christianities should look for the combined presence of both modern and late modern dispositions, and the kinds of subjectivities and institution-making that result from this dual identity. Second, talking of "modernity" in the abstract (as we have just done) works well for contextualizing discussions. But, thinking empirically about how modernity informs everyday life requires that we talk of concrete cultural conditions, not just the abstraction of "modern (or, late modern) culture." All too often modernity exists as an amorphous, hard-to-locate historical object that Christians are said to interact with. Throughout this book, whenever we speak of Emerging Evangelicals reflecting modern or late modern conditions, we will speak of specific discourses pertaining to those cultural eras and how the individual and collective lives of my consultants bear them out. Modernity, after all, ultimately exists as a set of lived realities, and they must be attended to as such. Third, the Christian-modern nexus is often investigated with respect to religious conversion (Keane 2007). While this is certainly a worthwhile effort, conversion is not the only aspect of Christian life impacted by modern and late modern dispositions. These cultural conditions are reflected throughout the entirety of Christian experience. This observation echoes Eva Keller (2005), who argued that the anthropology of Christianity must seek to understand not only the process of conversion but "the process of religious commitment" (7); that is, "what makes [adherents] remain committed to [their faith]" (6) long after they first felt transformed. Fourth, viewing Emerging Evangelicals as bearers of modern and late modern conditions opens a productive space to think about tensions in religious life. Be they tensions of practice or identity, thinking of Emerging Evangelicalism as a religious movement with a foot in two historical cultural periods makes it easier to see what tensions they struggle to resolve. Finally, placing Emerging Evangelicalism in this historical scope invites comparative opportunities with what the anthropologist Michael Fischer called "emergent forms of life generated under late modernities" (1999: 472). Fischer was suggesting that the twenty-first century will see numerous responses to "the reconstruction of society in the wake of social trauma" (457). As cultural critics of their social and religious climates, Emerging Evangelicals can certainly be understood as cultural architects, actively responding to a world deemed awry.

Fieldwork: Scope, Decisions, Priorities

I first encountered the Emerging Church on May 31, 2005 when doing fieldwork on the practice of Evangelical Bible study (Bielo 2009). This included a United Methodist men's group that met every Tuesday morning. The pastor, Bill, was the facilitator. That morning in late May the group was discussing chapter 2 of the Acts of the Apostles. One of the study guide questions asked them to "Describe the fellowship of the believers in [the first century] church." After others responded, Bill added:

> I've been even thinking in some radical ways, wondering whether a church ought to exist longer than about ten or fifteen years. . . I think some places are beginning to discover that. Some of the stuff I've been reading on the Emerging Church really talks about new congregations, it's a different model, it's kind of the model we're looking at [in Acts], where new congregations spring up almost as new churches inside the boundary of an existing church. And, there's this new congregation, and as another need arises there's, start another one. And, just different ways of looking at things and different ways of reaching people.

Bill's comment meant little to me at the time. I do not recall giving the slightest pause to the words "Emerging Church." As their study of Acts continued, Bill kept making these references. When he returned from the 2005 National Pastors Convention in San Diego, he referenced panels he attended on the "postmodern generation." The authors and books he seemed so enthralled with were ones I had never heard of: Rob Bell's *Velvet Elvis* (2005), Brian McLaren's *A New Kind of Christian* (2001), Dan Kimball's *The Emerging Church* (2003), and Chris Seay's *The Gospel according to Tony Soprano* (2002). I became increasingly intrigued.

By mid-2007 my analysis of Bible study data was over. It was time for new ethnography, and in October 2007 the fieldwork for *Emerging Evangelicals* began. I was living in Lansing, Michigan, teaching at Michigan State University, and so I began where I had left off. I interviewed Bill about his ongoing attraction to the Emerging Church. I then located other congregations in Lansing that, like Bill, were consuming and enacting knowledge produced by the Emerging movement. In August 2008 I moved to southwestern Ohio to teach at Miami University. From then until October 2010 I conducted ethnographic fieldwork with individuals and communities throughout the Dayton-Cincinnati corridor. This ethnography results from the data amassed during these three years.

My fieldwork was patterned on the idea of "multi-sited ethnography" (Marcus 1995), a methodological posture that

> examines the circulation of cultural meanings, objects, and identities in diffuse time-space. This mode defines for itself an object of study that cannot be accounted for ethnographically by remaining focused on a single site of intensive investigation. This mobile ethnography takes unexpected trajectories in tracing a cultural formation across and within multiple sites of activity. . . Just as this mode investigates and ethnographically constructs the lifeworlds of variously situated subjects, it also ethnographically constructs aspects of the system itself through the associations and connections it suggests among sites. (ibid.: 96)

The three theoretical points raised by this definition helped shape this book: the "circulation" of cultural material, the phenomenological "lifeworlds" of subjects, and the structural conditions that frame everyday performances. Marcus rightly distinguishes this approach of looking "across and within multiple sites of activity" from the familiar model of being immersed in one field site. Rather than focus on a single Emerging congregation I followed the presence of the movement across multiple locales. Within this methodological frame, I relied most heavily on four forms of data collection: interviewing, participant observation, collaborative ethnography, and textual archiving.

(1) I devoted significant energy to "informal" and "semi-structured" interviewing (Bernard 2006: 211–12). I sat in homes, coffee shops, restaurants,

pubs, and other public sites—sometimes with a tape recorder, sometimes not—with ninety Emerging Evangelicals. With the vast majority of this sample I conducted multiple interviews. The first meeting always combined a spiritual-religious life history with questions about what aspects of the Emerging Church attracted them and the details of their church community. Follow-up interviews explored key themes like "missional" and "ancient-future," and further explored their individual and collective Christian lives. The appendix surveys my Emerging Evangelical consultants.

As the following chapters progress, most of these individuals will become more than an Appendix entry. What is complex, intriguing, and revealing about their stories will become evident. In the meantime, consider some relevant observations about this sample. *Emerging Evangelicals* pulls together the experiences of individuals, and by extension the experiences of the church communities they are part of. Through these 90 individuals, 40 communities are represented. Through these 40 communities, 11 denominations are represented (United Methodist, Reformed Church of America, General Baptist Conference, Southern Baptist Convention, Vineyard Fellowship, Presbyterian Church of America, Presbyterian Church-USA, Church of Christ, Episcopalian, Anglican, and Church of the Nazarene). Because church planting and house churches are important in the Emerging movement, this sample includes 27 church planters and 24 house church members. As with American religion more generally, the book publishing industry is a significant mode of knowledge circulation for Emerging Evangelicals: this sample includes three editors representing two of the largest Christian publishers in America (Baker and Zondervan, both located in Grand Rapids, Michigan). The urban-suburban divide—foregrounded in chapters 1, 4, 5, 6, and 7—is an important structuring condition for Emerging Evangelicalism: this sample includes 56 urban dwellers and 34 suburbanites. In terms of social class, all 90 consultants are solidly middle-class, many with undergraduate and graduate degrees. All but two are white (one a Korean American male Anglican pastor, and one an African American female Vineyard worship director). Finally, all were born between 1952 and 1989, most between 1970 and 1980. Their ages of maturation help contextualize the argument that Emerging Evangelicals are both modern and late modern religious subjects.

(2) An ethnographer cannot live on interviews alone. In most cases interviews led to observations of place and collective religious practice. Some were exceedingly common for a fieldworker among American Christians: worship services, small group meetings, and informal gatherings. Others were closely linked to this particular project: missional practices, national

and regional Emerging Church conferences, ancient-future worship workshops, book promotion tours, and "pre-launch" meetings for new church plants.

These observations were valuable for many reasons. They allowed me to see the discourses of Emerging Evangelicalism performed. For example, reading and interviewing about being a missionary to your own society is one thing, but documenting how adherents go about doing this is another. Less obviously, because I conducted repeat interviews with most consultants, group observations generated useful questions for individuals who participated in those events; as well as for others, for whom I used an explanation of the event as an elicitation tool. These ethnographic observations provide an account of subject formation in process. To say that this book is about identity is not simply a claim about how Evangelicals talk about themselves; it is also about their lived subjectivity (Ortner 2005). Identity is not simply an ongoing discursive construction; it is an everyday, embodied, felt, and experienced self. The events I present are very much phenomenological rituals of religious becoming.

(3) My fieldwork included multiple forms of collaborative ethnography, where the anthropologist attempts some remove from authority by involving consultants in the making of research activities (Lassiter 2004). Consider an example that appears in chapter 8.

From early in my fieldwork it was apparent that "being missional" was closely linked with an attachment to place. The more I interviewed Emerging Evangelicals about their strivings to be missional, the more I heard about the localities they were in, and the more I realized interviews in abstracted contexts would not suffice. Hearing about a sense of place was not enough; I wanted them to show me. Moreover, I wanted them to control what they showed me, rather than me controlling the questions being asked. The result was a series of guided tours. Consultants created their own itineraries as they led me through the places they called their mission fields, told me stories, explained local history, took me to significant landmarks and street corners, navigated neighborhoods, and, ultimately, performed the link between being missional and being in a particular place.

(4) Lastly, this fieldwork included the compilation of a textual archive: published texts, virtual interactions, and items of material culture. Some were given without solicitation or recommended, others were publicly available, and others were found through my own investigative efforts. This archive includes books; articles and interviews from Christian media; articles and interviews from secular media; YouTube posts; personal, congre-

gational, seminary, and media podcasts; blogs; public flyers; conference and congregational handouts; small group study resources; paradenominational materials; and church planting resources. This diverse body of materials was a necessary complement for analyzing Emerging Evangelical knowledge production. One example, which appears in chapter 7, centers on the observation that planting new churches is nothing if not highly organized. Potential planters must typically convince several different sponsoring bodies that they are qualified, that a new church is necessary in the proposed context, and that they have definitive plans to make the church successful. To capture this reality I collected ten Church Plant Proposals (produced and used for fund-raising, among other reasons). As fashioned artifacts, they are revealing cultural documents.

The arguments and observations we consider in this book derive from my ethnographic work, but they address a movement active throughout the United States. However, accounting for the distribution of Emerging Evangelicals is difficult. How do you quantify a movement that does not exist under any umbrella institution(s)? Denominations and parachurch organizations are much more convenient in this way: they keep updated listings and provide a relatively clear sense of who is represented. What follows is, at best, a very rough mapping of the movement's widespread presence.

We can begin by establishing that there are about 100 million Evangelicals in America (Institute for the Study of American Evangelicals, Wheaton College). In theory, almost every Evangelical has at least been exposed to an institution, author, congregation, or idea that is distinctly Emerging. But, of course, exposure is not the same as acceptance, integration, or even a moment's entertaining.

Aaron Flores (2005) completed a Master's thesis in the Department of Religion at Vanguard University, a private, charismatic college in southern California. He assessed the Emerging movement from a missiological perspective, but as part of this work he identified 181 American congregations as definitely Emerging. Unfortunately, this count struggles on several fronts. It employs a far too restrictive criteria list. It does not include Emerging constituents in established congregations. It does not measure the number of practitioners in those 181 places. And it focuses only on the local, congregational model of religious belonging (excluding, for instance, online communities).

Michael Morrell is an Emerging Evangelical and the webmaster for an online resource hub that chronicles the movement. The site provides a state-by-state listing of "uncommon communities of faith" that are, by Morrell's and/or the community's designation, Emerging. As of March 2010 he had listed 724 congregations in 46 states. Morrell's effort is impressive and, in cases where the communities included in my ethnographic work are listed, he is accurate. However, this listing also has several problems (apart from being the subjective, voluntary effort of one individual). As with Flores, there is no measure of the number of practitioners in these communities, nor is there an account of Emerging constituents in established congregations.

Emergent Village, as an institution that Emerging Evangelicals connect and share resources through, lists communities that are self-consciously Emerging. The local gatherings organized under the Emergent Village name are called "cohorts" and the website lists 103 in 36 states. All these cohorts are included in Morrell's count. The debilitating problem with taking this listing as paramount is that it only includes Emergent Village cohorts, and most Emerging communities have no affiliation with this institution.

Acts 29, an interdenominational church planting network, also provides a state-by-state listing of its missional churches (210 in 42 states as of October 2010). Morrell excludes most of these congregations because of their strict theological requirements for admission into the network. As with Emergent Village, these communities are Emerging because they affiliate with an institution founded on Emerging priorities (namely, the desire to be missional). But again, the list is limited to that institution and provides no data on how many individuals are active in these communities.

While these listings cannot offer any percentage of American Evangelicals who identify as "Emerging" or who consume knowledge from Emerging Church institutions, they do allow some confidence. They provide some quantitative evidence to support what I am asserting qualitatively in this book—Emerging Evangelicalism is a viable form of identity on the American religious landscape and is present in nearly every region of the United States. And given the home cities of these communities, the Emerging movement seems to remain as it began, concentrated in urban and suburban America. Taken together, these listings help contextualize the ethnographic analyses in this book.

Postscript: Person-Centered Ethnography

I end this introduction with a reminder. For me, it is a crucial reminder and vital for theorizing. I stated upfront that this is a book about America's Emerging Evangelicals. Beginning with the opening vignette involving Larry,

Aaron, Becky, and D.G., and continuing through the remaining chapters, I hope one thing will be clear: there is no Evangelicalism without Evangelicals. In short, this book is a person-centered ethnography—an ethnography focused on individual lives and intersubjective gatherings, not on any superorganic version of Evangelicalism. I offer this reminder in the spirit of other anthropologists who have responded to a nonhumanist (antihumanist?) tendency among ethnographers and social scientists.

Writing as a phenomenological anthropologist, Michael Jackson (1989) argues for an ethnographic approach modeled in the spirit of William James's radical empiricism. He warns against treating conceptual abstractions as the end goal: "I do not want to risk dissolving the lived *experience* of the subject into the anonymous field of discourse" (1, italics in original); "Concepts do not transcend this life-world, mirroring its essence or revealing its underlying laws. They cannot get us above or outside experience, only move us from one domain to another" (1); "to investigate beliefs or 'belief systems' apart from actual human activity is absurd" (65). While this ethnography is not strictly phenomenological, I do take seriously the call to prioritize the lived realities of people over conceptual abstractions.

Writing toward a different theoretical standpoint, namely, the location and attribution of agency, Brenda Farnell (2000) echoes Jackson. She argues against a long scholarly history of assigning the ability to think, feel, act, make decisions, and mobilize to intangible, ineffable, and (ironically) unlocatable forces. Farnell places Freud's *unconscious*, Durkheim's *social structure*, and Bourdieu's *habitus* in the same pile (and we might add other favored concepts such as *culture, society, infrastructure, ideology, model, ritual*, and *system*). All these abstractions are treated as having "causal powers separate from the joint activity of persons" (406–7). She rightly concludes that such extrahuman forces "have no causal efficacy. Only people do" (404). In other words, things happen in the world because people produce, consume, circulate, and enact knowledge. Cultures do not act; people, individually and collectively, do.

This posture shaped both my fieldwork and my writing of this book. I work to illustrate several arguments about Emerging Evangelicalism in the chapters that follow, and I hope to do so without losing track of the Evangelicals who actually make this movement a reality.

1

Stories of Deconversion

I spent two hours on June 25, 2003 interviewing a man named Paul. He was in his late forties and a deacon at a rural Nazarene congregation. Paul was a conservative Evangelical, and there was nothing Emerging about him. I was doing fieldwork with three congregations, focusing on the circulation of moral discourses in local churches. Paul was an especially active member in several weekly prayer and study groups, so we arranged an interview about his experience with the church and cultural models of morality. I conducted fifteen interviews that summer, and always began by asking for a spiritual-religious life history. Paul's response was more elaborate than most, but it was typical. In nineteen minutes he methodically explained—detail-by-detail, memory-by-memory—the story of how he became a Christian. His chronology followed a six-part structure that organizes this narrative genre, no matter the length of any given performance. Paul explained his lifestyle prior to becoming a Christian, emphasizing his personal and existential struggles. Women and whiskey headlined his weaknesses. This was followed by the conditions surrounding his first encounter with the theological message that Jesus Christ is "the Way, the Truth, and the Life." After this came a period of reflection on that encounter, during which he scrutinized this theology in any way he could muster. Then he recounted a second encounter with this Christocentric message, which triggered his conversion. He continued by describing the vast differences between his old and new self. As a coda, he summarized his understanding of Evangelical theology and all its self-transformative effects. Paul peppered his story with a common born-again vocabulary: lost, sinner, flesh, convicted, death, life, saved, righteousness, blood, spirit, cross, gospel, light, Word, Good News, and Jesus, to name a few. In those nineteen minutes Paul told me his conversion narrative—the story of how he became Christian.

Paul's presentation of self is exceedingly common among American Evangelicals. One could easily argue that such stories are *the* typifying discursive act for this religious culture. I begin with Paul and the cultural fixity of this narrative genre to establish a contrast. Emerging Evangelicals, unlike their conservative brethren, rely on a different kind of storytelling when presenting their sense of Christian self: a narrative of deconversion.

Narrative and Christian Subjectivity

The intersection among Evangelical language, performance, and identity is busy (Meigs 1995). Social scientists from various disciplines have insisted that narratives are not just ways of telling, but ways of being. They do not simply inform about one's conception of self and experience, they are ways of enacting religious subjectivity. The ethnographic work of Susan Harding (1987) and Peter Stromberg (1993) are two widely cited examples of how the Evangelical conversion narrative can be culled for cultural insight. Harding examined how the born-again conversion is a process of acquiring a specific religious language, and how Evangelical speakers use the genre of witnessing to implicate their listeners in the narrated transformation. Stromberg examined how conversion narratives evoke preconversion emotional conflicts, and then reframe those conflicts in born-again language. Harding and Stromberg present religious subjects who seem to maintain unwavering faith. While their Evangelicals speak about experiencing doubt and questioning what responsibilities their faith demands, the narratives are marked by teleology, a straight line of change from rebellion to obedience. This is not the case when listening to Emerging Evangelicals.

It is not that Emerging Evangelicals lack this traditionalized conversion narrative, it is that they choose to replace it with a different kind of narrative. Invariably, when asked to tell their Christian story Emerging Evangelicals posit a distance between their sense of self and the conservative Evangelical subculture. They explain various elements of Evangelicalism that they no longer accept, how their distastes became realized, and how the details of their current life respond to those perceived shortcomings. The narrative of self they prefer enacts the cultural critique that animates the movement at large. Their frustrations, and their attempts to resolve them, provide a logic and direction to their storytelling. In taking this narrative stance Emerging Evangelicals re-create a historically consistent crossroads: how does one respond when dissatisfied with religious faith? To help understand the Emerging Evangelical response, consider two historical studies.

David Hempton's *Evangelical Disenchantment: Nine Portraits of Faith and Doubt* (2008) examines the religious lives of nine historically revered European and American artists and public intellectuals who lived (primarily) during the nineteenth century. All of his subjects were committed Evangelicals before "repudiating" this tradition. They "chafed at the restrictive dogmatism" (13) of Evangelicalism and decided their existential hopes and worldly aspirations would be best fulfilled elsewhere. Though they lived during a time of contentious relations between science and religion (for example, the cultural and epistemological battles that ensued from Darwinian evolutionary theory), the reconciliation that proved irreconcilable for them was between "artistic creativity and Christian orthodoxy" (12). Hempton offers the nine portraits as "Evangelical disenchantment narratives," which he metaphorically describes as "referrals to the complaint department of the evangelical tradition" (3). To make the metaphor work properly, we should say that they dropped off their complaints and left the building permanently. Hempton's subjects stood at the crossroads and opted for a wholesale change of religious identity. This is not the case for Emerging Evangelicals.

John Barbour's *Versions of Deconversion: Autobiography and the Loss of Faith* (1994) is a much better fit (cf. Harrold 2006). Barbour argues that Western spiritual autobiographers have relied heavily on the idea of a "loss or deprivation of religious faith" (2). As opposed to the "turning to" orientation that characterizes conversion narratives, deconversion is marked by a "turning from" (3) orientation defined by self-conscious critique. Barbour identifies four themes that animate deconversion writing from St. Augustine to Malcolm X: doubt or denial of a belief system; moral criticism of an entire way of life; emotional upheaval; and rejection of a community of belonging.

Not surprisingly, considering the eminence of *The Confessions* in literary history (Stock 1996), Barbour sees Augustine as the best early example of the genre. Troubled by epistemological uncertainty and intellectual doubt, the focal point of Augustine's deconversion narrative is a spiritual crisis followed by the sudden embrace of orthodox Christianity. The seventeenth-century Puritan John Bunyan, in his *Grace Abounding to the Chief of Sinners*, offers a different kind of deconversion, one based on moral criticism. The focal point here is an "intensification" of religious identity, or "the revitalized commitment to a faith with which converts have had a previous affiliation" (16). This revitalization is defined by the "struggle to become more than a superficial Christian" (17). It is this Bunyan-style deconversion that characterizes Emerging Evangelicals.

Their deconversions are not a matter of jettisoning faith altogether; they are a matter of self-consciously heightening religious devotion because they deem their religious lives wanting. Their crossroads question does not lead to Hempton's disenchantment. They are still compelled by the hope and effectiveness of Evangelicalism; just not in the form that they have learned it. The deconversion stories presented below follow a narrative structure based on moral criticism and, like Bunyan's "struggle to become more than a superficial Christian," are grounded in the desire for authenticity that organizes the Emerging movement. In their terms, they want something more real, more genuine, more meaningful, more relevant, more honest, more biblical—something more. The role of desiring authenticity in these narratives reveals, following Lindholm (2008), a deeply modernist disposition at the center of Emerging Evangelical subjectivity.

Emerging Stories of Deconversion

There is no single problem with the conservative Christian subculture from which Emerging Evangelicals want to distance themselves. In most cases, consultants integrated several critiques that culminated in their desire to separate from the conservative tradition. Nearly all of my consultants are lifelong churchgoers, and most have had a lengthy relationship with Evangelicalism. Their stories of deconverting usually involve a time in their lives when they realized that they "just don't fit [as a typical conservative Evangelical]." This realization was either prompted by, coincided with, or followed by an encounter with the Emerging Church. Many expressed the same feeling of "I'm not the only one!" when recalling a book they had read by an Emerging author, a conference they had attended, or a local congregation they had connected with. The following six individuals—Cathy, Chris, Jeff, Ford, Lilly, and Ben—provide a representative look at the varieties of Emerging deconversions. Taken together, we see in them a composite of the cultural critique that fuels the Emerging movement.

"I don't want to make lace covers for Bibles"
Cathy was surprised, even pleased, that I had requested to interview her. Whenever someone has wanted to know about the house church network she planted with her husband, Glenn, he has always been the public voice. Having someone "take notes" on her story was a novelty. Sponsored by the Southern Baptist Convention, they planted the church in 1999 in Oxford, Ohio; a small college town thirty-five miles northwest of Cincinnati. Cathy and Glenn are both "bivocational" (a common signifier among Emerging Evangelicals, and itself a point of separation from the conservative expectation of "paid staff"). She teaches in a public elementary school in Oxford; he teaches and does academic advising at a nearby Christian college. Cathy

is short and petite, and speaks with a heavy east Tennessean accent. Her face—full of small, delicate features—is framed by a heap of tight, loosely knit brown curls.

She relied on two themes to organize her deconversion narrative: "figuring out who Cathy is" and "never being comfortable in traditional church" (the latter was her chosen signifier for the conservative Christian subculture). She has been a Southern Baptist her entire life. This began in rural, northeast Tennessee where her family was steeped in local church life. Cathy's "journey" of self-discovery is bound tightly to her family relations. While she and Glenn were in college at East Tennessee State University they decided that they were willing to move anywhere to pursue ministry together; it was the first time she had seriously considered living more than an hour's drive away from home. When she was a young girl Cathy's brother spoke for her. This is not figurative. She struggled to overcome a severe speech impediment throughout adolescence and her older brother, quite literally, would communicate on her behalf. "Figuring out who Cathy is" meant creating distance from her family.

She also sought distance from being Southern Baptist: she had matured in the denomination, remained with it through college, and continued when Glenn attended Southern Seminary in Louisville, Kentucky. During those seminary years, as she and Glenn socialized with other married couples, Cathy realized that she "did not fit the mold" of being a pastor's wife. "I don't sing. I don't want to run the children's ministry. I don't want to make lace covers for Bibles. I didn't dress like they did." This tension persisted at Glenn's first pastorate with a rural church in central Kentucky. Unlike previous pastors at this church, Glenn did not speak for Cathy when interviewing for the job. She spoke for herself.

In 1997 Cathy and Glenn had an unsettling realization: they were the only ones from their generation active in their church; no one else was younger than fifty. After several months of difficult consideration, they decided it was time to plant their own church. That same year, 1998, the Southern Baptist Convention launched the Nehemiah Project, which focused exclusively on planting new churches throughout North America. Cathy and Glenn attended the requisite church planting classes together and accepted the suggestion to plant in Oxford, a hundred and fifty miles north of their first church, where Southern Baptist churches had continually failed to succeed.

They spent a year observing the town, with its mixed demography of college students and local residents. Both populations were predominantly white, but an intensely marked economic divide separated the mostly upper-middle class students and the mostly working class locals. In concert with the Nehemiah guidelines and in step with conservative Evangelical practice, they focused most of their energies during the first year on the weekly worship event. Despite constant pressure from the regional denominational staff to increase membership, their church size remained stable. Glenn and Cathy both realized they were investing most of their efforts in an event that only about thirty people attended. Most of those thirty were not eager givers of time or money because they had negative histories with other churches. The formulaic model of church growth with which they had been supplied, and thought would work, was failing. Something had to change. In 2002 they ended the weekly worship event, stopped renting the building space where services were held, and reorganized their community into a house church network.

Cathy took on two main roles after this transition. For the first time in her life she was being positioned as an authority figure, mentoring college-aged women. She also dedicated herself to performing everyday acts of hospitality. Their home became grand central station for house church members. Those struggling financially would stay at Glenn and Cathy's house for a night, sometimes a week, and on several occasions for months at a time. This marked a major difference between "traditional church and house church." In the former it was easier to "separate church life from the rest of your life." Now, "everything is tied up together," which Cathy described as harder emotionally and spiritually, but far more rewarding. Hospitality was familiar to Cathy, which she attributed to her rural upbringing, but she soon began thinking about hospitality in a new way: as a monastic discipline. She and Glenn, publicly with house church members in witness, accepted a vow of stability, which pledged their commitment to live in Oxford for the remainder of their life (a vow patterned on the *Rule of St. Benedict*, c. 540 C.E.). Cathy is "in love with this commitment to a place and a people," as well as the formal performance of vows, which she likened to her marriage oath. She has been heavily influenced by a widely circulated text among Emerging Evangelicals, *The Celtic Way of Evangelism: How Christianity Can Reach the West . . . Again* (Hunter III 2000), which accepts the missiology of fifth- and sixth-century Celtics as a model for being a missionary in twenty-first-century America. Cathy rereads the book twice every year: "I love the story of St. Patrick and the idea that, 'I'm here to live with you, and that's a conscious choice I make every day.'"

"For the longest time, I didn't know how to capture what we were doing." Explaining this to her family is still a struggle. "It messes with them because it challenges their ideas about what it means to do church." For now, she settles for a hopeful, if imprecise, description: "I just tell people to come join this big mess with us. It's the best thing ever."

"All about money"

In 2000 and 2001, when Glenn and Cathy's frustrations with church growth models were moving toward outright disavowal, they connected with several church planters in Cincinnati who were experiencing the same cultural dissonance. They bonded quickly and remain close friends and ministry colleagues. (Deconversion, I guess, loves company.) Chris is one of those church planters. He and Glenn teach at the same Christian college, and he lives with his wife and three children in West Chester—a largely affluent, new growth exurb of Cincinnati, twenty miles north of the city's downtown. Chris's narrative relies heavily on this locale, though he has not always lived on the crabgrass frontier.

He was raised in inner-city Philadelphia by Evangelical parents and moved to Cincinnati when he was fourteen. His born-again conversion, which he characterized as a dramatic, Paul-on-the-road-to-Damascus type experience, occurred as a senior in high school. At the time he was "mister youth Evangelical," and chose to attend a Christian college near Chicago, Trinity Evangelical Divinity School. During college he was a youth minister for a megachurch in Lake Forest, a wealthy suburb on the west side of Chicago. This was his first encounter with the spiritual-emotional problems of suburbanites: "People are miserable [in the suburbs]; they get addicted to all kinds of things." During the time he lived and worked there, he cited Lake Forest as having the second highest suicide rate in the country (second only to California's famed Beverly Hills). The main culprit, Chris explained, is the "huge pressure to succeed" among kids with successful parents.

After two years in Lake Forest Chris took a job as a youth minister in Kalamazoo, Michigan. It was here that he experienced his first serious disenchantment with Evangelicalism. It began when the church froze his annual youth program budget because of financial difficulties. He saw this setback as a challenge, and started hosting weekly youth gatherings at his house. The meetings grew quickly and, with other youth pastors in the city, he rented out public centers to accommodate the two thousand people who were attending. Eventually, the church admitted the money troubles to be more of a scare than reality, and that their spending on other programs had never abated. Every discussion he had with his church elders seemed to begin and end with dollar signs. This was during the late 1990s, and overlapped with a string of high school shootings in Colorado, Arkansas, and elsewhere. Chris was conflicted about the jarring difference between what was going on "in the culture" and the church board's conversations, which were "all about money." His outward success as a youth pastor clashed with a feeling of "dying inside." He needed to "escape."

In 1999 he enrolled at Asbury, a United Methodist seminary in central Kentucky. He organized a "nontraditional" degree program, taking classes primarily in missiology and anthropology. At Asbury he committed himself to being bivocational, and to the missional stance of "fitting into the scene of the culture." In 2001, following seminary, he planted a house church network in West Chester with "no agenda," except "to be in relationship with each other." They joined the General Baptist Conference in 2003—a decision that secured financial help for them, and a move on the denomination's part to build a "postmodern" church plant portfolio. Chris's network now maintains three house churches, each with a dozen members.

For Chris, planting a house church is a response to the "consumerism" of Evangelical churches, embodied most clearly in the suburban megachurch. He described this as the premier artifact and "last wave" of "modern Evangelicalism." "They are not sustainable," citing energy bills and other maintenance costs. "It's hard to be genuine about money because they really do *need* it to stay afloat. Eighty percent of what people give financially goes back into the system."

Chris's desire has been to "live simply" amongst suburban largesse, "in the belly of the beast." He considers conspicuous consumption a sin that their house church can address as a community. "One thing I stress to people is 'don't live on 100 percent of the money you make.'" Living on the "margins" of income allows house church members to give more and to maintain "freedom from the system." Unlike megachurches, they give 90 percent of their tithing to local, national, and foreign mission work. "I want to help people see an alternative to the story they have been given. My goal has always been to subvert wherever I am." He gave the example of house church members who are upwardly mobile in their companies, and whose experiences Chris likens to Old Testament figures like Joseph and Daniel who had "success in foreign kingdoms. But, we can subvert it if we don't belong to it."

"I read banned books"

Chris's deconversion meant staying in suburbia. Other Emerging Evangelicals want physical and cultural distance from suburban America. They desire an urban life, placing the city and the sprawl into extensive symbolic orders. Jeff was among the more vehement of my consultants that this move from suburbia is non-negotiable.

I first interviewed Jeff in September 2009. I had found his online weblog, "CincyMissionary: dispatches from an urban missionary," and was intrigued. My interest turned to sheer bemusement after our first email exchange. He suggested we meet at a Starbucks in West Chester because his house was right next to it. This was odd. Why did an "urban missionary" live deep in the heart of an exurb?

Longevity did not prompt Jeff's claim to be a "CincyMissionary." He had moved to West Chester in 2008, with his wife and four kids, from Dallas, Texas. Dallas had been home for thirty-five years, his whole life. Like Cathy, Jeff had been a Southern Baptist for all of that time. He graduated from Dallas Baptist Seminary with a degree in philosophy in 1994, and immediately became a pastor. His first church was small, but it grew to over two thousand members in just a few years. He moved to a different congregation and spent three years repeating this growth process. Jeff was called to West Chester by the denomination to help a suburban megachurch that was in financial danger, the very kind Chris warned of. The church was $15 million in debt after purchasing 180 acres of undeveloped land and constructing a 108,000 square foot building. Jeff stressed that it is precisely this cycle of spending and debt, as well as the consumption system it celebrates, which exemplifies the problem with conservative Evangelicalism. He was "sick of living" in suburbia and felt "convicted" for having done so his whole life.

Jeff's unapologetic critique of suburbia has several sides. Megachurches do "19,000 Bible studies during the week," which "tears families apart" instead of keeping them together. Suburban Christianity cannot help but be "self-centered," because doing things with "no self-interest" would not allow them to sustain themselves. These churches "look the same as the culture," debilitated by the same problems of being overstressed, overfed, and divorced. The suburbs "do not create culture, they just follow and react to culture." Megachurches might be reaching "soccer moms," but they are not "changing culture." One of his preferred allegories for Evangelicalism's suburban haze is a 1999 Hollywood film, *The Matrix*. For Jeff, Evangelicals are like Neo, the movie's central character: they must "unplug, see things as they really are." There are too many "unthinking" Evangelicals who resemble the unknowing pods in the Wachowski brothers' blockbuster. As he painted this public image of Evangelicals Jeff quipped, "I want one of those T-shirts that say 'I read banned books.'" He did not want to be mistaken for an anti-intellectual preacher and pulpit pounder.

His reprieve came in May 2009. He was teaching a church planting seminar near downtown Cincinnati. One of the seminar participants was Tim, the pastor of a one-year-old church plant in the city. Tim wanted to hire an assistant pastor to help with "vision and leadership." Following the seminar, he offered Jeff the job. Jeff's first order of business was to move his family out of suburbia. In October 2009 he and his wife found a hundred-year-old apartment, four miles from where his new church rents a space for weekly worship. Jeff understands this move to the city as a biblical mandate. He highlighted the Book of Acts, where Phillip, Stephen, and Paul all sought to reach the most influential people in their respective urban settings.

Jeff's deconversion gravitates around the close coupling of suburbia, consumerism, and the conservative Evangelical megachurch. Though similar to Chris in this critique, his response is quite different. He was not content to "subvert wherever he is" and so became an "urban missionary."

Jeff revamped his blog in January 2010. He changed the title to "Lost in the Noise," an overt reference to the dizzying conditions of late modern life, but almost everything else remained the same. His description of himself and his family stayed the same. His lists of "How I Play," "Interests," "What I Listen To," "What I Watch," "The Silver Screen" (*The Matrix*, included), and "What I Read" are the same. His explanation for why he is an urban missionary is the same. But there was one striking change: his picture. The former blog featured a posed portrait of Jeff and his family set against a brown canvas backdrop. They were all dressed in white, beaming immoderate smiles. It looked perfectly suited for a suburban fireplace mantel. The new picture is in black-and-white. Still posed, it is now just Jeff, looking intent and serious, nearly squinting. Dressed in a long-sleeved T-shirt and scarf, he is standing in front of an old-stone church. It is singularly devoid of anything suburban.

"Jesus was not a church planter"

Jeff's transition to being an urban missionary was tied closely to a concern with church planting. For him, these are not just coincidental bedfellows, they work incredibly well together. This is not a stable association for all Emerging Evangelicals.

Ford describes himself as a "kingdom builder," and he is interested in "mapping the city for the movements of the kingdom." He wants to "connect people so they can share and be released to impart." The Christian role Ford commits himself to is "discipleship," which he defines as spiritual mentoring. Since May 2007, Ford has been doing the work of discipleship through a curriculum he developed with his copastor: "The Story-Formed Life" (SFL), a ten-week course designed to fashion religious subjectivity. Using teaching materials they developed together, Ford trains other church communities around Cincinnati to use SFL in their congregations. He explained SFL as "a mix of narrative theology and midrashing. You argue with each other to discover what you believe, rather than working together to find consensus." Each week of the program confronts a new topic: "Creation, the Fall, the Gospel, Lordship, Sonship, the Holy Spirit, the Disciplined Life, Being the Church, the Kingdom, and Re-Creation." Ford wants to "steward SFL to the city," and sees it as a "foundation necessary for community."

The first time Ford explained SFL to me, in late September 2009, I suspected he would eventually frame it as a means of planting new churches. I was wrong. We were sitting on the outdoor patio of a downtown Cincinnati coffee shop, although Ford could easily have been transplanted to a beach in southern California. He wore a pair of tattered Vans sneakers, equally exhausted blue jeans, a generic faded brown T-shirt, and a blue bandana that barely managed to hold a mass of intricately curled blonde hair. His easygoing smile was framed by a neatly trimmed dark blonde beard. He concluded his explanation of SFL unexpectedly: "Jesus was not a church planter. Jesus was about making disciples." How did Ford come to internalize this model of discipleship?

Born in Oregon, he moved to Los Angeles with his mother after his parents divorced. She remarried and they moved to Florence, Kentucky, ten miles south of the bridges to Cincinnati. This was his first encounter with suburbia and suburban Evangelicalism. In seventh grade he joined a Bible study group with a friend, but he "did not really hear the Gospel" until high school when he saw a staging of the Passion Play at Easter. "It unraveled me." He became a regular churchgoer, but his faith did not "mature" until college at Northern Kentucky University, twelve miles southeast of Florence. For most of his college years he was active in Young Life, a nondenominational, Reformed, Evangelical, parachurch organization that ministers exclusively to high school students. A few months before graduating, in 2004, he read Brian McLaren's *A New Kind of Christian* (2001)—a canonical Emerging Church book, and one of the most often-cited as formative by my consultants. A mentor loaned him the book, presenting it to Ford as both "dangerous and healthy." The book resonated with Ford's "deconstructionist" tendencies and ignited his deconversion; he began asking himself "what is the Church" and started to challenge the answers he had already learned.

After graduation Ford joined a Vineyard church in northern Kentucky where he knew and respected the pastor. Early in his time there he observed that members were only active together on two occasions: Wednesday night Bible study and Sunday morning worship. In the terms he uses now, they lacked "effective discipleship." At the time, he was beginning to realize that the Seeker-Sensitive megachurch model they used for church growth did not align with his desires. It was too formulaic, too suburban, too impersonal, too detached from peoples' everyday lives. As a self-described "starter of things," Ford responded by calling a meeting for young men in the church (the same night, the pastor's daughter held a separate meeting for college-aged women). The message he presented that evening was simple: he wanted all of them to "heed the New Testament command to turn over your life and give everything to Jesus." He did not offer any precise forms that this heeding would take, but he promised them that all of their lives could "change in a fundamental way." The following week he was "shocked"; everyone returned to hear more. Four months later he and the pastor agreed that forming any kind of "subgroup" in the church was not healthy for the congregation, and Ford left.

He did not leave alone. While at the Vineyard he met Jeremy, codesigner of SFL and now his copastor. They shared the same frustrations and decided to plant a church together. They invited twelve couples from the Vineyard, all of whom were small group leaders, and re-presented Ford's message from six months earlier. No one seemed interested. But, after a week, the first married couple responded. For Ford, they were the least likely: a corporate CEO and his wife living in an affluent Cincinnati suburb. Then two more couples committed. Then two more. In December 2004 they planted in Ft. Thomas, a largely residential neighborhood fifteen miles northeast of Florence, and a ten-minute drive away from downtown Cincinnati. Why Ft. Thomas? Ford described the community as "not on the way to anywhere," as a "walking" neighborhood, and "safe," a value for the couples who were parents, which was most of them. The group that Ford and Jeremy had gathered, following the missional logic of acculturating into a local context, sold their houses and moved to Ft. Thomas. They began "experiencing community like never before." They were meeting in homes, but Ford explicitly distinguished their congregational structure from being a house church. He was uninterested in pinning what they were doing to any identifiable institutional form. For everyone involved, it was an "intense" spiritual time. They quickly grew to sixty members, and had to "restructure" every two months to figure out "the best way to organize" themselves. Each time they restructured, members left.

In 2007 they reorganized so that the community structure overlapped with the idea, first design, and first teaching of the Story-Formed Life. Ford's intertwining narrative of his personal transformations and those of their church in Ft. Thomas culminated in the final stage of his deconversion. The Church in America, he laments, suffers from a crippling commitment to "tribalism." When he first explained this to me, he borrowed my fieldnote pen and pad to illustrate. He drew two images. The first was a small, closed circle, surrounded by a larger, closed circle. The second image was an even larger, dotted-line circle. The Church universal, he explained, should be the only closed circle and all smaller circles should be dotted. Americans have it "backwards from what God intended." "Local expressions [of church] should be permeable and people should be able to come in and go out" at will. His critique of Christian tribalism was not over. He drew another diagram. This one had a circle with "Training" written in the center, a series of smaller circles next to it labeled "local expressions," and a few slightly larger circles in the remaining open space called "ministries." The goal, he continued, is to organize a city where everyone interacts and people stop working solely within narrow theological camps. SFL is intended to achieve this ecumenism. In September 2009 there were ten SFLs happening throughout Cincinnati, with several others planned.

"Why do we want to worship in Wal-Mart?"

Discipleship, Ford's main concern, is present in some form in every Christian community. Of course, evidenced by Ford's critique, Christians do not agree about what discipleship is or how it should be institutionalized. The same is true with another foundational practice in Evangelical life: worship. This has been the motivating interest, and deconversion impetus, for Lilly.

A bundle of contagious energy, Lilly smiles relentlessly, big, and laughingly. It is unceasing. She smiles when explaining, when listening, when telling stories, when answering questions. She speaks with a slight Tennessean accent. She has short, dark hair with strategically placed blonde highlights. And every time I have seen her, irrespective of the occasion, she has worn a small, wooden Celtic cross on a tightly fitting necklace around her neck.

Lilly moved to Cincinnati in 1996 when she and her husband accepted jobs at a suburban megachurch, the region's first and still its largest congregation. Their positions were eliminated due to funding after just a few months and Lilly took a brief hiatus from professional ministry. In 1998 she accepted a job as a youth pastor at a small, "Anglo-Catholic" Episcopalian church. Her experience there catalyzed her deconversion.

Lilly had spent her entire religious life as an Evangelical, including the neo-charismatic Vineyard megachurch that brought her to Cincinnati. The liturgical, mainline Episcopalian atmosphere was "another world." Maturing in the Protestant culture that she did, Lilly was unaware that she "spoke Evangelical." The senior pastor cautiously questioned some of her language, such as "having a personal relationship with God," which is beyond commonplace in Evangelical communities. She remembers her time at this Episcopalian congregation as a mutual learning experience. For her part, she slowly coaxed the pastor into saying "Jesus" instead of "Christ." She narrated her experience there as the start of her religious self-consciousness. For the first time in her life, she was constantly and consistently aware of the kind of Christianity she had learned. The highly structured liturgy, Anglican symbolism, and lectionary readings were foreign, but strangely attractive. Something clicked: "Here we were living in an image-based culture, and places like the Vineyard had thrown out all the images." Her critique of church aesthetics and worship started Lilly on a search to find others who perceived the same contradiction.

She immediately connected with Emerging Church bloggers in England who practiced "alternative worship" styles. Lilly visited her long-distance advisers in 2000, observing their experimentations, and learning what they meant by "alternative worship." She returned to Cincinnati, full of ideas and convinced more than ever that contemporary church worship needed to change. In the fall of 2001 she started "Sacred Space," an alternative worship service, at the Episcopalian church. This continued every week until she left the position, four years later. The service consisted of "multisensory, experiential, and participatory" ways to "encounter God." For Lilly, the biggest adjustment in this new approach to worship was her revised role and responsibilities. Instead of being at the front of the room directing everyone, as she always had been, she moved to the back of the room and existed as a resource for congregants (for example, if they wanted someone to pray with).

Lilly's critique of Evangelical worship defines her deconversion. "In Christian land we equate worship with singing." She juxtaposes this with Old and New Testament examples where "God communicates through stuff" and "experiential" moments such as Jesus' use of the "lilies in the field." For her, this is about more than just an inherited worship culture, it is about personhood: "This is the way God created us to be." In late June 2009 Lilly taught an all-day seminar on "creating sacred space" at St. E in Norwood. During the morning session, as she explained her transition to alternative worship (essentially performing her deconversion narrative to the audience), she asked rhetorically: "Why do we want to worship in Wal-Mart?" The narrow definition of worship that Lilly sees as operative among American Christians prompted a related critique: the lack of opportunity for reflection. Restricting "worship" to preaching and singing "tells the story too directly. We need room for contemplation. Churches are really loud, and there's one speaker after another. Yet we're told to hear God."

Lilly is no longer employed by a congregation. Instead, she works freelance as a worship consultant, advising congregations, organizing retreats, and teaching workshops at conferences across the country. In Cincinnati, she "curates" a series of experiential worship events. She calls the events "Thinplace," a term she borrowed from the Celtic Christian tradition. It references the idea that there are certain locations in the world where the line between heaven and earth is at its thinnest, making it easier to feel God's presence. Rather than locate those places and go to them, Lilly wants to create them. On a glossy advertising card she makes available at her workshops and retreats, Thinplace is described as "a pilgrimage of discovery and creativity, integrating ancient and future forms of worship to bring liturgy new life." Thinplace events are ostensibly open to the public, but they are mostly attended by a collection of fellow Christians in the area whom Lilly keeps informed through email and Facebook. During my fieldwork, there were about fifty people on the email list.

"Why do we always have to be studying something?"

Every deconversion story includes a breaking point. For Lilly, it was her experience working in an Episcopalian church. It is a time remembered—a brief moment for some, a lengthy period of slow realization for others — when one's critique of the Evangelical subculture becomes clear for the first time or finally becomes too intense to continue unaddressed. Ben's breaking point happened in February 2004.

For those who keep tabs on American popular culture that date might be familiar. The first day of the month was the National Football League's 38th Super Bowl, and the half-time show was arguably more memorable than the game. It was the scene of the Janet Jackson "wardrobe malfunction" controversy, where one of her breasts was exposed and the broadcasting network (CBS) was fined a record $550,000 by the Federal Communications Commission. Ben watched the entire spectacle, but he missed it all. He was too busy "banging" on his laptop keys, furiously and without expletive censor. The email he was typing ("composing" would belie Ben's retelling of the frenetic writing) was intended for the pastor of his house church network.

November 2009. As Ben told his story from nearly six years before, I sat pinned against the back of my chair. The whole interview was intensely captivating. It was not the trajectory or mileposts of his narrative; these were all unsurprising, given the other deconversion narratives I had collected.

It was his demeanor. His outward aesthetic and mannerisms conveyed a working-class toughness. He was dressed simply: faded blue jeans, white sneakers, a New York Yankees baseball jersey with "Gehrig" stitched on the back, and a tan Kangol cap. His head was shaved bald. He looked strong, but not overly or intentionally muscular. And he walked with an incredible sense of purpose, each stride as determined as its predecessor. We were in a favorite coffee shop of his, and he had ordered a single-shot espresso in a small red cup. It appeared dainty, until he gulped it in one, abrupt motion. I asked my standard opening interview question about his religious biography, which prompted a nonstop, hour-long response. He struggled to find exactly "where to begin." Rubbing his forehead and shifting in his seat, stopping, and starting: "Man, I'm dusting off words I don't use anymore."

Why was he banging so ferociously on his computer that night in 2004? The house church he committed to in 2002 was changing into something he did not want. For one thing, they had outgrown their living room meeting space and had bought a church building. Church buildings were the kind of thing he had joined the house church to escape. The solution he and the pastor worked out was for Ben to lead a group at his home: "We used to joke that we were a support group for recovering Fundamentalists." The same week he agreed to this plan he read Brian McLaren's *A New Kind of Christian* (the same book that facilitated Ford's deconversion). It was a "big, big deal" for him. He repeated the oft-described Emerging Evangelical experience: "It's not just me. Maybe this thing I hate [the conservative Christian subculture] is worth hating." Soon after reading McLaren he read Dallas Willard's *The Divine Conspiracy* (1998) and David Dark's *Everyday Apocalypse* (2002); both furthered his "not just me" moment. (It was extremely common to hear consultants rattle off titles and authors of books to structure deconversion narratives. But there was something different, something more intentional with Ben. He did not recall them from memory; he read the titles from a monthly planner. Organized by month, it was a printed list of every book he had read since July 2002. He had not brought it for the purpose of our interview; he simply always had it with him: "This thing is the closest I've got to a journal.") As a house church leader, Ben knew what he did and did not want. He wanted to avoid formalities: "Why can't we just *be*? Why do we have to always be studying something? Everything becomes a thing. I just want to *be*."

Ben's desire to "just be" jettisoned an important Evangelical institution of subject formation, the small group Bible study. This jettisoning had a long history. He began his deconversion narrative in adolescence, with Evangelical parents and an inability to "fully buy into the conservative Evangelical worldview." His father taught at a Christian university in Cincinnati and, despite his own preferences, Ben took advantage of the free tuition and spent five years finishing an education degree. He "always felt like an outsider," and described the decision to attend there as "the path of least resistance." After graduating in 1995 he accepted a job as a youth minister in rural Kentucky, an hour south of Cincinnati. He remembered the church as "small, highly Fundamentalist, traditional, old school, everybody wore suits and sang hymnal music; the kind of Baptists who don't like other Baptists." As with college, despite having a conscious aversion to the entire scene, he promised the church elders he was not going to use the position as a stepping stone to go elsewhere (as several youth pastors before him had done). He paused to indulge a self-reflection: "I don't leave things. The whole leaving thing seems really violent. I'll live in Cincy for the rest of my life." This is a difficult emotion to square with deconversion, and I would venture is part of Ben's intensity.

Ben left the Fundamentalist church in the summer of 1999. It was a matter of cumulative dissonance. He recalled a particularly trying example. Part of his ministry work involved hospital visits to older, dying patients. He would play the guitar, sing worship songs, and pray with them. For him, it was a highlight in an otherwise dreary job. During a staff meeting he "got reamed out" for not wearing a suit on these hospital visits. The elders thought it reflected poorly on the church. Ben thought it the height of triviality. Soon after, he returned to Cincinnati.

The house church Ben led in 2004 continues today, but in a much altered form. The initial group of fifteen used to meet every week. Now, seven of them have dinner every other week. They do not pray together. They do not read religious books together. They eat together and share the joys and frustrations of each others' lives. Their affiliation with the larger house church network is mostly loose. Ben described the present as a time to "let the waters settle. The more I thrash, the muddier the water gets. For thirty-five years I was in church three times a week. I need some distance." Time to just be.

An Anatomy of Deconversion

What do we hear in the intricate life details of these six deconversion narratives? Most explicitly, we hear a striving toward authenticity and confident ideas about what authentic Christianity means. Toward the end of his comparative analysis of religious autobiographies, John Barbour reflects on the significance of the deconversion genre and the kind of subjectivity it encourages:

deconversion is a subtle yet pervasive impulse and theme not only in autobiographies but in a great deal of modern and postmodern thinking. Deconversion is a metaphor for our times that expresses modernity's search for authenticity, which so often takes the form of a flight from authority, from inherited paradigms of thought, and from various forms of pressure to conform. (1994: 210)

As Barbour explains the cultural work performed by deconversion it is difficult to not recall the sweeping ethnological analysis of Lindholm (2008); namely, the claim that authenticity is a defining value of modernity. The search for what is "original, real, and pure" (ibid.: 2) compels the modern subject, and we now have several explanations as to why this is. Lindholm highlights the "condition of living among strangers" (3), and the isolation, uncertainty, and fear that travel with it. Parish (2009) favors modernity's "way of living among symbols" (143), the unsettling feeling of being forever separated from what is really real by significations that are nothing more than social contracts. Barbour adds to these explanations three more aversions: the weight of authoritarianism, the burden of established ways of thinking, and the seductive pressures of social conformity. All five of these endangerments to authenticity are part of the anatomy of Emerging Evangelical deconversion.

Emerging deconversions are oriented toward recovering a lost sense of Christian authenticity. Cathy spoke about not separating "church life from the rest of your life," Chris about "subverting," Jeff about "unplugging," Ford about "discipling," Lilly about creating "Thinplaces," and Ben about wanting to "just be." If their narratives seem self-elevating, if it seems they want to author their own hagiography, it is because the deconversion genre compels a sense of revelation. This register of modernity is necessarily about desiring and moving closer to the authentic. In no particular order, these six stories tell us that the conservative Evangelical subculture:

> does not allow for silence and contemplation,
> is regrettably consumerist and money-driven,
> prioritizes megachurch growth over spiritual growth,
> has become overly suburban, both geographically and culturally,
> functions tribally, not ecumenically,
> is overly invested in being Seeker Sensitive,
> is dogmatic and rigid,

stifles creativity for the sake of role expectations,
allows for complacency and a lack of commitment to faith,
is self-centered and motivated by self-interest,
follows "culture" blindly, but constantly fails to create it,
inadequately disciples its adherents,
stays disconnected from Christian history,
has a skewed sense of what "worship" means,
and assigns importance to trivial matters.

This list recalls the challenges to authenticity predicted by Lindholm, Parish, and Barbour. Living among strangers (the anonymity of the megachurch), feeling disconnected (the lack of silence and contemplation), authoritarianism (dogmatism and theological rigidity), inherited paradigms (the devotion to being Seeker Sensitive), and fears of conformity (the critique of suburbia) all help structure these deconversion narratives. We could add the conditions of living among conspicuous consumers and living among bureaucracies, which Emerging Evangelicals also identify in their cultural critique as distortions of authentic Christianity. Understanding Emerging deconversion as a modern disposition is furthered by looking beyond authenticity as a value and toward the primary "moral narrative of modernity" (Keane 2007: 4), the emancipation of the human subject achieved through self-transformation. As they seek authenticity, Emerging Evangelicals seek freedom—from loneliness, convention, unwanted authority, dominant paradigms, the prevailing social climate, and impersonal bureaucracies. Ironically, in this sense, their preferred narrative and their desired subjectivity are just as modern as what they seek to distance themselves from: the conservative Christian subculture, including its born-again narrative of awakening and transformation.

Emerging Evangelicals do not narrate their sense of self through the kind of conversion genre we have come to expect from conservative Protestants. Theirs is a narrative of deconversion: a narrative of critique, of contrast, of rethinking, of recovery, of revelation, and ultimately of keeping the faith. The inseparable ties between deconversion and desiring the authentic reveals this narrative as a distinctly modern presentation of self. Yet, while Emerging Evangelicals are convinced that authenticity has been lost and must be regained, they are equally convinced that regaining authenticity is an extremely difficult prospect. It is this flip side of desiring authenticity that we will examine next.

---

2 ─────

Ironies of Faith

March 25, 2008: East Lansing, Michigan. Tonight I witnessed one of the oddest scenes I can recall in eight years of fieldwork with American Christians. It was ten o'clock on a weekday night. A tall, lanky man stood in front of a pulpit. His hair was short and neatly trimmed. He wore nondescript glasses, and a plaid button-up shirt tucked perfectly into iron-pressed beige khakis. He did not look the part of a celebrity, but he seemed to be playing one. A throng of preteen boys and girls with arms extended surrounded him, all waving the same book. They were clamoring, always inching forward. I was standing at the back of the sanctuary, watching the crowded scene grow, shrink, and grow again for nearly fifteen minutes. The man stood head, shoulders, and part of a torso above the young gathering. He was fixed in the same spot, smiling, signing front pages. It was a most unlikely mob scene.

The event was a book release party for *Why We're Not Emergent (By Two Guys Who Should Be)* (2008). Kevin, the senior pastor and unlikely celebrity, coauthored the book with one of his congregants, a professional sportswriter. In alternating chapters they deliver a measured, but unrelenting response to what they deem the theological, liturgical, and ecclesiological flaws of Emerging churches. (The book would later win the 2009 "Church/Pastoral Leadership" award from *Christianity Today*, American Evangelicalism's flagship periodical.)

Kevin's celebrity moment happened at the evening's end. It was preceded by a question-and-answer session with the audience (about two hundred people, half of the congregation's weekly worship attendance at the time), a free pizza dinner, brief speeches from the two authors about their motivations for writing the book, and worship singing. The event began with a video projected onto two large screens. It was filmed in the spirit of MTV's *Cribs*, a popular show that features celebrities giving guided tours of their lavish homes. The opening scene introduced Kevin in his kitchen. In a conversational, discernibly playful tone Kevin told viewers that "pastors" have "ordinary" houses, "just like everybody else," and that "nothing special" happened there. The camera then followed him through different rooms, upstairs and then back down. Along the way he pointed out different household features: the fireplace, good for burning cards with sins written on them; bathroom soap, the milk and honey variety "like the Promised Land"; the shower, good for perfecting baptismal techniques; a toy globe, perfect for keeping track of missionaries; and so on. The video was received uproariously by the crowd, myself included. It was all, of course, farce. It was—by parroting a recognizable pop cultural form and delighting in reflexive humor—irony for the sake of spoof. Coincidentally, and unintentionally, the fame Kevin mocked in the video reappeared earnestly in the book signing. Irony, we might say, enjoyed the last laugh.

July 18, 2009: Cincinnati, Ohio. Tonight I witnessed a unique event in my fieldwork with Emerging Evangelicals. The event was a book promotion; one stop on a six-city tour. The book, *A Christianity Worth Believing: Hope-Filled, Open-Armed, Alive-and-Well Faith for the Left Out, Left Behind, and Let Down in Us All* (2008), was (at the time) the most recent from Doug Pagitt. Pagitt has been a public persona in the Emerging movement since its institutional beginnings in the mid-1990s. My consultants consistently treated Pagitt as a symbol, for the movement itself (because of his respective venerability) and the movement's ecumenical, boundary-pushing theological voice.

An independent coffee shop next to the University of Cincinnati hosted the event. Lilly, whom we met in the previous chapter, is the reason Pagitt included Cincinnati in the tour, and why this location played host. She and Pagitt have been close friends since 2002, and he knew she could facilitate lodging and a venue. The coffee shop was owned and operated by a local pastor, with whom Lilly had collaborated on several ministry projects. The event lasted from 8 p.m. until 10:30, and was truly a multimodal performance. Pagitt spoke in a lecture format for part of the evening, but he also read excerpts from the book, guided multisensory activities, and interspersed short media and video clips. He was accompanied by a friend who played an acoustic guitar to lead worship songs.

One video clip garnered an inordinate amount of audience attention. Unaware at the time, I would later identify it as the second episode of a webshow/podcast called *Mr. Deity*. The episode, lasting not quite five minutes, was entitled "The Really Big Favor." The gist of the episode was Mr. Deity (the show's index for *Yahweh*) trying to convince Jesus to be crucified as the atoning sacrifice for humanity's sinfulness. Pagitt showed the clip to extend an analysis he had been building for several minutes: how representations of

Jesus are always inherently cultural. He concluded this rather weighty theological discussion with the thick satirical coating of *Mr. Deity*. The episode begins with Mr. Deity and Jesus sitting in uncomfortable silence. Jesus is looking with bemused discomfort at an exaggeratedly silly pencil drawing of a man nailed to a cross. Mr. Deity speaks first: "So, um, yeah, that's, obviously that's the downside." Mr. Deity is a middle-aged white man with neatly cut silvery hair, a silver goatee, hip spectacles, a Hawaiian shirt, and a distinctly nasally voice. Jesus is younger, also white, and very handsome with a 5 o'clock shadow beard, short dark hair, thin dark goatee, and the kind of shirt one expects at an urban night club. As they haggle over the "really big favor," the humor shifts idioms. When Jesus hesitates about being "down" for three days, Mr. Deity compromises: "You know, I said three days in the prophecies, but you know there's fudge room. We could put you down late Friday, all Saturday, and then you know raise you up at the crack of dawn on Sunday. So, what would that be, 36 hours tops; 35 if we did it on the week they set the clocks forward." Elaborating his offer, Mr. Deity adds: "Plus, this could be a really good career move for you, you know, get you in on the ground floor." When Jesus questions why "you can't just do it yourself," Mr. Deity stumbles, starts, stops, hedges, and finally blurts: "It's time, is what it is, trying to get the time off, can't do it." The episode ends with Jesus convinced he is being "punked," looking under a table for cameras, and Mr. Deity confused as to what "being punked" means. Most intriguing was not the clip itself, but the audience's reaction. There were about thirty people present, many of whom I knew from my fieldwork. Everyone, and I mean everyone, laughed with appreciation and gusto for the entire clip. Many gave it a salutary round of familiar applause and anticipatory laughter when the show's title first flashed on the screen.

Irony in Late Modernity

These two vignettes introduce two ideas: that irony is increasingly pervasive in contemporary life, and that Emerging Evangelicals use irony in a particular way. The first has been asserted *ad nauseam* by philosophers and literary critics. Ernst Behler (1990) writes that modernity, since its philosophical "[origins] with Bacon and Descartes," encouraged a "self-reflective consciousness" (3). To be modern is to be introspective, and irony is an inevitable by-product. Self-reflection prepares the ground for indirectness, inversion, circumlocution, satire, parody, pretense, and other ironic forms to flourish. The argument is not that modernity invented irony, but that it ignited a special appreciation for it. Colebrook (2004) suggests that the impulse for irony is exaggerated in late modernity. Echoing Baudrillard (1981), she addresses irony's current status: "We live in a world of quotation, pastiche, simulation, and cynicism: a general and all-encompassing irony" (2). Purdy (1999) writes polemically against the destructive nature of this ubiquitous irony: "The ironist expresses a perception that the world has grown old, flat, and sterile, and that we are rightly weary of it. There is nothing to delight, move, inspire, or horrify us. Nothing will ever surprise us. Everything we encounter is a remake, a rerelease, or a rerun. We know it all before we see it, because we have seen it all already" (xii). Examples abound in contemporary American popular culture. Think, for example, of the extraordinary popularity of news media send-ups like *The Onion* and *The Daily Show* (Boler 2006).

It is in this context that we should read the opening vignettes. Contemporary American Evangelicals, like other late modern subjects, are apt to be ironists and so it is no surprise to find irony as a centerpiece of both public performances. However, Emerging Evangelicals harbor a different relationship to irony than their conservative counterparts. Kevin, a published critic of the Emerging movement, and Doug, a published icon of the Emerging movement, use irony differently. In his mockery of MTV's *Cribs*, Kevin uses irony as a farce, poking fun at himself, but with no serious intent. It is all for a good laugh. With *Mr. Deity*, Doug uses a product defined by its irony to make a substantial theological point about how our representations of Jesus affect our understanding of Jesus. It is a valued strategy in his repertoire of teaching tools. Irony is not like deconversion; it is not a defining cultural trait in the Emerging movement. However, unlike their conservative counterparts, Emerging Evangelicals tend to take irony very seriously and value it as a resource in their broader cultural critique. Read alongside each other, deconversion and irony capture a central theme of this book: the intertwining of modern and late modern dispositions in Emerging Evangelical subjectivity.

But why irony? The answer begins with the value of authenticity. Whereas the previous chapter illustrated how Emerging Evangelicals desire the authentic, here we consider the flipside to this desire. Just as they are committed to the need for authenticity, they are equally convinced of its difficulty. The search for authenticity can fail. It is an elusive, problematic pursuit, notoriously tough to achieve.

The difficulties that Emerging Evangelicals assign to authenticity arise from a general anxiety of mediation. As the anthropologist Kathleen Stewart (1988) said of late modernity, "we are tourists whose constituting practice it is to read things *as* signs" (230). Of the endangerments to authenticity we considered in the previous chapter, it is Parish's (2009) observation that lingers most destructively: the condition of living among symbols where "knowing one's place in the world and defining a self become progressively harder as both 'reality' and 'self' are defined as consisting of arbitrary symbols, objects of cognitive and social manipulation, whose meaning is a matter of convention and negotiation" (144). This interpretation draws our attention to a popular theme in the anthropology of Christianity and the study of religion more generally, "the inescapability of material and social mediations" (Keane 2006: 322; cf. Engelke 2010). For Emerging Evangelicals, two problems feed this anxiety of mediation most vociferously: commodification and the limits of language. These problems are not thought to make authenticity impossible, but they do seem to be always in the way, forever muddying the waters. It is in response to these muddy waters that irony becomes an especially attractive resource. If authenticity cannot be achieved, can it be hinted at? If direct access is denied, can circumlocution help?

Commodity Trouble

Emerging Evangelicals are acutely aware that nothing is exempt from the capitalist impulse to brand, price, sell, and buy. Once economic value is assigned, authenticity is endangered (if not altogether compromised). This does not mean that they practice any wholesale rejection of capitalism. It means that they foster a self-conscious aversion to treating matters of faith as commodities (see Coleman [2006] for how Prosperity charismatics address a similar tension). Marxist scholars have debated this dynamic for a long time. As one version of the argument goes, alienation defines the commodified life. We are distanced from the things we purchase: detached from acts of production, we know only consumption. Calling something a commodity asserts a sense of irrevocable separation. As modernity marched on, goods and services were not the only targets of this economic logic. For example, indigenous populations entering the global marketplace experience and promote the commodification of their identity, history, traditions, and places (Graham 2002). To begin exploring how Emerging Evangelicals view their commodity troubles, we return to this book's opening scene: the afternoon at 1801 with Aaron, Larry, Becky, and D.G.

We were 98 minutes into the interview. Everyone had introduced themselves, and I had asked two questions. The words "authenticity," "authentic," and "real" had been used numerous times and I wanted to elicit a definition.

D.G. and Larry responded briefly, focusing mainly on issues of transparency and integrity, before Aaron entered the exchange:

> One critique I heard recently was that some of whatever is happening in, [brief pause] Churchdom, is a reaction against [stops mid-sentence], oh it was in Mike Bishop's book *What Is Church?* and he used the term, which I just really thought was insightful, which was "spiritual technologies."

The book Aaron referenced, *What Is Church?* was published in 2008 and is a guide to planting new missional church communities. The author, a church planter on the east coast of Florida, describes in the Introduction his own search for community:

> What is Church? (Or what did Jesus intend his church to be?) What does it mean to be a follower of Jesus? (Or what does it mean to be an authentic Christian?) What is the gospel Jesus preached? What does it mean to be authentically spiritual (In light of cultural definitions of being *spiritual*)? What does it mean to be a leader in Jesus' church? We discovered that questions such as these have been asked throughout church history. However, the answers to these questions were not going to come quickly or resolutely. We would have to work out answers in community, over a long period of time, with the witness of Scripture and God's people through the centuries as our guides. Throw out the typical church planting timeline. Trash the two-year-plans and marketing campaigns. This was more like the work of jungle missionaries. Break out the compass and map; all of us were suddenly in vastly unfamiliar territory (8, italics in the original).

This excerpt is packed with symbolism that resonates with Emerging Evangelicals. For now we will focus on its use of authenticity and its derision of "marketing campaigns." The concept Aaron found useful, "spiritual technologies," appears later in Bishop's book and describes the tendency of American Christians to turn resources for spiritual formation into portable, marketable commodities. Aaron's response, continuing where I interceded above, offers some examples:

> I can see that in Bill Bright's "Four Spiritual Laws," in some of the Willow Creek, Saddleback, *Purpose Driven, Prayer of Jabez*. . . . I mean, all these, like video series after video series, workbook after workbook [that say] here's the next spiritual technology by which we'll orchestrate something.

This requires some decoding. All the examples Aaron lists are iconic among Evangelicals. Bill Bright founded Campus Crusade for Christ in 1951, a college ministry through which he began distributing en masse the evangelistic booklet containing the Four Spiritual Laws. Willow Creek pioneered the megachurch movement in the late twentieth century, and is famous for mass producing small group, Bible study, discipleship, and other teaching materials. Saddleback is a Southern Baptist megachurch in southern California. The senior pastor, Rick Warren, authored the megaselling devotional manifesto *The Purpose Driven Life* (2003). The book quickly birthed a series of small group curricula that continues to be used in thousands of U.S. congregations. *The Prayer of Jabez* (2000) incited a similar phenomenon, though geared more toward personal devotion than group study. These examples are also iconic in the Emerging cultural critique. They were commonly woven into deconversion narratives, as indices of authenticity gone awry. Aaron's reference to the exhausting appearance of teaching materials recalls Ben's desire to "just be" and disinterest in "always studying something." Aaron's use of the word "orchestrate" reiterates the sense of a contrived, micromanaged, arranged, artificial spirituality. He concluded by extending his critique to the very object of his desire:

The antithesis, oddly, of "real," "authentic" is when it becomes, when even those words, become a spiritual technology; a way by which we manipulate people. "Hey, we're a real place for real people," as though saying it makes it so.

Aaron's mocking intertextual reference is also significant. At the time of the interview a nearly identical phrase was the frontispiece displayed by a non-denominational megachurch located only three miles east of the 1801 building. He offers the megachurch's claim to being "a real place for real people" as proof that nothing is beyond commodification. For Aaron, religious language is just as easily merchandised as "workbooks" and "video series," the signifier polluting his desired signified.

Glenn, whom we met in the previous chapter via his wife Cathy, voiced a similar critique of consumerism and what happens when religious earnestness is made into a marketable good. Since my first interview with him in August 2008 two things have been unambiguously obvious about Glenn: he was profoundly changed by the Emerging movement, and he has grown profoundly skeptical of the movement. In 2001, when his deconversion crystallized, the influence of Emerging authors, pastors, and local congregations aided his transition to being a house church pastor. By the time I met him he was suspicious of anything trafficking under the label "Emerging Church": books, authors, conferences, and celebrity pastors. For Glenn, the movement had become "a brand." He distinguished between "talkers and practitioners"; the former are individuals who "make a living" debating movement concerns and he considered them complicit in making "authenticity" a talking point, a mere expression of "the Emerging brand."

Glenn had grown suspicious of the blogosphere for the same reason. Reading blogs and regularly maintaining his own blog were important in Glenn's deconversion. He described blogging as an act of "risking openness": sincerely and intimately disclosing matters of faith. This ideal was corrupted by the increasing number of bloggers who accepted sponsors: "Anytime you introduce that kind of consumerism the sincerity of it is going to be doubted." In July 2009 he posted a single, seemingly rhetorical, question: "Does anyone really blog anymore and not get paid for it?" Glenn's concern with the crippling impact of commodification has been evident since his first blog post in September 2002, "Don't Put My Faith on a Tee Shirt: The Domesticated Jesus in a Feral Culture." I have italicized his many references to consumerism:

(This article—my first blog attempt—is a result of the cringe factor experienced upon perusing the *trinkets, paraphernalia and apparel* found in almost any Christian book store; staples of the Christian *mass marketing monolith . . .)*

What the modern 20th century *churchianity* experiment has left us with is nothing short of a rebellion—or better—a pilgrimage of the rejected masses to fend for themselves in the dark woods. The Jesus that the feral culture sees (when it looks) is a carnival mirror distortion of another bygone reflection—an echo of an echo. We obviously no longer live in a churched culture (if we ever did) and emerging cultures have little or no authentic Christian "memory."

Establishment *churchianity* accuses the surrounding culture, crying, "you're anti-God," when, in reality, they are just anti-whatever-the-Church-as-institutional-demagoguery-substitutes-for-authentic-biblical-spirituality (read, *pre-packaged Jesus by-products*).

I confess; I bought them. When I first discovered them, they were a cool way for me to express something that, as a new believer, I was still trying to figure out how to communicate—and there are some clever ones out there. But now, my "Won By One" tees (and their ilk) remain in the bottom of my drawer. My *Christianized tee shirts* are not going to convince the 24 year-old Satanist with the tattooed pentagram to whom our church gave out a free pack of gum and a hemp necklace last week. Nor will the neo-pagan, crew-cut, lesbian college freshman be swerved by *screen-printed Christian cliches*. It may have made one a bit more chummy with oneself for having the gusto to wear it in the presence of the heathen (and thank God we have a few of those); but that's about it. Relational mutts though we may be, I never cease to be amazed that the desire to *publicize our affiliation* is only surpassed by our longing TO affiliate.

Are *all of the tee-shirts, the W.W.J.D and F.R.O.G. bracelets* really doing more than unifying the already-convinced? A self-described pagan dabbler in both Hinduism and Buddhism (but reared Jewish) has started hanging out with us. He has an antidote in the form of a bumper sticker on his car. I can't tell if it's a sacrilege or just a plain funny indictment on the *Christian marketing juggernaut* of which I bemoan; it reads, "667, Neighbor Of The Beast." This one puts in its place the veritably *un-Christian bumper adornment*, "God Is My Co-Pilot."

So we further segregate ourselves from an unregenerate culture and become an unapproachably peculiar people for no real redemptive reason.

From his first foray into the blogosphere, Glenn has pitted religious-spiritual commodification as an obstacle to authentic faith. For him, this particular problem is central to the failings of the Evangelical establishment. And it is clear from his closing sentence, with its subtle shift to "we," that this problem is not easily solved. Commodification is not just inevitable, it is the sea Glenn swims in, even if his desire and efforts are aimed against the tide.

Language Trouble

Commodification is one form of mediation that Emerging Evangelicals see as perpetually in the way of authenticity (in turn, one reason why irony holds special appeal). A language ideology that emphasizes the limits of communication is a second. Irony is deemed helpful because human semiosis is deemed cloudy, an inherent bulwark to transparency. We begin with two influential theologians in the Emerging movement.

LeRon Shults is an American-born author and professor. He spent the first part of his career teaching at an American Evangelical seminary before moving to a Theology and Philosophy department in Norway. In May 2006, the Emergent Village Board of Directors issued a public call to address a refrain in the discourse of conservative Evangelical critics: the need for some institution to write a "statement of faith" on behalf of the Emerging Church detailing what theological beliefs were non-negotiable for movement insiders. Many responses to this call read as reminders that the Emerging movement does not work like this (with a select individual or institution speaking for everyone). Shults's letter, circulated widely through the Internet and lauded by many Emerging Evangelicals, argued against adopting any such "statement" for a different reason:

> [The] fixation with propositions can easily lead to the attempt to use the finite tool of language on an absolute Presence that transcends and embraces all finite reality. Languages are culturally constructed symbol systems that enable humans to communicate by designating one finite reality in distinction from another. The truly infinite God of Christian faith is beyond all our linguistic grasping . . . and so the struggle to capture God in our finite propositional structures is nothing short of linguistic idolatry.

With this statement Shults participates in the familiar Emerging critique that Evangelical theology is tainted by modernist assumptions. Belief statements ("propositions") are depicted as linguistic constructs, and the transcendence of God is stressed as ultimately outside the reach of human language. An ordered "statement of faith" is rather useless because it cannot achieve what it promises (claims defining the nature of God that individuals accept in order to signify belonging).

Peter Rollins was born in Belfast and is the founder of "Ikon," a Christian community in Northern Ireland internationally recognized as one of the first self-consciously "Emerging" churches. His first book, *How (Not) to Speak of God* (2006), was immediately influential among Emerging Evangelicals in the United States. The book is divided into two sections: an opening theological exegesis ("Heretical Orthodoxy: From Right Belief to Believing in the Right Way"), followed by descriptions of Ikon's weekly life presented as practical applications ("Toward Orthopraxis: Bringing Theory to Church"). Part I is replete with claims about the proper place of language in Christian thinking:

> Talking about Christian mystics, Rollins writes, "[Their] God whose name was above every name gave birth, not to a poverty of words, but to an excess of them. And so they wrote elegantly about the brutality of words" (xii).
> Describing Christianity's Jewish heritage Rollins writes, ". . .the Old Testament contains numerous warnings about placing the divine into representational form, making clear that God cannot be revealed through human *logos*" (14).

Praising the use of icons in worship Rollins writes, "Instead of saying anything positive or negative regarding God, [an icon] provides a way of avoiding idolatrous talk in favor of heartfelt praise. In this iconic understanding, our thoughts concerning God are directed towards God in love rather than enslaving God with words" (40).

Returning to his opening salvo on mystics, Rollins writes, "So in a sense, when it comes to God, we have nothing to say to others and we must not be ashamed of saying it. Our approach must be a powerless one which employs words as a way of saying that we have been left utterly breathless by a beauty that surpasses all words. This does not mean that we remain silent—far from it. The desire to get beyond language forces us to stretch language to its very limits" (42).

Rollins articulates a clear and consistent posture toward language: it will always fail if the task is to use language to adequately communicate divine realities. This fundamental suspicion of language does not result in despair, but in a call to creativity and "excess" (of which irony is a premier example).

The language ideology articulated by Shults and Rollins, that language is not a transparent medium for theological discourse, occurs in direct contrast to the language ideology of conservative Evangelicals. At least since John Calvin in the sixteenth century (Keane 2007), many Protestants have promoted a posture toward language that assumes a relatively unobstructed relationship between language, world, belief, and self: "The focus on propositions is part of a larger semiotic ideology, the belief that language functions primarily (and properly) to refer to or denote objects in a world that lies apart from it, in order to communicate ideas that lie within one person to another listener or reader" (ibid.: 67).

In 2008 I tested the possibility that Emerging Evangelicals have a distinct language ideology from their conservative counterparts, the latter favoring linguistic clarity regarding the divine in a way the former do not. I asked consultants to read and respond to two quoted excerpts. The first was from LeRon Shults's public letter. The second was from Dr. John MacArthur: an author, pastor, and public voice for Fundamentalist Christianity (for example, as a guest on national media broadcasts like *CNN's Larry King Live*). In 2007 he published *The Truth War: Fighting for Certainty in an Age of Deception*, a strident rejection of all things "postmodern" and "Emerging." In May 2007 MacArthur was interviewed on the equally Fundamentalist XM broadcast, *The Way of the Master Radio*. The show's host, Todd Friel, asked MacArthur to comment on the hermeneutic claims of Emerging Christians:

FRIEL: Dr. MacArthur, they deconstruct. Now, they call it a breakthrough and not a breaking down. What are they doing to the Bible hermeneutically?

MACARTHUR: When we talk about hermeneutics from the Greek word *hermeneu*, which means to interpret, we're talking about how do you interpret the meaning of the Bible? It's really not that hard. It's not brain surgery. You use the normal sense of language. You just see what the language says like you do, how do you interpret a conversation? Or, how do you interpret an old document? We're talking simply about how we discern what it means by what it says. These guys want to come at the Bible with some culturally informed, esoteric approach and reinterpret the Bible based upon more contemporary cultural attitudes.

The first two individuals I asked to compare the quotes from Shults and MacArthur were Jeremy (a church planter in urban Lansing with the Reformed Church of America) and Jack (an Anglican pastor in suburban Lansing).

Jeremy was a thirty-three-year-old doctoral seminary student and founding pastor of a self-consciously Emerging church. He began his ministry career in 2001, dividing his days between two positions. He worked for Youth for Christ, a conservative nondenominational parachurch ministry with "clubs" in public high schools. His main responsibility was to design after-school activities for non-Christian kids. His other job was as a youth pastor for an Evangelical congregation, and he worked exclusively with "well-churched" kids. Living in "two worlds," Jeremy saw a discrepancy between "the culture of the church and presenting the Gospel in ways that those [high school] kids needed." During this time, 2002–2003, he encountered Emerging Church authors who explicitly wrote about "how to reach the postmodern generation." Excited by the realization that he was "not alone" and that practical solutions were available, Jeremy began implementing Emerging ideas about postmodern witnessing at his congregation. For example, in response to the dual assertion among Emerging authors that Evangelicals need to recover elements from pre-Reformation Christianity and that the postmodern generation prefers multisensory learning (Webber 1999), he used material forms of historic Christian iconography during youth worship services. Every change he proposed or attempted was met with sharp "resistance" from the senior pastor and the elder board. He eventually resigned—willingly, though not without pressure from the other staff. After six to eight months of praying for direction, Jeremy and eleven others planted a church in downtown Lansing, where the working-class culture of a GM-dependent economy sharply contrasted with its university-centered neighbor. Their church plant materialized in 2005 and, as of 2010, they maintained a weekly worship attendance of fifty people and three "neighborhood groups."

The following transcript is the close of my second interview with Jeremy. It begins just after he read the Shults and MacArthur quotes:

JEREMY: [Laughs] I mean, I would definitely sympathize with the first one more.

JAMES: And, again, the point is not to pigeonhole you into one or the other. It's just to get your reaction.

JEREMY: Right. Um, I choose (a) [Shults].

JAMES: [Laughs]

JEREMY: I will say, though, that there is a danger in making hermeneutics a professionalized thing that lay people can't do. I want people to feel confident in their ability to hear from God through the scriptures without me being there to tell them. In that sense, I sympathize with (b) [MacArthur] to some extent as well.

JAMES: What's wrong with (b) otherwise?

JEREMY: Um, it's anti-intellectual. [Laughs]

JAMES: [Laughs]

JEREMY: And, far too simplistic.

[FIVE-SECOND PAUSE]

JEREMY: Okay. The statement, "You use the normal sense of language," is pretty limiting. You know, I think the normal sense is the most important sense. But, there are, historically there's been a lot of talk about the different senses and the different layers of meaning. So, scripture is so obviously polyvalent, that to say there's one sense and you use that sense. And, it's just, you know, the test is, it'll fail the test of, you know, my sense and your sense are going to be different senses. There's no way that we can adjudicate that. And, it'll fail that test every day of the week. So, yeah.

JAMES: So, anything about (a) that's particularly disturbing?

[SIX-SECOND PAUSE]

JEREMY: No, I think I agree with it 100 percent. [Laughs] I mean, if this statement were taken to mean that we couldn't know God through language or that God couldn't communicate to us through scripture, then I would definitely see that as a dangerous idea. But, I don't hear him as saying that at all. I hear, his critique is of the fixation, not propositions. But, the fixation of propositions. And, I agree. I mean, you know, as a, in terms of like my craft of preaching. I see how that plays out, and how the fixation on propositions leads to really bad sermons a lot of the time. You know, people latch on to what they think the idea being communicated is, rip it out of context, or totally misinterpret it, and just preach a horrible sermon. But, they're, you know, stridently confident about it being the Word of God. So, I'm definitely in camp (a).

Jack was thirty-four years old and had been in the Lansing area for less than two years. He began his ministry career as an army chaplain before changing to congregational ministry. He considers himself a "three streams Christian: high sacramental, high evangelical, high charismatic." He has been conversant with the Emerging movement since 2002, when he began reading books and blogs on theology and worship. The following is Jack's response to the Shults and MacArthur quotes:

> JACK: I would lean toward (a). As far as, and I really like this "truly infinite God of Christian faith is beyond all of our linguistic grasping and the struggle to capture God in our finite propositional structures is nothing short of linguistic idolatry." So, I don't know where this puts me in the pail.
>
> JAMES: I can tell you where it comes from if you want.
>
> JACK: Yeah, sure.
>
> JAMES: After you finish. [Laughs]
>
> JACK: Okay. So, for me, and I don't think it's, I'm not trying to say there's some kind of hidden meaning in the scriptures, Bible code or anything like that or otherwise, but I think that we do a disservice in trying to put such firm definitions to an infinite God with our little vocabulary. I think we're always doing violence to the scriptures in preaching. We're giving people a glimpse. And, I try to explain that every so often when it comes up. We're giving you a glimpse into the eternal, into the holy, and I'm doing it the best that I know how with the vocabulary that we have on this earth. But, we're not going to fully understand the bigness of God with the smallness of our vocab. And, so I gravitate toward that, as far as that's the way I approach it. But, I would also say that I did like "it's not brain surgery," as far as this is the Bible. I have a hard time with the hidden meanings and all this other stuff. Where, you know, Jesus was very clear about us being sheep. I think the imagery there is pretty clear, is we're not that clever. We're not that smart, though we think we are. And, really, that's kind of a blow to our ego, when it's really not the smartest animal that ever lived. And, that's who Jesus compared us to. It's not brain

surgery, nor should it be, especially given the fact that we are so easily led astray. And, like I said, not the smartest animals ever in the kingdom. But, we act like there's a lot of hidden meaning in the scripture and that's the thing. I think it had to be plain as day because of our propensity to be so easily led astray.

JAMES: So, would you say there's any danger in (a)?

JACK: Oh sure. Oh, there's definitely danger in (a), because I think you can also take that to its logical end where, you know, none of these words make sense. That makes me a little uncomfortable. You know, we're constantly redefining what a Christian is or what salvation is, because these are very flexible kind of terms. So, I can see the danger coming from it in that way.

Jeremy and Jack lend much support to the possibility that Emerging Evangelicals operate with a different language ideology than conservative Protestants. Their only hesitancy in completely eschewing MacArthur is that they appreciate the sentiment that biblical hermeneutics is "not brain surgery" because it keeps scriptural interpretation from being the sole purview of elite theologians (historically, an exemplary Protestant notion). Otherwise, they have little patience for MacArthur's simplifications and they celebrate Shults's posture toward the theological limits of language.

Alongside commodification, this language ideology helps explain why irony is an appealing resource for Emerging Evangelicals. This affinity aligns with what historians of irony have said. For example, Behler (1990) writes: "It is precisely here, at the breaching of the limits of communication, that postmodern thinking and writing begin to operate through circumlocution, indirectness, configuration, and ironic communication" (36). And, "The ironic manner of expression can be described as attempting to transcend the restrictions of normal discourse and straightforward speech by making the ineffable articulate, at least indirectly, through a great number of verbal strategies, and accepting what lies beyond the reach of direct communication" (111). Similarly, Colebrook (2004) writes: "Those who feel that they simply know the ultimate truths of life have forgotten or repressed their own location and position within life. Instead of a style of speech that simply asserts the truth . . . irony emphasizes the processes of dialogue, thinking, and expression from which truths are given" (112). In short, for those who do not accept language's ability to directly, clearly, unambiguously, or unproblematically communicate, irony becomes a treasure.

Taking Irony Seriously

We have examined two reasons that feed Emerging Evangelicals' anxiety of mediation and complicate their search for authenticity: the inescapable, deadening effect of commodification and a language ideology that emphasizes the limits of communication. We turn now to the consequence of this anxiety of mediation: taking irony seriously. Doug Pagitt's use of *Mr. Deity* was one example, and we consider several others below. The first comes from an Emerging Evangelical working in the Protestant Mainline.

Irony as Introspection

Ed moved to Cincinnati in December 2008 with his wife and three kids. Actually, they moved to Wyoming, an affluent neighborhood twelve miles north of the city's downtown and directly south of its northern exurbs. Previously a Presbyterian Church-USA pastor in South Dakota, Ed accepted the senior pastorship at a PC-USA congregation in Wyoming with a stable membership of about four hundred people.

Ed grew up in Colorado and converted to Evangelical Christianity in 1990 through a PC-USA church near the University of Colorado that was "culturally and theologically Evangelical." He attended Princeton Theological Seminary, where he met his wife Amy, herself a seminary-trained, ordained hospital chaplain. At Princeton Ed was challenged, "and not in a good way," by theological issues such as source criticism in Old Testament hermeneutics. The conservative Evangelicalism he was socialized into did not mesh well with this seminary training. It also did not mesh with his experience as a hospital chaplain intern. He realized in those "death and dying" situations that the "catch phrases" he had learned (for example, "God works everything out in the end") sounded empty when he offered them as comfort. Ed summarized his period of deconversion in our first interview: "I knew what I believed, and it did not quite work." Much like Ford and Ben whom we met in the previous chapter, Ed's deconversion coincided with his reading of Brian McLaren's *A New Kind of Christian* (2001). McLaren, and other Emerging Church authors, helped Ed straddle the two worlds of Evangelicalism and Mainline Protestantism.

A major influence that the Emerging Church has had on Ed is a "willingness to engage culture," by which he means a willingness to use non-Christian cultural productions for Christian purposes. This is a bedrock quality of taking irony seriously because it does not require that cultural resources be used in a single, literal fashion. He cites different forms of media as a concrete way of doing this and describes it as "seeing what traces of God are out there." The premier example in Ed's ministry career of using media in this way is a small group series he and Amy led together in South Dakota: "Theology @ the Movies." 〔handwritten text〕

The series' premise was fairly straightforward: watch a popular movie as a group and talk about its theological implications, assumptions, and representations of Christianity. Ed developed study guides for twenty movies, ranging in genre from documentaries (*Bowling for Columbine*) to the unflaggingly serious (*Hotel Rwanda*), comedic (*Bruce Almighty*), fantastic (*Gattaca*), and romantic (*Chocolat*). Ed described two of the movies they chose as particularly challenging for the group: *Dogma* (1999) and *Saved!* (2004). Both are ironic parodies of conservative Christian subcultures, one Catholic *(Dogma)* and one Evangelical *(Saved!)*, and Ed's use of them is an exemplary case of taking irony seriously as a practice of faith.

I asked Ed why they chose these two movies: "We had gotten to a point that Amy and I felt the group was ready to be stretched a bit. We felt both of these movies raised some excellent questions/thoughts/ideas and presented a picture of faith that we felt very challenged by when we first saw them." I asked Ed to elaborate on both parts of his answer:

> We wanted to push them to look critically at their own faith. Quite often we become so insulated by our own circumstances that we might not realize or think a great deal about how the rest of the world beyond those circles experiences us. For *Dogma*, the questions raised [on the study guide] were around how much the church is or is not willing to change in order to speak the Gospel in a connecting way in the present day. This was particularly evident in the depiction of the Buddy Christ. Some of the imagery used, especially that of God being presented as a female. Also, questions of how the story [Bible] came to be written and what was left in and what was left out. And, some of the specific conversations between characters really show a significant wrestling with matters of faith. With *Saved!* the big question I was pushed by was authenticity in faith. We can portray one thing on the outside, but on the inside be vastly different. We can say we're all about love and grace and forgiveness, but when one commits the "unforgiveable sin," in the case of the movie the one girl getting pregnant, then they are cast out.

아이러니 라기 기둥끔까는 역할이지만
이 영화들을 통해 기둥들이 대해 meaningful 같은 Questions
들을 물어 보는기라가 됨.

In Ed's explanation irony functions as a tool of introspection. Both films are sardonic, unapologetic, and unmerciful in their send-up of Christianity. Yet Ed finds in them a productive way to ask himself, and his congregants, to think seriously about their religious identity and how popular culture represents Christianity. The ironic idiom of the two films is precisely what makes them attractive, irrespective of other, less redeeming qualities (for example, frequent profanity and gratuitous violence).

Ed singles out "the Buddy Christ" in *Dogma* as an example. This figure first appears in the film during a press conference scene. A New Jersey cardinal, played by George Carlin (a recognized ironist extraordinaire in late modern America), is unveiling the first of many symbols as part of his "Catholicism Wow!" campaign:

> Thank you, thank you. Now we all know how the majority and the media in this country view the Catholic Church. They think of us as a passe, archaic institution. People find the Bible obtuse, even hokey. Now, in an effort to disprove all that, the Church has appointed this year as a time of renewal, both of faith and of style. For example, the crucifix [Carlin motions toward a waist-high, copper-looking Christ nailed to the cross]. While it has been a time-honored symbol of our faith, Holy Mother Church has decided to retire this highly recognizable, yet wholly depressing image of our Lord crucified. Christ didn't come to earth to give us the willies. He came to help us out. He was a booster. And, it's with that take on our Lord in mind that we've come up with a new, more inspiring sigil. So, it's with great pleasure that I present you with the first of many revamps the Catholicism Wow! campaign will unveil over the next year. I give you the Buddy Christ! (Smith 1996)

십자가는 원래
의미없이 왜비
재미 시각의
이미지
10여개위에서

Two priests pull a red cover off a life-sized, brightly colored Jesus: beaming a Colgate-grin, looking very plastic, winking, with one hand pointing its index finger and the other flashing a thumbs-up. In the movie plot, as Ed indicates in his explanation, the symbol is intended as a gesture of relevance for "the present day." The Buddy Jesus image is blatant mockery, but the impulse it mocks is central to the Emerging movement. Recall that this was a founding purpose for Young Leaders Network in 1995: how to connect Evangelicalism to "postmodern generations." Ed uses *Dogma's* ultraironic displays to engage a hotly debated question among Evangelicals.

The Buddy Jesus, in all its ironic glory, has become something of a calling card among Emerging Evangelicals. One is apt to find desk-sized ver-

이같은 것들이 마티 핀박다고
Emerging Evangelicals
들이 사회들. 좋나 바쁘 통 북유
북나 바라에서 서권 하나 것임 -

sions of it alongside more earnest religious artifacts in homes and offices. Jack, the Anglican priest we met earlier, proudly keeps one fixed on his office desk at home. It was the first thing he showed me when we met there for an interview.

Ed and Amy have yet to restart Theology @ the Movies at their church in Wyoming. For them, it is a more risky small group curriculum than conventional Bible studies. They wanted to spend their first year learning "the culture" of the congregation (an extremely common trope in discourses of "being missional"). But they both assured me that they planned to start the series as soon as they felt comfortable.

Irony as Self-Deprecation

Emerging Evangelicals also take irony seriously by making a joke of it. The butt of the joke is sometimes conservative Evangelicalism, and in these cases the joke performs the cultural critique that organizes the movement. Other times, the butt is the Emerging Church movement, poking fun at themselves and performing a self-conscious religiosity. Still other times, the butt is both. Consider two examples of this latter case.

In December 2007 the online "webzine" *The Jesus Manifesto* published an article, "First Ever 'Emerging' Amish Church." The author, Mark Van Steenwyk, is the general editor of the site and a founding member of an Anabaptist intentional community in Minneapolis, Minnesota. The article satirizes both the cultural quirks of Emerging churches and the typical criticisms leveled against the movement by conservative Evangelicals. The article's dominating picture, an overly serious looking young Amish man clutching an electric guitar on a soundstage, hints at what is to come. The following are three excerpts from the article's text that continue the ironic play:

- "The church, calling itself 'Solomon's Barn' blends cutting edge worship with Amish sensibilities." Doug Pagitt's church in Minneapolis, considered one of the earliest self-consciously Emerging churches, is called Solomon's Porch (a reference to Acts 5:12–13).
- Quoting the fictional pastor about his sources of inspiration, "I mean, there I was, settling with 'church as usual' when I stumbled upon the writings of Brian McLaren. I felt like his words were coming right from my own head, you know? I realized that I was a postmodern Amish person. . . . I needed to reject premodernism for a more authentic faith." The

"you know" moment when reading McLaren is an oft-cited experience in the deconversion narratives of Emerging Evangelicals (recall Ed, Ford, and Ben from earlier). "Premodernism" is the Amish substitute for Evangelical modernism and "authentic" is deployed as cliché.

- "Not everyone is happy with these changes. Hiram Grebel—a local Amish Bishop—believes that this new 'emerging' church is coming close to heresy: 'This is just a neo-English cult.'" The fictional Grebel represents the voice of conservative Evangelical gatekeepers who publicly denounce the Emerging movement.

Examples abound in the brief article (less than four hundred words), but they all reiterate the same balance of self-deprecation and cultural critique. The symbolic use of the Amish is significant in and of itself. On the one hand, Anabaptist communities are often hailed in Emerging discourses as Christian communities who have maintained an authentic faith in spite of the late modern cultural conditions of constant consumerism and commodification. On the other hand, by separating from mainstream American society Anabaptist communities defy the Evangelical logic of witnessing and the Emerging logic of being missional. "The Amish" become the perfect ironic vehicle for double-edged satire.

In January 2010 an Emerging Evangelical blogger posted a text, "The Emerging Church: a controversial movement inspiring many the past 10 years, dies at 21," which was reprinted in the January 2010 edition of the Emerging Church "e-zine" Next-Wave: Church and Culture. The author, Rick Bennett, is a former church planter. Consider three excerpts from the blog post cum article:

- "The Emerging Church, the controversial Christian movement that inspired many to plant churches, leave behind their faith and question authority, died in her sleep Thursday following a short illness. She was 21 (according to some sources)." The closing parenthetical indexes the ambiguity of the movement's beginnings.
- "Mrs. Church was instrumental in the advent of many advances in the Christian church, including facial hair, tattoos, fair trade coffee, candles, couches in sanctuaries, distortion pedals, Rated R movie discussions, clove cigarettes and cigars, beer and use of Macs, as well as the advancement of women's issues, conversations about sexuality, environmentalism, anti-foundationalism, social justice and the demise of the Republican party's stranglehold on young Christians." The use of "Mrs." references

the divisive role of gender (for example, female ordination and inclusive biblical translations) among contemporary Evangelicals. The laundry list of "advances" covers the range of aesthetic, discursive, and political stereotypes associated with Emerging Evangelicals.

- "She is survived by her parents, the Seeker Church, and Sojourners; her paternal grandmother, the former Deconstructionism, now Postmodernity; her maternal grandmother, French Nihilism and her paternal great-grandparents, the Social Gospel and Fundamentalism." This list of surviving kin (which goes on further, naming other institutions and individuals) calls attention to the same kind of genealogy we traced in this book's Introduction, in particular its confluence of seemingly opposing sources (for example, "Social Gospel and Fundamentalism").

Bennett's satirical obituary occurred as a direct response to a discursive flurry on the Internet beginning in 2008 that proclaimed the end, or at least the beginning of the end, of the Emerging movement. These proclamations came from both critics and movement insiders. Critics suggested the movement never was more than a fad and those initially attracted to it had grown tired. Advocates suggested the movement was never meant to be an institutional establishment, had served its purpose, and those influenced by it were ready to start their own kinds of institutions. Bennett, much like Van Steenwyk, is an equal opportunity ironist: riffing simultaneously on the cultural signifiers of Emerging and conservative Evangelicals.

These two examples illustrate how Emerging Evangelicals use irony as a means of self-deprecation. They do not, however, just poke fun at an imagined Self. The net they cast includes an imagined Other, namely, conservative Evangelical critics. As with Ed and Amy's introspective use of Theology @ the Movies, irony as self-deprecation is used to engage self-conscious struggles of religious identity.

Taking Irony Too Far?

The Emerging Evangelical practice of taking irony seriously is not always well-received, roundly appreciated, or inexhaustible. Conservative Evangelicals find this reliance on irony infuriating. It is interpreted as a smokescreen for theological waffling and a lack of spiritual reverence.

John Piper pastors a megachurch in Minneapolis, Minnesota, and is a popular author and orator among conservative Protestants. Since 1988 Piper has hosted an annual conference at his church, "Desiring God," which routinely attracts several hundred pastors from around the country for a long weekend of speeches, seminars, prayer, and conversation. For his keynote address at the 2006 conference Piper spoke about a biography he had read, and loved, on the life of William Tyndale—the English Reformer who was burned alive for producing and circulating vernacular scripture. Roughly halfway through the eighty-minute speech Piper reached a crescendo in comparing Tyndale with his two most famous Catholic opponents, Erasmus and Thomas More. When he concluded Piper was interrupted by applause from his audience, the only such occasion in the talk:

They were elitists. They were nuanced. Their language had layers of subtlety. They were entrapped in kinds of church tradition. Erasmus and Thomas More satirized the monasteries. But, they were playing games. It had the ring of gamesmanship about it. I am SO familiar with this from conferences to which I have gone, or academic societies where I have visited, or lectures I have listened to on the Internet, or sat under. And you get the distinct impression when this Ph.D. is talking, IS THERE ANY BLOOD ON HIS HANDS? IS THERE ANYTHING THERE? DOES HE REALIZE WHAT HELL IS? Can there be any reality between that tone, between that gamesmanship of language, that nuancing and layering and that lack of corners, that ambiguity, that FOG? [Brief pause] Today, there are notable Christian writers, when you read them, sound just like Erasmus. They write for the Emergent Church. . .with its slithering language. . . . It is ironic and sad today that supposedly avant-garde Christian writers can strike this cool, evasive, imprecise, artistic, superficially Reformist pose of Erasmus and call it "postmodern," and capture a generation of unwitting, historically-naïve, Emergent people who don't KNOW that they are being duped by the same old verbal tactics of elitist humanist ambiguity. . . . It is NOT postmodern. It is PREmodern because it is PERPETUAL. And the only people who don't know that are people who don't know HISTORY.

Piper's objection to irony begins with a critique of language. Indeed, his problem is precisely what makes irony attractive to people like Jeremy and Jack, who affirmed Shults's critique of linguistic clarity. For Piper, this is not just about language. Language indexes theology (or, in his critique, a lack thereof). In naming "Emergent" as the culprit, Piper is focusing on institutions like Emergent Village and individuals like Doug Pagitt.

We hear a different objection to overindulging irony from Charlie, an Emerging Evangelical in Cincinnati. He is not a pastor. He owns his own business as an athletic trainer. Charlie grew up Jewish and converted to Evangelicalism through a nondenominational church located in one of the city's northern neighborhoods. He described himself during our first one-on-one interview as "pretty banged up spiritually and emotionally" when he began attending a house church network in 2002. At first, this emphatically Emerging congregation fit what he desired from a spiritual community. But after three years, he grew tired. In particular, he tired of the kinds of interactions he had participated in and overheard on a daily basis, all laced with the characteristic irony of the Emerging Church. For Charlie, people in this house church stayed too focused "on who they are not." This created a "cycle of dysfunction" where people were "reliving the same hurts over and over again." The ironic discourse, itself a response to seeking authenticity, was for Charlie the very thing that ended up seeming inauthentic. He offered a poignant example, implicating himself in his critique. In 2007, a year after he left the house church, he reread the journals in which he used to make daily entries of spiritual reflection. He was "turned off" by the way his journals "repeated the same things" and sounded "fake." His journals reflected the ironic tone of which he had grown weary. He was so upset with this finding that he shredded the journals—literally, physically shredded them to pieces. Charlie may have experienced what the literary critic Will Kaufman, in his study of American comedians, called "irony fatigue" (1997). While initially attractive, irony can be tiresome. It can take its toll. One can dwell too long in the land of inversion. If not checked, irony fatigue produces "intolerably unfunny pessimists" (13, quoting Kurt Vonnegut). Did Charlie sense this in himself? Did he distance himself from the ironic discourse of Emerging Evangelicals to avoid the spiritual equivalent of Kaufman's disenchanted humorists?

Irony—as a resource, a backdrop, and a source of frustration—figures into the lives of Emerging Evangelicals. Their attraction to irony should not be surprising, given their status as late modern subjects. As they engage in forms of verbal and conceptual play, Emerging Evangelicals take irony seriously as a way to engage matters of faith. In particular, it allows them to self-consciously reflect on their sense of Christian self. Ultimately, irony is attractive to Emerging Evangelicals because of the troubles surrounding their pursuit of authenticity, namely, the anxiety of mediation associated with commodification and linguistic representation. Anxiety, however, is not the only relationship they cultivate with the process of mediating religious experience. In the next chapter we will see a different response to "the inescapability of material and social mediations" (Keane 2006: 321).

3

Ancient-Future I

Experiencing God

The December 2007 issue of *U.S. News and World Report*, one of a few widely circulated news periodicals reliably perched in grocery store check-out aisles, was entitled: "A Return to Ritual: why many modern worshipers, including Catholics, Jews, and evangelicals are embracing tradition." The cover photo hints at the story's contents: priests in formal, brightly adorned robes blessing a sacrament in front of an altar, complete with sacred texts and a white stone, winged angel (Figure 3.1). The article suggests that Jewish, Catholic, Protestant, and Muslim communities are increasingly attracted to older expressions of faith. To illustrate the Evangelical incarnation, the author takes us to a nondenominational church in Texas:

> The congregation of Trinity Fellowship Church participates in something that would have been considered almost heretical in most evangelical Protestant churches five or ten years ago: a weekly Communion service. An independent, nondenominational church of some 600 members, Trinity Fellowship is not the only evangelical congregation . . . doing [things] that seem downright Roman Catholic or at least high Episcopalian.

Two months after the *U.S. News* release, the feature story for *Christianity Today* was: "Lost Secrets of the Ancient Church: how Evangelicals started looking back to move forward." The cover photo differs from its secular counterpart (Figure 3.2). A shovel is implanted in sand, signifying a completed excavation. A gold, Eastern Orthodox cross is mostly dug out of the sand. And a Centauresque excavator kneels by the cross: the body of an I-Pod, the head of a twenty-something white male. The article reports various ways in which Evangelical communities are "embracing tradition." It begins with a montage of scenes from the 2007 Wheaton Theology Conference, "The Ancient Faith for the Church's Future":

They joined their voices to sing of "the saints who nobly fought of old" and "mystic communion with those whose rest is won." A speaker walked an attentive crowd through prayers from the 5th-century Gelasian Sacramentary, recommending its forms as templates for worship in today's Protestant churches. Another speaker highlighted the pastoral strengths of the medieval fourfold hermeneutic. Yet another gleefully passed on the news that Liberty University had observed the liturgical season of Lent. The *t*-word—that old Protestant nemesis, *tradition*—echoed through the halls. Just what was going on in this veritable shrine to pragmatic evangelistic methods and no-nonsense, back-to-the-Bible Protestant conservatism? Had Catholics taken over? (italics in original)

The shared reference to Catholicism in both articles—*U.S. News*'s "almost heretical" nod and *Christianity Today*'s somewhat earnest, somewhat rhetorical take-over inquiry—is revealing. These two reports suggest that Evangelicals are worshiping God in ways that seem patently non-Evangelical. A partial list of such worship activities from my ethnographic fieldwork includes: heightened emphasis on public creedal recitation, public reading of monastic and Catholic prayers, burning incense, replacing fluorescent lighting with candles, setting early Protestant hymns to contemporary music, chanting Eastern Orthodox prayers, using icons, creating prayer labyrinths, following the church calendar for sermons and lectionary readings, using *lectio divina* to read the Bible, and increasing the role of silence. What do we make of all this?

We begin with these two mass-produced moments to establish that by 2008 "ancient-future" had entered the Evangelical mainstream. It was no longer merely an ideal promoted by scattered theologians, such as Robert Webber, but had become a widespread phenomenon that legitimated front page news. We observed earlier that ancient-future is an integral part of the Emerging movement's genealogy, and in this chapter we examine the cultural work performed around this trope with respect to an enduring question that confronts all Christians and Christianities: what is the best way to experience God? For Emerging Evangelicals, ancient-future performances tell us a great deal about the intersection of religious experience, mediation, and late modernity.

Presence and Mediation in Evangelical Subject Formation

In the previous chapter we considered one response to the anxiety of mediation: the strategic use of irony. Ancient-future worship demonstrates a different response: the strategic use of varied semiotic channels for religious expe-

Treating Depression • Iraq Status Report

U.S.News
& WORLD REPORT

DECEMBER 24, 2007

A Return to
Ritual

Why many modern
worshipers, including
Catholics, Jews,
and evangelicals,
are embracing
tradition

www.usnews.com

Figure 3.1. *U.S. News and World Report* cover, December 2007.

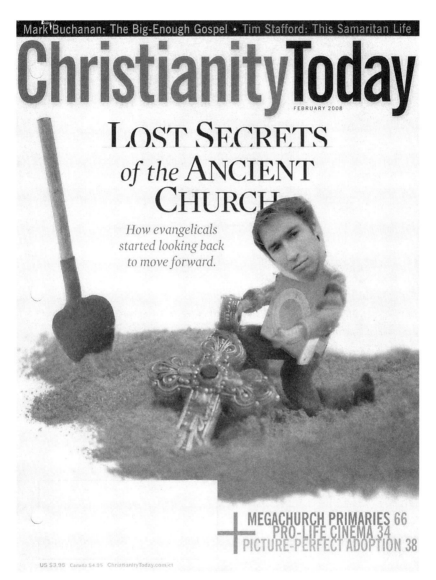

Figure 3.2. *Christianity Today* cover, February 2008.

rience. This phenomenon—"embracing tradition" and remembering "lost secrets of the ancient church"—is one means by which Emerging Evangelicals are formed as religious subjects. Adherents do not arrive on the scene of their faith as fully developed practitioners. They must learn how to participate as competent members. Two anthropological examples help clarify this quality of religious subjectivity. Saba Mahmood (2005) describes how female Muslims in Cairo's Islamic Revival organize their theological pedagogy, and how they learn to embody their ideologies. She illustrates how, in contrast to Western assumptions about personhood and agency where beliefs produce action, these women create interior states of faith through exterior rituals. For example, they learn to heighten their religious commitment through forms of intellectual and bodily discipline. Tanya Luhrmann (2010), shifting from the urban Middle East to suburban America, describes how charismatic Christians learn to be, and to recognize, successful "pray-ers." She argues that religious experience entails elements of practiced proclivity. For her consultants, "hearing God" is reflected in "how hard religious practitioners work, how they labor to develop specific skills and ways of being" (67). Studies like these prompt us to ask what kinds of religious subjects are formed by specific kinds of ritual practice.

Through ancient-future worship Emerging Evangelicals learn an answer to the enduring question of how best to experience God. In his celebrated ethnography Matthew Engelke (2007) frames this question as "the problem of presence . . . how a religious subject defines and claims to construct a relationship with the divine through the investment of authority and meaning in certain words, actions, and objects" (9). Christians always seek to interact with their God, but they are apt to pose different solutions to this problem across cultural contexts. The space of deciding what does and does not foster a connection with the divine is not just theological, it is ethnographic. As Engelke (2010) discusses elsewhere, this requires an inquiry into the role of mediation in religious life, the material and immaterial channels by which experience becomes possible and meaningful.

The supposed rap on Evangelicals is that, as religionists of the Word, they encounter God through reading, teaching, praying, listening, and otherwise engaging their sacred texts. And there is ample evidence that they do this in everyday and ritual contexts (Bielo 2009). The emphasis on text and language, following Calvin more than any other prominent European Reformer, reflects a Protestant theological tradition that opposes materiality (Keane 2007: 67). However, in practice, the notion that Evangelicals are a-, non-, or anti-material in their religious life is quite wrong. Colleen McDannell (1995) illustrated how Christians of various theological stripes incorporate religious artifacts into their everyday lives: family Bibles, art displayed in domestic space, bumper stickers, kitschy clothes, and miscellaneous accoutrement. Simon Coleman (1996), in his ethnographic work with Prosperity-oriented charismatics, demonstrated how the body, the physical environment, and mass media are all used as sites for objectifying language and experience. Grey Gundaker (2000) showed how scriptural texts are materially recontextualized in her account of African American yard displays in the U.S. South. When studied empirically, it turns out that Protestants are apt to meaningfully incorporate material items in their efforts to experience the presence of God.

Materiality is but one channel that mediates religious experience. The human sensorium is another. Engelke (2010) notes that the respective senses rarely receive equal treatment in this regard: "sensual hierarchies often discipline and direct the religious subject" (376). How have Evangelicals ranked and meted out smell, taste, touch, sight, and sound? Leigh Eric Schmidt's wonderful history—*Hearing Things: Religion, Illusion, and the American Enlightenment* (2000)—provides an answer. For Schmidt the senses, like God's presence more generally, pose an enduring problem: "Christian devotion has always been deeply bound up with the refusal and deflection of the senses, whether plugging the ears, averting the eyes, or avoiding the touch, constantly negotiating the temptations of the body through the body" (viii). His specific interest is "the pitched battle over modern hearing" (6) and his base argument is that sight became "the dominant sense of modernity" (16). The triumph of vision was primarily a matter of knowledge and reason: "seeing (and only seeing) is believing" (28); a picture is worth a thousand words; eye witnesses send you to jail the fastest; and smell, taste, and touch were too subjective, too ineffable, and too unruly to organize religious devotion. The stratification of vision and hearing put Evangelicals in a bind. At least since the Reformation, hearing had unequivocal value: "Martin Luther famously declared: 'God no longer requires the feet or the hands or any other member; He requires only the ears. . . The ears alone are the organs of a Christian'" (13). While sermons, prayers, confessions, creeds, songs, revivals, and scripture reading kept Protestantism a very talky religion, sound was also the primary source of deception and spiritual confusion. As a result, twentieth-century Evangelicals toned down their public expressions, lest they be confused with loud and rowdy Pentecostals (Wacker 2001).

Emerging Evangelicals, through ancient-future worship, rethink the role of both materiality and the senses in religious experience. Ancient-future practices encourage them to use both these forms of mediation in ways, as

U.S. News and *Christianity Today* predict, we might not expect from Evangelical worship. Many of my consultants made materiality central in their attempts to feel God's presence, and they disrupt modernity's sensorial hierarchy that downplays all but sight.

Thinplaces

In chapter 1 we met Lilly. Her deconversion was primarily about worship. Having spent most of her life in conservative Evangelical churches, including years as a youth and worship pastor, she was clear and organized in her critique of how Evangelicals imagine and conduct worship. Lilly was equally opposed to overemphasizing the spoken sermon, deemphasizing structured liturgy, stripping down the aesthetics of worship spaces, reducing "worship" to music, disembodying and dematerializing theology, and cluttering worship with too much noise and too little silence for contemplation.

Beginning in 2008, Lilly organized a loosely knit community of ancient-future worshipers in Cincinnati. She called the group "Thinplace," borrowing a Celtic Christian term. Thin places originally referred to physical spaces on the earth where God's presence could be most readily felt (where, as it were, the line between heaven and earth was thinnest). Lilly's reinvention redirects the pursuit from one of pilgrimage to one of creation, where any place can be made Thin. During my fieldwork, Thinplace consisted of three regular events: a biweekly "Artwalk," a weekly journaling group, and a monthly "Maproom." For Lilly, the focus of all three events is "experiencing God." She would be the first to tell you that other things happen at Thinplace; for example, the implicit and explicit reproduction of theology. However, these are always downplayed in favor of, and only happen within the broader frame of, what it means to be in the presence of God.

Artwalk

The Cincinnati Art Museum is quite venerable among its American kin. It opened in 1881 ("the Met" in New York City, by comparison, opened just eleven years earlier), and the current building is for the most part the original one. It is located in Mt. Adams, an affluent residential-commercial neighborhood set on a substantial hill overlooking the city's downtown. The art museum is about halfway up Mt. Adams's northwestern slope. A wrong turn, like the one I made on my first visit to the Art Museum for Thinplace, takes you into Over-the-Rhine, the city's most reviled neighborhood for poverty, violent crime, and a general disparity between despair and hope. My wrong turn happened just before 11:15 a.m., when Artwalk was scheduled to begin. I phoned Lilly, but she is a "landmark" driver and could not orient me using street signs alone. Sans a GPS or city map in the car (an ethnographic blunder), I stopped at a gas station. The cashier accepted payments and answered questions from behind a locked door and bullet-proof glass barrier. On my way to ask for directions, a middle-aged African American man approached me. His body looked frail and slight. Before he could ask me for money (as he had just done with another customer), I asked if he could direct me to the art museum. His directions were impeccable.

It was Saturday, June 20, 2009. The sky was clear blue. The sun was warm, but not stifling. I arrived five minutes late, which proved not to be a problem. Lilly was outside, waiting on the large, ornate entrance stairwell for myself and other tardy Thinplace members. Since 2003 the museum has been free to the public, so the only expenditure was a four dollar parking fee. By 11:30 everyone had assembled in the museum lobby. There were six others besides Lilly and myself (two men, four women), a smaller-than-average Artwalk group.

Lilly began the event with a brief preamble. She welcomed everyone, noting this was the first Artwalk for several of us present. Her introduction had four points. She emphasized that God is the "ultimate creator" and that "all good things," including "all the art in the museum," are part of "His creation." She emphasized that Artwalk is a way to "spend time with God" through his creations, and to "allow the Holy Spirit to teach us." She added that Protestants are not accustomed to using images in this way. She highlighted "the Reformation" as the main culprit in divesting art from worship. One of the women, a Missouri-Synod congregant from northern Kentucky, offered the slight correction that this was less true for Lutherans than other Reformed traditions. This did not phase Lilly much; she acknowledged the comment, but did not accept or reject it. Lastly, she described the Artwalk process: we would "find a corner," read a chosen text of scripture, spend an hour walking the museum alone, journal our thoughts ("there is no right or wrong way, just journal"), then meet for lunch and "share what the Holy Spirit taught us."

The corner they normally use for reading and prayer is in the lobby, but it was occupied by a tourist group. We found a circle of chairs in a different room. Once we sat down Lilly explained how biblical texts are read at Artwalk. They used *lectio divina*, or "divine listening," a monastic method of reading. She stressed the monastic origins of *lectio*, juxtaposing it to "modern" ways of reading that prioritize comprehension. Three different individuals would read the text in turn. For the first reading she instructed us to listen for "a word or a phrase" that "jumps out at you." On the second reading we were to listen for "an idea or a feeling" provoked by the text. And on the third reading we were to listen for "an action." Lilly emphasized that *lectio* is meant to be "a process," not a singular act of absorbing what is read. The text, Matthew 6:19–24, was printed on a sheet of white paper and distributed to everyone:

> Do not store up for yourselves treasures on earth, where moth and rust destroy, and where thieves break in and steal. But store up for yourselves treasures in heaven, where moth and rust do not destroy, and where thieves do not break in and steal. For where your treasure is, there your heart will be also. The eye is the lamp of the body. If your eyes are good, your whole body will be full of light. But if your eyes are bad, your whole body will be full of darkness. If then the light within you is darkness, how great is that darkness! No one can serve two masters. Either he will hate the one and love the other, or he will be devoted to the one and despise the other. You cannot serve both God and Money.

Lilly noted, almost apologetically, that this was not the lectionary verse for the day. She usually followed the lectionary calendar reading for Artwalk, but that day's text was "too hellfire and brimstone." As Lilly explained this, two potters worked a potter's wheel in the opposite corner of the room. They were museum employees, busy making small artifacts and demonstrating techniques for the passing crowd. Lilly remarked, in a regretful tone, that if she had known the potters were going to be there she would have selected a text related to pottery.

Prior to the first reading Lilly asked us to "sit for a moment in silence." Not quite a minute passed before the first reader began. After a six-second pause, the second reader began. Five seconds, then the final reading. Following the last reader Lilly added, "The Word of the Lord," and several others added in unison, "Thanks be to God." We ended at noon and all eight of us departed, everyone going in a different direction.

During the hour I made my way steadily through the museum. I saw almost everyone else at least once, all still on their own. There were small, silent recognitions that we were there together, but the journaling-walking hour was definitely a private experience.

We rejoined for lunch at the on-site restaurant promptly at 1 p.m. There was very little of the "sharing" Lilly had described during her preamble. Talk was directed toward the food, the art, the museum, and Cincinnati. Lilly tried several times to ask people what they had journaled about, but never with much success. When she asked me how my first Artwalk had been, I said it was enjoyable, but there was an irony to reading a biblical text about not storing up treasures, then walking around a museum filled with the kind of treasure the text seemed weary of. Others agreed; they had also entertained this thought. Lilly did as well, but added "another way to look at it": these treasures are God's creations and provide a means to connect with God, express our thoughts, and clue "nonbelievers" into "God's glory." The others immediately nodded. A man in his early thirties, a house church member who had known Lilly for several years, recalled a quote from St. Augustine that he thought might resolve this tension: "even in sin God redeemeth." The others affirmed his sentiment. We continued eating, talking, making little mention of the hour we had spent walking, and left for our separate destinations at 2 p.m.

The Journaling Group

The Sunday before my first Artwalk was my first Thinplace journaling group. We met in Norwood, five miles north of the art museum, at the 1801 Building (the site of this book's opening vignette). The journaling group was the most consistent Thinplace event, meeting every Sunday night for two hours. It was also a highly fluid group, with between eight and twelve people present on any given Sunday. Thirteen different people attended (eight women, five men, mostly white), a half dozen of whom attended regularly. All were between twenty and fifty-five years old. There were five people there, including Lilly, on my first night observing the group. A twenty-one-year old woman, a junior at the University of Cincinnati, introduced herself to me as a pupil of Lilly's. She would leave a few days later for a six-week anti–human trafficking campaign in Thailand. She was a member of the Vineyard Central (VC) house church network. She joined because on her first visit to Sunday worship the pastor had closed his sermon by inviting questions—an invitation that was never extended in the conservative church in which she had matured. There were two men in their early thirties, also VC members. And there was Charlie, whom we met in the previous chapter. He had met Lilly when he was a VC member, and though he had not been part of the house church for several years, he regularly attended Thinplace events.

Two large windows let in the fading, late afternoon sunlight. Otherwise, the space was dimly lit by differently designed and scented candles spread throughout the room. We sat in a tight circle, some on chairs and couches and some on the floor. After everyone had introduced themselves, a gesture largely for my benefit, Lilly introduced the evening's readings, both from the day's lectionary. Psalm 20:

May the LORD answer you when you are in distress; may the name of the God of Jacob protect you.

May he send you help from the sanctuary and grant you support from Zion.

May he remember all your sacrifices and accept your burnt offerings.

May he give you the desire of your heart and make all your plans succeed.

We will shout for joy when you are victorious and will lift up our banners in the name of our God. May the LORD grant all your requests.

Now I know that the LORD saves his anointed; he answers him from his holy heaven with the saving power of his right hand.

Some trust in chariots and some in horses, but we trust in the name of the LORD our God.

They are brought to their knees and fall, but we rise up and stand firm.

O LORD, save the king! Answer us when we call!

And Mark 4:21–34:

He said to them, "Do you bring in a lamp to put it under a bowl or a bed? Instead, don't you put it on its stand? For whatever is hidden is meant to be disclosed, and whatever is concealed is meant to be brought out into the open. If anyone has ears to hear, let him hear." "Consider carefully what you hear," he continued. "With the measure you use, it will be measured to you—and even more. Whoever has will be given more; whoever does not have, even what he has will be taken from him." He also said, "This is what the kingdom of God is like. A man scatters seed on the ground. Night and day, whether he sleeps or gets up, the seed sprouts and grows, though he does not know how. All by itself the soil produces grain—first the stalk, then the head, then the full kernel in the head. As soon as the grain is ripe, he puts the sickle to it, because the harvest has come." Again he said, "What shall we say the kingdom of God is like, or what parable shall we use to describe it? It is like a mustard seed, which is the smallest seed you plant in the ground. Yet when planted, it grows and becomes the largest of all garden plants, with such big branches that the birds of the air can perch in its shade." With many similar parables Jesus spoke the word to them, as much as they could understand. He did not say anything to them without using a parable. But when he was alone with his own disciples, he explained everything.

As with Artwalk, we read in the same *lectio divina* style. (During the introductions there was some brief reflection on *lectio*. One of the men used an abbreviated deconversion narrative to introduce himself. He grew up in the Church of the Nazarene, a conservative Evangelical denomination, and described Nazarenes as "the kind of people who think *lectio divina* is heresy. They don't like anything that smacks of Catholicism." Lilly responded, more amused than exasperated: "It just means divine listening, and started because there was a shortage of Bibles in the monasteries. People don't like it because I'm not playing the role of telling people what to think; I'm letting the Holy Spirit teach.") After the third reading, Lilly instructed that we would have forty-five minutes to journal on our own, think about these texts, and "just be with God." After that, we would come back together and "share what God had taught us."

Lilly turned on a portable radio, from which soft, instrumental Celtic music played. Charlie and the other two men moved to a different room. Once they were settled, the music, overhead fan, and occasional scribbling of pens on paper were the only breaks in the silence. Lilly had laid out a cadre of art supplies (colored markers and pencils, scissors, colored construction paper), and the young woman made ample use of them. A couple of people consulted the surrounding books: pulling them off the shelves, reading briefly, and either returning them to their original place or leaving them on a nearby table. Most used well-worn journals to write in, seemingly devoted specifically to Thinplace events. Everyone was cognizant of the time, returning to the circle after forty-five minutes without any signaling from Lilly.

The discussion lasted forty-five minutes. This time frame was the same each evening I observed the journaling group, as was the discussion style and content. Seven things characterized their reading of scripture. (1) The frame was open-ended, with little in the way of an explicit agenda (for example, there was no list of study questions to answer). (2) Humor, often the type of irony-infused joking discussed in the previous chapter, was foregrounded. (3) Substantial attention was given to differences in translation, often prompting the same verse to be read from three or four different versions. (4) Participants were apt to dwell on the minutia of passages, frequently questioning why small details were included in the text or what motivated various biblical characters' speech and action. (5) While back-and-forth exchanges were common, it was extremely rare for individuals to debate questions of textual meaning, challenge the appropriateness of a textual application, or in any way criticize someone else's reading of the text. (6) The dominant hermeneutic method employed by the group was to establish the relevance of the text for personal, local, and global circumstances—a characteristic interpretive practice for Evangelicals (Bielo 2009). This was also true of the questions Lilly distributed to each participant for consideration while journaling. On the first night I observed the group there were four sets of questions, all geared toward personal application:

> How's your flavor as a follower of Jesus? Are you leaving a bitter taste or a good one when you encounter other people? What type of mustard is your life of faith? Spicy, regular, international like Grey Poupon?
>
> Often living out the kingdom of God involves process . . . it takes time, it takes work, you aren't always in control of what happens. How does that make you feel? What frustrates you the most about the planting process?
>
> What things would you like Jesus to explain to you in your life right now? Talk to him about this.
>
> Is there any light in your life that you are hiding right now? Any kingdom gifts that you have a problem sharing with others? Why?

(7) Lilly closed the meetings with a multisensory lesson. The first week I attended this lesson was designed to parallel the parable of the mustard seed (Mark 4:30–34). In the middle of our circle of chairs there was a small table with several items on it: a container of mustard seeds, an aluminum pan full of planting soil, three small plants, and four kinds of mustard (for example, Frenchs' brand yellow mustard and a pricier "stone ground" version). Lilly instructed us to place a few mustard seeds in our palms. We took one of the seeds, crushed it with our teeth, closed our eyes, and thought about its taste. We could then do one of three things with the remaining seeds: scatter them in the dirt and pray about what we wanted God to "grow in us"; take them home and pray about "what seeds we need to plant in our life"; or scatter them in the dirt, pick a leaf from the plant, and take it home to pray about "what God has already grown in our life." The multisensory exercise was always followed by a brief prayer, a few minutes of idle talk, and everyone's departure from 1801 Mills.

Maproom

The flyer advertising Maproom was printed on a single-sided, 8½ x 12 sheet of paper. There was always an image invoking some connotation of "ancient" faith: for example, an Early Middle Age painting of Madonna and Child (think of Duccio di Buoninsegna's thirteenth- and fourteenth-century art). The image was complemented with two sections of text. The main portion read:

> *Maproom* is an experiential worship gathering where you can spend five minutes or three hours.
>
> *Maproom* is a place where you engage God on your own . . . interacting with prayer stations set up around the room. Each station involves one or more of your senses.
>
> *Maproom* is a place to be still, and a place to create your prayers in art.
>
> Come experience worship beyond preaching and singing.

The brief secondary text read: "Maproom: An Open House for God . . . Experience God using all your senses." The details for date, time, and location were, of course, variable. The first and second Maprooms I attended were in January and February 2010. Both were held at a coffee shop (the same site of the Doug Pagitt book tour from the previous chapter). The pastor who owned the shop is a friend and ministry partner of Lilly's, and was pleased to offer it as the host for Maproom. Its size, and the fact that it was closed on Sundays, made it a good fit.

Unlike Artwalk and the journaling group, Maproom is a labor-intensive event for Lilly and requires a relatively large, rearrangable meeting space. She designed her first Maproom in Cincinnati in early 2005, and was able to make it a monthly event with the availability of this coffee shop. Like Artwalk and the journaling group, Maproom is open to the public, but is mainly attended by those in Lilly's Thinplace network. The instructions for Maproom are simple: come whenever you want, stay as long as you want, and leave whenever you want.

Every Maproom has a theme. In February 2010 the theme, aligning with the church calendar, was "Lenten Hobo Honeymoon." A take-home sheet available as you first entered described the theme:

> The title of our journey is "Lenten Hobo Honeymoon," inspired by a book by the same name by Edward Hays.
>
> What is a Hobo Honeymoon you may ask?
>
> A Hobo is a pilgrim working his/her way Home . . .
>
> A Honeymoon . . . it's a special time set aside exclusively for the one you love.
>
> So what if we actually take time to FALL in LOVE with JESUS during Lent . . . the days between now and Easter.
>
> Where could we be by Easter on our journey with God?

This theme was repeated iconically throughout fourteen prayer stations, with hiking boots, camping gear, bandanas, and heart-shaped items. Slow, soft, instrumental music played on overhead speakers as attendees proceeded through Maproom. The detailed and complex semiotic nature of the stations makes them a bad candidate for narrative portrayal. What follows is a photo essay, captioned with ethnographic interventions. You move through the stations as you would walk counter-clockwise around the room.

The opening station welcomes you to Maproom. It provides the organizing metaphors of hobos and honeymoons, as well as several symbols that repeat in later stations: boots, maps, hearts, walking sticks, and backpacks. The sheets of text also set a tone for the remaining stations, relying primarily on introspective questions (for example, "Where do you want to go with Jesus?").

Station One plays on the phonetics of Lent. The dryer lint was from Lilly's home dryer. The blending of everyday domesticity with religious experience questions the divides of public/private and sacred/profane. Refusing these binaries is common among Emerging Evangelicals, and is a base assumption for Lilly's interpretation of the Celtic model of thin places. The interactive portion of this station asks you to roll the lint brush on your clothes, the removed lint symbolizing the removal of sin. Two scriptural texts frame the exercise: Isaiah 1:18 and Psalm 103:12–14.

Station Two asks you to "pray for Hobos around the globe." The scattered photos, all of impoverished and nondescript Africans, are meant to encourage ideas for prayer. Using the pen provided, you are instructed to write your prayers and place them on the globe. The heart-shaped Post-It notes on the globe when this photo was taken included: "Refugees in Palestine," "anyone lost . . . ," and "fatherless everywhere." The prayers at this and other stations followed this pattern of ranging from the precise to the generic.

Station Three asks you to remember that "you are loved by God." You are instructed to look in the mirror and read the following prayer: "I am God's Beloved. God loves me . . . GOD LOVES (say your name!). God is PLEASED WITH ME! God is pleased with (your name)." You are then asked, "How does this make you feel? Can you really believe it?" The tendency toward questions of personal relevance and application we saw in the journaling group continues in Maproom.

Station Four, the "Desert Station," begins with a reference to Jesus' period in the wilderness. You are prompted to "Sit down . . . play in the sand. Consider how you view the desert." You are then told to write your prayers in the sand, and reflect on "the wilderness in your own life." The sand, which was cold and wet, had been purchased that day from Lowe's. This combina-

Figure 3.3. Maproom Welcome Station

Figure 3.4. Maproom Station One

Figure 3.5. Maproom Station Two

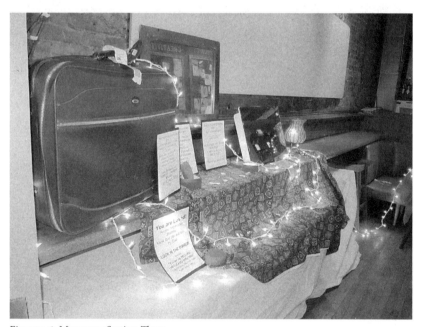

Figure 3.6. Maproom Station Three

Figure 3.7. Maproom Station Four

tion of scriptural reference, personal reflection, and sensory engagement was repeated throughout the stations.

Station Five asks: "What is weighing down your pack today? What things are making you slow and heavy, slowing you down on your journey? Stuff like fear, anger, worry, frustration, unforgiveness [*sic*], distrust . . . What else?" You are then instructed to pick up the backpack on the photo's right, which is filled with bricks. The station informs you that the weight of the pack represents your own spiritual-emotional-psychological baggage. You are then asked to remove one of the bricks and place it at the foot of the wooden cross, just out of the frame to the right, symbolizing the act of giving your worries to God. Matthew 11:29–30 contextualizes the exercise. Iconicity, here referring to weight, is a common technique in Maproom stations.

Station Six, in the photo's forefront, begins with two lengthy scriptural texts: Luke 3:7–15 and Philippians 4:10–13. You are then instructed to pray about your level of contentment "on your journey," and to take one of the plastic bags home, fill it with unneeded "stuff," and deliver it to a local church or Goodwill. The blue squares of paper are to be taken home so as to remind you to complete the exercise. This strategy of providing a take-home

Figure 3.8. Maproom Station Five

reminder is often a part of individual stations and the Maproom theme. Note, again, the presence of quotidian items (for example, the plastic bags).

Station Seven advises that "It is OK to rest on your Journey!" The prayer instruction here is open-ended and dialogic: "Talk to Jesus, Let Him talk to you." Psalm 46:10, Exodus 34:21, and Exodus 20:8–11 contextualize this prayer. The Bible, in this case, is less for reading than for signification. As with many other stations, places to sit have been provided, encouraging participants to rest and move through the stations slowly.

Station Eight celebrates the honeymoon element of the organizing metaphor with hearts, candy, and roses. The open heart-shaped box contains small, differently colored, Styrofoam hearts that you are instructed to hold when praying and take home to remember the exercise. The closing sign instructs you to: "Check your calendar . . . Is there a day you can give to have a date with Jesus? Is there a day or even a half a day between now and Easter that you can have a 'Minimoon' . . . a special time for you to just be with God? Get out your phone or your calendar and make an appointment." Each of the texts stresses that this honeymoon is an "opportunity" for participants to renew their relationship with God.

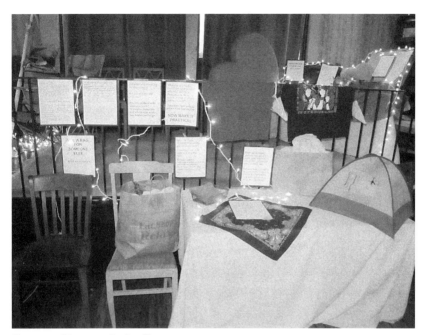

Figure 3.9. Maproom Station Six

Figure 3.10. Maproom Station Seven

Figure 3.11. Maproom Station Eight

Station Nine plays on the "temporary tattoo" that occurs on Ash Wednesday, the cross drawn on one's forehead. One sheet asks: "Just wondering what tattoo we can wear everyday to say that we are a follower, a creature acknowledging our Creator . . . a dust speck filled with possibilities?" Another sheet tells you: "When you see a tattoo between now and Easter, be reminded of God's tattoo of love for you! . . . the cross of Ash Wednesday and the piercing of Jesus on the cross." You are instructed to use one of the available stamps— a cross, a heart, a pair of feet—on your hand. The physical embodiment of stamping your hand, and the link between the station and the connection with a future event, are common in Maproom.

Station Ten was the only truly topical station, dealing with the massive earthquake in Haiti in January 2010, one month earlier. Referencing current events was not uncommon in other Maprooms. Your taste buds are targeted in this station: "Taste the Sugar. As you taste the sweetness of the sugar, pray for the sweetness of God to be present in the lives of everyone in Haiti today and that all those who suffer around the world and in our neighborhoods will feel God's sweetness and love today." The prayer is provided for you on one of the sheets of text. The scattered pictures came from an unidentified weekly news periodical. Note that the use of a prewritten prayer, like the meaningful use of materiality, conflicts with the Protestant semiotic ideology depicted by Keane (2007: 1–2).

Figure 3.12. Maproom Station Nine

Station Eleven is meant as a preparatory exercise: "We have the opportunity to go on an amazing journey with Jesus over the next 40 days. But before anyone starts a journey, they must get ready, they must prepare. How are you feeling today? How is your heart? Is it soft like a sponge ready to absorb more of God? Is it more like a rock feeling heavy and weighted down? Is it like dry sand . . . a desert in need of water? . . . in need of refreshment?" All three options are available, and the instruction directs you to "Put your symbol in the water." Again, note the iconicity ordering the connection between material objects and the interior spiritual condition.

Station Twelve featured a basket full of cards, just below this photo's frame, each with different scriptural texts. You are instructed to pick one and take it home: "Let the Holy Spirit lead YOU! Let the Holy Spirit choose." The card I pulled from the basket had three texts: Psalm 119:33–34, Luke 9:23–24, and Luke 5:10–11. Deuteronomy 11:18–21 frames the exercise. This was one of the only stations that was not explicitly multisensory, and did not involve a specific spiritual exercise.

The last two prayer stations were on the second floor. Both are open-ended, with no explicit instruction, just room and supplies to "create your prayers in art." Station Thirteen had a sample, which sits in this photo behind the Ziploc bag. The picture is of Jesus holding a young boy in his arms, framed by a fragmented scriptural recontextualization of John 3:16: "For God So Loved." Note also the Bible, *The Message* paraphrase version, on the small table available for reading.

Figure 3.13. Maproom Station Ten

Figure 3.14. Maproom Station Eleven

Figure 3.15. Maproom Station Twelve

Figure 3.16. Maproom Station Thirteen

Figure 3.17. Maproom Station Fourteen

Aside from the Bible, Station Fourteen mirrors Station Thirteen. Note the pencil sketch of a treasure box with "Where?" written in red ink, prompting the participant to ask how great is the distance between him- or herself and God.

Lilly described the Lenten Hobo Honeymoon Maproom as one of her favorites. "Falling in love with God" has been a powerful trope in her Christian life, and she is convinced that everyone who attends this Maproom leaves with a new way to think about Lent. Roughly thirty people came and went that February evening, most staying for at least an hour. A few weeks earlier Lilly had driven all these stations, except the Desert Station, to Nashville, Tennessee. She had been hired by the regional district of the United Methodist Church to teach a Maproom workshop for a youth pastors' conference. Ideally, for the denomination and for Lilly, some of those pastors will create Maprooms in their local contexts.

Ancient-Future Mediations

Lectio divina, pre-Reformation art, contemplation, using the lectionary, following Lenten season, reimagining the Stations of the Cross, and creating thin places—all these function as indices of "ancient" Christianity for Lilly. Ancient-future worship, however, is not simply a collection of practices; it is also a means of subject formation. To conclude, we return to three questions that introduced the ethnographic representations of Thinplace. What kind of religious subjectivity is encouraged by ancient-future worship? How are material mediations used? And what sensorial hierarchy is evident?

Three qualities are most evident about Thinplace's process of ancient-future subject formation. This is a highly individual spirituality, where the focus stays fixed on one's personal relationship with God. The readings of scripture are likely the best illustration of this, such as the journaling group discussions that pose only questions of relevance and allow for multiple, idiosyncratic interpretations of the same text. In this way ancient-future departs little from the conservative Evangelical model of faith, a sense of "radical inter-subjectivity, an experience of continuous subjection to and reliance upon [God]" (Elisha 2008a: 58). In a related fashion, it is a highly introspective spirituality, one which displays great interest in interrogating the status of one's own emotional-cognitive condition. The practice of journaling, made explicit in Artwalk and the Sunday night group and encouraged in Maproom, best illustrates this. Taken together, these two qualities suggest the lingering of Western individualism, the kind of "inwardly individual" described by Dumont (1985: 114) in his historical review of modernity. Moreover, they can work against Lilly's Thinplace aims, such as the stifled discussion following Artwalk. Ancient-future is also a highly expressive spirituality, where acts of creativity are valued. This is evident throughout Thinplace events, as in the consumption and production of art, and Lilly's designing of Maproom stations. As suggested for other Emerging-influenced churches, this may reflect the impact of the "creative class" (Marti 2005: 152) on American religion, a labor force prized in late modernity. Mirroring the tensions of desiring and doubting authenticity, the religious subjectivity in ancient-future worship involves both modern and late modern dispositions.

Thinplace involves materiality in two ways. The reliance on quotidian items—lint brushes, globes, sand, bricks, bags, sugar, stones, and sponges—refuses distinctions between public and private, sacred and profane. Nothing is too banal or too worthy to facilitate the experience of God. Second, the physicality of these items is marshaled through the logic of iconicity. Lint brushes roll off sin, prayers are placed onto their destinations, bricks are lifted and removed, and sponges soak while stones sink. Still, it is the signifying quality of these items that is taken seriously, not the items themselves. They are utilized during worship, but they are not transformed. Just as they are not dismissed, they are not special. Lilly is constantly on the lookout for items to incorporate, but none are retained for very long or treated with any reverence. While Thinplace worship does not invest material items with any particular authority, they are valued as mediators in the attempt to experience God. Their physical qualities are made explicit in the process, not downplayed or refused. Confession, for example, is not accomplished only by verbalizing interior states of conviction, but is complemented by rolling a lint brush on your clothes. By reordering the respective value of words and things, this engagement with materiality largely (though not entirely) departs from the semiotic ideology Keane (2007) assigns to Protestants.

We can also make two observations about the involvement of the sensorium in ancient-future worship. First, the senses are considered important for their powers of memory. Tasting sugar, for example, implants an association: "As you taste the sweetness of the sugar, pray for the sweetness of God to be present in the lives of everyone in Haiti today and that all those who suffer around the world and in our neighborhoods will feel God's sweetness and love today." The memory power of multisensory acts helps explain Lilly's regret in not knowing that potters would be working in the museum; if she had known, she would have chosen different scriptural texts for the Artwalk reading. Second, recalling Engelke (2010: 376), not all the senses are valued equally. Sound, in particular, is thought to be more hurtful than helpful in the attempt to experience God. Silence is deemed necessary. But it is not a Quaker silence, collectively awaiting revelation from the Holy Spirit and ready to be broken at any time (Bauman 1974); it is a monastic silence dedicated to contemplation. This both recalls and departs from the modern religious sensorium. Ancient-future hearing, like the auditory world described by Schmidt (2000), is less valued than the other senses. But the problem with hearing is not the likelihood of deception or the dangers of becoming overly ecstatic. Rather, the ancient-future problem with sound is one of clutter. It gets in the way of God. Many of my consultants, including Lilly, described this spiritual noise as a recent problem, a product of living in the dizzying multimedia age of late modernity.

We have explored here a thick ethnographic description of ancient-future worship. I hope to have conveyed what these worship events consist of—if not a little of what it is like to participate in them. The real significance of ancient-future worship is its role in Emerging Evangelical subject formation.

And issues of material and sensorial mediation are crucial to understanding this process. Worship, however, is not the alpha and omega of ancient-future as a cultural category. For many of my consultants, being connected to older expressions of faith is not a desire confined to ritualized gatherings. We will take up how this desire is performed in everyday life in the next chapter.

4

Ancient-Future II

Everyday Monastics

In late October 2008 I waited in a coffee shop for Glenn. It was a Friday afternoon and the atmosphere was bustling, nearly frenetic. The activity was explained by the start of weekend socializing, the unseasonably warm, sunny weather and a fast approaching presidential election. Political talk filled the air alongside the permanence of coffee smells and the occasional, halting grind of an espresso machine. I had not talked with Glenn for over a month and was excited at the prospect of another follow-up interview.

Glenn is an east Tennessee native and retains a thick, Appalachian drawl. It complements the half-smile he mostly prefers. He is fit and well-built from marathon training. His closely shaven head keeps a receding hairline barely visible, and he usually hangs a small, gold hoop from his left ear. Glenn arrived that afternoon in dress slacks, a short-sleeve button-down shirt, and silk tie. This was unusual. Previously, I had seen him in strictly casual, sporty attire. My memory returned: he had recently started a new job. For several years Glenn had worked as a public bus driver in the small, university town where he and his wife planted their church. He described being a bus driver as an invaluable way to "learn this culture" and to "be around students in a unique way." But the pay was not sustainable. His new job—twenty-five miles away—was as an academic advisor and part-time teacher at a Christian college.

We spent the first few minutes talking about his new job. He explained the daily routine, the rhythm and nature of the workday. He seemed genuinely delighted with the change. Thinking nothing of it, I quipped that he probably didn't "miss being a bus driver." Kindly, but quickly, Glenn corrected my gaffe:

> Actually, I do. I miss the extreme simplicity of it. There's something about driving around all day in a circle that really forces you to learn discipline. It allows you to learn to be content with what you're doing.

The interview continued for nearly two hours. Toward the end, prompted by the electoral season, Glenn asked if my research addressed the Evangelical-political nexus. I used his question to ask my own. Had he watched the "Leadership and Compassion Forum" two months earlier? The event was the first of its kind: two leading presidential nominees answered questions posed by an Evangelical pastor, hosted at that pastor's church, and broadcast for a national television audience. The pastor was Rick Warren, who several months later would give the invocation at Barack Obama's inauguration. Glenn watched the Forum and was "revolted." He thought the whole production suffered from the same problem that plagues all public Evangelicals: attention had shifted to issues other than "who Jesus was and what he did" as definitive of "orthodox Christianity." He continued: "Everyone has an agenda in politics and Christians should not be beholden to anyone." Glenn never told me who he planned to vote for, only that he was not registered as a Democrat or a Republican.

Glenn's reflections on bus driving and politics were not delivered with happenstance words. They trace the contours of the kind of Christianity he desires. References to "simplicity," "discipline," "contentment," and being "beholden" are building blocks for incorporating monastic values and traditions into everyday life. Many Emerging Evangelicals, like Glenn, emphasize acts of remembering and practicing monasticism in their individual and congregational lives. Integrating monastic elements is an extension of the ancient-future phenomenon, distinct from worship but issuing from the same logic: reclaiming a lost sense of authenticity in their faith by connecting with church history.

New Monasticism as Lived Religion

Emerging Evangelicals attracted to monasticism have used the term "new monastic" since at least the late 1990s. New monastics do not live in the confines of monasteries, but they regularly practice values and traditions derived from monastic Christianities, the histories of which date to the Patristic era. Being a new monastic is a self-conscious act of embodied social memory, and can take several forms. Some individuals do this remembering in a bricoleur fashion, appropriating only selected practices. Others participate in loosely knit collections of individuals who work together to remember. And still others live in intentional communities in order to make this remembering definitive for their lives. We might say that while all New Monastics are Emerging Evangelicals, not all Emerging Evangelicals are New Monastics.

One of the more outspoken individuals for new monasticism's public personae has been Shane Claiborne. In 1998 Claiborne cofounded "The Simple Way," an intentional community in inner-city Philadelphia. Claiborne's first two books—*The Irresistible Revolution: Living as an Ordinary Radical* (2006) and *Jesus for President: Politics for Ordinary Radicals* (2008) —were both published by Zondervan, one of America's largest Christian publishers, and have been consumed widely as new monastic testaments. The Simple Way maintains an online register of "Community of Communities" that, as of October 2010, listed sixty-four like-minded groups in twenty-five states. In May 2007 Claiborne was the focus of National Public Radio's "Speaking of Faith," a weekly documentary broadcast that reports on American religiosity. In the interview, Claiborne framed his new monasticism as a deconversion:

> I felt like the Christianity I grew up with really sort of looked at the world and said, "Yeah, it's falling apart, but there is life after death." While a lot of us were really asking, "Is there life before death?" You know? And, "doesn't our faith have just anything to speak into the world that we're living in?" I became pretty disenchanted with a lot of the church culture that I grew up with and just felt like I was asking bigger questions than they were willing to trust me with.

He "grew up with" Southern Baptist Evangelicalism in east Tennessee, precisely the kind of "church culture" many of my consultants used as a deconversion foil. New monastics rely on much the same cultural critique as the broader Emerging movement. Two indictments have been especially resonant: a critique of late modern consumer capitalism, and a critique of the institutional congregational structures that dominated twentieth-century American Christianity. If these are the problems, then the practices and ideals of monasticism spearhead the solution.

The pre-Reformation origins of monastic Christianities create automatic appeal. The cultural logic at work here is that because monastic traditions predate the modern era, they are unspoiled by the problems endemic to conservative Evangelicalism. As a form of social memory, the new monasticism relies on this logic of an Evangelicalism increasingly troubled and inauthentic with the passage of time. This temporality (that the passage of time is marked by worsening conditions) is not peculiar to new monastics, and could easily be read as a species of the broader eschatological impulse among Protestants (Bialecki 2009).

What exactly is "new" about the new monasticism? The answer empha-sized by my consultants is that "traditional" monasticism is largely insular, forming in relatively isolated communities and living relatively isolated lives. They are not easily visible to, and not particularly engaged with, the rest of society. This remove from public life conflicts with the evangelistic sensi-bilities of my consultants, for whom "reaching the lost" still takes priority. We can roughly sketch this priority as Max Weber's (1922) classic distinc-tion between *weltablehnende Askese* (world-rejecting asceticism) and *inner-weltliche Askese* (inner-worldly asceticism). In the latter, one seeks to attain a level of spiritual commitment while still participating in the institutions of contemporary life, even if that attainment is difficult or unlikely. As one commentator of Weber puts it, inner-worldly ascetics have "a program of disciplined spiritual living within the realm of every day life and business" (Pals 2006: 173).

Extending this theme of "every day life," we can locate the new monasti-cism as an expression of "lived religion" (Hall, ed. 1997). This term evokes an interest in how religiosity is "expressed and experienced in the lives of individuals" (McGuire 2008: 3) and an emphasis away from "the prescribed religion of institutionally defined beliefs and practices" (ibid.: 12). Adherents often perform their faith outside the authoritative reach of religious authori-ties and institutions of belonging, and sometimes at odds with them. View-ing religion as lived asserts that religious experience cannot be reduced to a belief system, a formal creed, a set of rituals, or regular engagement with spaces deemed sacred. While the relevance of these familiar categories is recognized, religious identity includes much more: specialized language, embodied practices, internalizing and displaying emotions, and doubting, to name a few. Lived religion prioritizes the unceasing efforts of religious adherents to map meaning onto the details of the life-worlds they inhabit (D. Hall 1997: ix).

This interpretive frame also refuses a distinction that has been part of sociological thinking at least since Durkheim's sacred-profane separation. A strict Durkheimian logic tells us that adherents declare certain mediations—texts, words, practices, spaces—as being for religious purposes, while others are excluded from the realm of faith. The vantage of lived religion disinte-grates sacred/profane, religious/secular, and physical/metaphysical distinc-tions in the experience of adherents (Orsi 1997: 6). People are able to, and are often apt to, sacralize all of life. They take their faith to work, to play, to relationships, and to the most mundane activities. From a theoretical per-spective lived religion is convincing, but it also interests me because of my ethnographic experience. My consultants were extremely quick to refuse any separation between the sacred and the profane. In interviews they often called attention to this dualism before I had a chance to ask about it. As late modern subjects, and in many cases as well-educated people who have read *The Elementary Forms of Religious Life* (Durkheim 1912), Emerging Evangelicals are quite self-conscious about the idea that everything is sacred. Moreover, many insist that this is not news. They consider it an old fact, a biblical fact, and a fact lost by conservative Evangelicals, making the fiction of sacred-profane part of their cultural critique.

In his ethnography of American religious tourism, Aaron Ketchell (2007: xvi) describes lived religion as a matter of "impart[ing] everyday experiences" with sacred meanings. Quotidian matters matter. This everyday aspect of lived religion carries a phenomenological torch: even the most macro level reading of society, culture, and history must spring from the smallest intra- and interpersonal experiences. Religion is about public rituals, but it is also about the behind-the-scenes/off-the-radar/out-of-view meaningful preparations and reflections on those rituals. Religion is about authorized practices, but it is also about the practices that adherents authorize. Religion is about addressing life's grand questions, but it is also about using the least grand of experiences to do so. For new monastics, no experience is too banal to be spiritual.

Lived religion is particularly well-suited for understanding new monasticism, given the kind of knowledge produced by the movement's public voices. Mary Douglas, the eminent anthropologist, remarked in her classic study of comparative religion *Purity and Danger* (1966), "People do not necessarily listen to their preachers" (196). This seems exceedingly obvious, but looking again, it indexes an extremely important theoretical stance. Knowledge produced is not necessarily knowledge consumed. Even in religious contexts, where certain speakers are granted moral, spiritual, or theological authority, listeners are apt to hear different meanings and act differently because of what they hear. Consider Shane Claiborne and his discourse of being an "ordinary radical." In his books and public lectures Claiborne references numerous ways to be a new monastic: living communally with other Christians, maintaining the bare minimum of material possessions, driving a tour bus that uses recycled vegetable oil instead of gasoline, making his own hand-sewn clothes, growing his own food, transforming "abandoned" public spaces into edifying creations like community gardens, and "rescuing" discarded items in public dumpsters for community use. Claiborne never mandates these practices, but he certainly frames them as desirable and attainable for everyone. But not every new monastic who reads or listens to Claiborne follows his example to the letter. Given the difficulty of sustaining such a drastically different lifestyle compared to the American mainstream, how could they? A lived religion approach allows us to see how everyday monastics actually listen to figures like Claiborne.

Finally, note that lived religion affirms what we described in the Introduction as person-centered ethnography because it operates on the base assumption that the lives of people and the institutions they create provide the makings of religion (Orsi 1997: 7). There is no ritual without a ritual performer. There is no sermon without a sermonizer and audience. There is no creed without a reciter. There is no everyday imparting of meaning without an imparter. And there is no new monasticism without new monastics. How do new monastics take the idea of new monasticism seriously? How do they live as inner-worldly ascetics? How do they make the profane sacred? How do they assign meaning to the everyday? How do they bring monasticism to lives lived outside monasteries?

"Unpimp and Remonk"

Simplicity

Every new monastic I encountered during my fieldwork stressed the value of simplicity. As they often said, they nurtured "a desire to live simply." What do they mean by this? How is it practiced? A common response, one that echoes the cultural critique of megachurch Evangelicalism, is to apply the principle of living simply to local institutions of church belonging. Many new monastics have left familiar congregational models in favor of house churches.

Since its inception in 2000, Jamie and her husband Todd have been members of the house church network led by Chris (whose deconversion narrative we heard earlier). They both grew up in the exurban area north of Cincinnati where Chris planted the church, but lived nearly all of the 1990s in a condition of white-collar industrial transience: as an executive for General Motors, Todd was relocated every few years. Wherever they were living, Jaime and Todd sought a local megachurch that offered ample children's resources and allowed them to participate in congregational ministries as much or as little as they wanted. They returned to Cincinnati in 1999 to care for Todd's ailing mother, and knew Chris as a family friend. At the time, they were not familiar with the house church model, but trusted Chris as a pastor and joined the group of founding members.

When I first asked Jamie why she, Todd, and their two teenage children have stayed with this house church for ten years, she gave the following reasons:

1. She has "grown spiritually like never before."
2. Members "carry each others' burdens."
3. It is unlike "any other church experience" they have had: "it's not a place you go, but a life you live together."
4. When members have difficulties, for example when married couples have considered divorce, they mediate the problem as a group. This is fundamentally different from "other church experiences" where "experts determine advice."
5. It does not have a "one-sized-fits all" mentality.
6. They live in walking distance of eleven other families in the church.
7. "Overhead costs," such as a paid pastor or money spent on maintaining a building, are minimal: "We give away 96 percent of [our tithes]."

Three logics organize Jamie's response: a cultural critique of "other church experiences"; simplicity encoded as proximity to other members, relational commitments, and the handling of tithing; and the lived religion spirit of refusing sacred-profane distinctions. For Jamie, the simplicity of the house church is not only the reason for continued commitment, it is also an incubator for new ideas. Beginning in late 2008, she started a "kids' church" for the children of house church members. They meet on Sunday mornings, unlike the house church meetings which take place on weeknights, and usually about fifteen kids attended. She recalled one Sunday as an exemplary moment. The weather was ideal and they drove all the kids to a nearby public park for prayer and Bible reading. Refusing to anchor religious practice in a particular space, Jamie remarked: "I want these kids growing up understanding that *that* is church." Returning to the frame of cultural critique, she used a familiar Sunday school project as a foil for their house church version of "kids' church": "we are not just coloring Noah's Ark."

New monastics also apply the value of simplicity to less institutional, more individual concerns. Consider Virgil.

My most startling memory of Virgil is from a theology conference he organized and hosted in May 2009. On the conference's opening morning, Virgil approached the podium to deliver some welcoming remarks. An unlit, rotund Cuban cigar was perched in his right hand. He wore an Army-green Che Gueverra T-shirt with a Cuban military cap. A large tattoo of a Celtic cross was emblazoned on his left bicep. His aesthetic invoked the conference title, "Subversion," and the new monastic trope of being an "ordinary radical."

Virgil was born in communist Romania in 1972. He grew up attending an Eastern Orthodox church and converted to Evangelicalism in high school via Southern Baptist missionaries. He migrated to the United States in 1992 to attend a Baptist university in central Ohio, though he did not complete his degree. With two semesters remaining, he accepted a job as a computer security engineer with a nearby corporation in Dayton, a position he still occupies. Virgil shared all this with me during my first interview with him, but I had sought him out initially because he was the organizer for the Dayton Emergent Village cohort. Given the important status of Emergent Village as a resource-sharing institution and a cultural symbol in the Emerging movement, I was anxious to include Virgil and others affiliated with the cohort in my fieldwork. As it turned out, this was the least interesting thing about Virgil. First off, the cohort itself was not particularly thriving. In April 2009 there were roughly forty people on Virgil's cohort mailing list. About ten of those forty met monthly, and everyone who attended did so as a supplement to active membership in a local church. They did not practice any form of structured religious inquiry. The group functioned primarily as an opportunity for informal dialogue. By November 2009 the cohort had stopped meeting regularly and Virgil had stopped sending group emails. He was unsure whether they would rejoin, and seemed indifferent about the possibility. For Virgil, the meetings had grown tiresome with too much dwelling on the problems of conservative Evangelical churches. Echoing Charlie's distaste for overused irony that we heard earlier, the cultural critique that fuels Emerging Evangelicalism seems preferable as a shared context, but not as the overt focus of regular dialogue. Finally, Virgil's association with Emergent Village was both recent and fairly single-minded. His involvement in the Emerging movement began in 2005, and his interest stemmed almost exclusively from theological debates about the nature of God's kingdom. We focus on Virgil here not because he waves the Emerging Church flag, but because of the way he has embraced the desire for simplicity.

Beginning in mid-2008 Virgil and his family started seeking "an escape from the world of corporate consumerism." His job with a computer security corporation is in that world, but he does not want his life to be organized by that world. The effort began when he and his wife Jamie bought a five-acre plot of rural land east of their exurban home outside Dayton. They sold their $300,000, three thousand square foot house, and lost $12,000 on the mortgage. They sold and donated half of their belongings, then moved into a nine hundred square foot apartment halfway between Virgil's work and their future home site. Their plan is to build a straw bale house on the rural property. It is slow going because they are intent on completing the transition from exurb prefab to rural straw bale without any debt: they work in segments, paying for everything outright, $10-15,000 at a time. They began by clearing the property and preparing the grounds for a permanent home. Virgil cites three motives for this ruptured life: living debt-free ("free from the system"); teaching their three daughters certain values ("things like hard work and responsibility"); and living simply, closer to God ("the way people used to do").

On a late afternoon in late March 2010 Virgil showed me their vision. I arrived at the transitional apartment home, a nondescript one-story house in a quiet working-class neighborhood. It was the best day of the new season: warm but not hot, with the faintest of breezes. Spring was springing, but had not yet sprung. There were two cars in the driveway: a Honda minivan and a red, slightly rusting pickup truck. Both vehicles bore a familiar Evangelical bumper sticker: "Love Wins." On the truck, it was pasted next to a sticker announcing Virgil's libertarian politics: "Don't Tread on Me," complete with the iconic coiled, hissing snake.

Virgil greeted me as I approached the door. He was just home from work, but had been there long enough to change out of his corporate attire into jeans and a T-shirt. The tattoo dominating his left arm was on full display. He immediately apologized, pointing out the chaotic collection of household items piled in the storage area directly inside the entrance. Despite their substantial downsizing, moving from three thousand to nine hundred square feet meant that some piles were still necessary. The kitchen and living room were cluttered but clean, and the stamp of three young daughters was evident: Barbie dolls and coloring books were scattered without design. The air in the house smelled delicious. Jamie had made a Romanian stew that afternoon, Virgil's mother's recipe, and it had been cooking all day. We enjoyed a bowl while Jaime and the kids readied themselves for a trip to the five-acre property.

The drive took only about fifteen minutes, but a lot was said. Jamie had first found the property searching for rural land in local real estate listings. It fit their vision and was the right price. Virgil and Jaime spoke excitedly, even dreamily, about the future move and the new lifestyle it promised. Jaime planned to get a pygmy goat for each of the girls, as well as some chickens. They wanted a dog, but Virgil still needed convincing. Now that the weather

Figure 4.1. Virgil and Jamie's two oldest daughters standing on the building site of the pole barn.

was improving, regular work on the property would resume. The season's task list included finishing the driveway and building a pole barn, which would replace the apartment as their temporary housing. Jamie laughed at her own excitement: "If you had told me two years ago that I wouldn't be able to wait to live in a pole barn, I would have told you you were crazy. But, here we are!" The adjacent property, an additional ten acres, had recently gone on the market. Virgil wanted to buy this as well, and hoped to plant a blueberry farm. Ideally, the income from operating the blueberry farm would allow him to quit his job as a computer engineer, severing all ties with suburbia.

We arrived, and Virgil parked at the top of the property so as not to disturb the gravel that had been laid last season. The five of us walked up the driveway, Jamie carrying their infant daughter. Talk of future plans continued: they wanted a wood-burning stove to minimize heating costs; Virgil wanted to build two bat-houses to combat the mosquito population. As we proceeded back toward the minivan, Virgil framed the entire effort: "We really want to live out the kingdom the way we think God wants us to. This is a lot of work, but in the end it will be much simpler." As he trailed off, Jamie added: "And the girls really love it here."

Virgil's aspirations—for blueberries and all that comes with them—are animated by a cultural critique of capitalist consumption and its incongruities with authentic faith. Scholars have detailed at length the cultural conditions that typify late modern capitalism (Appadurai 1996). The movement of people, capital, ideas, and commodities is both rapid and global. As an economic experience, there is a fragmented and expendable work force. As a socio-psychological experience, there are increased levels of anxiety, alienation, dislocation, and a threat of constant rupture to self and social bonds. While Virgil did not use these terms, the pressures they indexed were evident in his words and in the decisions he and Jamie had made. On our drive to and from the property they both discussed the sins of mass accumulation, being singularly focused on economic advancement, and the general consumptive impulse of living in a service economy. Their discontents were explicitly directed at the cultural conditions of late modernity.

There is a certain Weberian irony to all this. In Virgil's case, while he sought to withdraw from certain institutions (corporate America) and places (the exurbia he formerly called home), his asceticism was still very inner-worldly. As he phrased it to me, their family was not interested in "the extreme of complete removal from society, like some Amish." His hoped-for blueberries would embed him in a local and transnational economic market. He maintained a regularly updated weblog, a technological form not part (imaginable?) of Weber's thinking, but nonetheless a means of remaining connected. Leading up to the summer of 2010 Virgil campaigned for public office (a county commissioner seat, which he did not win, though he did receive 25 percent of the vote). As Weber (1904<N<5 [1930]) famously argued, striving for inner-worldly asceticism fueled the Protestant ethic which in turn spurred the spread of modern capitalism. And then there was Virgil, whose inner-worldly asceticism fueled a cultural critique of late modern capitalism.

Virgil's embrace of simplicity should not be mistaken as the same kind of spiritual renewal efforts described by Rebecca Kneale Gould (2005) in her historical ethnography of homesteading. Virgil and Jaime wanted to build their own straw bale home. They wanted to grow some if not most of their own food. They wanted to feed an agrarian sensibility. But their guiding logic was not one of going "back to the land," nor was it an attempt to recreate a romanticized early America. Theirs was a different nostalgia: for monastic Christianities deemed unspoiled by late modern obsessions.

Virgil's case is extreme. Most new monastics in my fieldwork were not measuring blueberry plots. Others found more isolated, more easily managed ways to enact their discontents with mass consumption: church communities organized the sharing of resources (for example: food, money, housing, clothing, and transportation); individuals and communities prioritized becoming debt free; groups ate communally on a daily basis; church members were encouraged to not live on 100 percent of their income, decreasing their reliance on "the system"; communities eliminated ownership of a church building, freeing time and resources to devote to other expressions of faith; individuals worked together to eliminate various addictions, from alcohol to shopping; and individuals and small groups regularly went on weekend or weeklong silent prayer retreats. Like Virgil, they framed their efforts as acts of taking the monastic value of simplicity seriously and escaping the consumptive life of late modern America, while remaining active participants in capitalist structures.

Stability

Kevin maintains a weblog where he writes about matters of religious faith. This, of course, is unexceptional among Emerging Evangelicals. Blogging has been crucial for the development and spread of the Emerging movement. Nearly half of my ninety consultants maintained their own blogs and nearly all of them read blogs as part of their Christian life. Blogging, much like all social practice (Bourdieu 1977), confronts the tension of conformity and creativity. It is a shared resource with relatively stable conventions (Doostdar 2004), yet blogs still allow for individualized expression. In the spirit of the latter, consider the subtitle of Kevin's blog. It pithily captures this chapter's theme: a cultural critique of conservative Evangelicalism grounded in an embodied social memory of monasticism. "Unpimp and remonk." The monastic value most central to Kevin's ongoing practice of faith is stability. Indeed, it is not just valued; it is vowed.

Kevin is a house church pastor, a husband, a father, proprietor of an automotive body shop, and a native Cincinnatian. Recall this book's opening vignette, the neighborhood setting of Norwood, and the reference to a Vineyard house church network (VC) and their ornate building (St. E). Since 1995, Kevin has been part of this network, mostly as a lead pastor, and he was instrumental in facilitating their purchase of St. E.

Kevin's body shop is located a half mile from St. E. Along with his wife and children, they live next door to St. E. But they do not live there alone. They live communally, with a fluid collection of six to eight housemates. Nightly meals are eaten together as a house. Along with other VC members, they conduct "fixed hour prayers" together: fifteen-minute scriptural recitations performed every morning, noon, and evening. Roughly eighty other VC members have bought and renovated houses within a three-block radius of St. E. Emphasizing a sense of permanence, Kevin describes their community as "owners, not renters." Several other members have started businesses in the neighborhood. Jeremiah, a VC assistant pastor, is convinced that a central motivator for this immigration has been the taking of a vow.

Shortly after VC was established in Norwood, Kevin, his wife, the founding pastor, his wife, and another married couple publicly accepted a "vow of stability." They patterned it on the *Rule of St. Benedict* (~540 C.E.). References to "stability" are found throughout the *Rule,* but perhaps the most explicit directive comes from Chapter 58: Of the Manner of Admitting Brethren:

> If he promises stability and perseverance, then at the end of two months let this rule be read through to him, and let him be addressed thus: "Here is the law under which you wish to fight. If you can observe it, enter; if you cannot, you are free to depart." If he still stands firm, let him be taken to the above-mentioned novitiate and again tested in all patience. And after the lapse of six months let the Rule be read to him, that he may know on what he is entering. And if he still remains firm, after four months let the same Rule be read to him again. Then, having deliberated with himself, if he promises to keep it in its entirety and to observe everything that is commanded, let him be received into the community. But let him understand that, according to the law of the Rule, from that day forward he may not leave the monastery nor withdraw his neck from under the yoke of the Rule which he was free to refuse or to accept during that prolonged deliberation. When he is to be received he promises before all in the oratory stability, fidelity to monastic life and obedience. This promise he shall make before God and His Saints, so that if he should ever act otherwise, he may know that he will be condemned by Him whom he mocks. Of this promise of his let him draw up a document in the name of the Saints whose relics are there and of the Abbess who is present. Let him write this document with his own hand; or if he is illiterate, let another write it at his request, and let the novice put his mark to it. Then let him place it with his own hand upon the altar; and when he has placed it there, let the novice at once intone this verse: "Receive me, O Lord, according to Your word, and I shall live: and let me not be confounded in my hope" (Ps. 118[119]:116). Let the whole community answer this verse three times and add the "Glory be to the Father." Then let the novice prostrate himself at each one's feet, that they may pray for him. And from that day forward let him be counted as one of the community.

Following this text to the letter was never the intention. Kevin and the others did not vow to never leave their house, St. E, or the neighborhood. What they vowed was to never move away, to maintain Norwood as their home until they died. Irrespective of their occupational fates, the fates of their families, or the fate of the VC community, they would live there.

For Kevin, this vow of stability is the bedrock of his lived religion. He describes his everyday embodiment of faith as "incarnational," invoking the biblical presence of Jesus on earth, and uses it to connect his roles as resident, pastor, and business owner. He considers his auto body shop a premier example. Every car that he helps restore is an enactment of faith. Similarly, every house that VC members restore is an enactment of faith. Restoration—of cars, houses, lives, and relationships—is only truly possible for Kevin when there is stability. In good Evangelical fashion Kevin frames these efforts by recontextualizing individual scriptural texts, citing Isaiah 58:12:

> Your people will rebuild the ancient ruins and will raise up the age-old foundations; you will be called Repairer of Broken Walls, Restorer of Streets with Dwellings.

Isaiah 61:4:

> They will rebuild the ancient ruins and restore the places long devastated; they will renew the ruined cities that have been devastated for generations.

And Luke 4:18:

> The Spirit of the Lord is on me, because he has anointed me to preach good news to the poor. He has sent me to proclaim freedom for the prisoners and recovery of sight for the blind, to release the oppressed, to proclaim the year of the Lord's favor.

Kevin and others in the VC community see themselves as fulfilling biblical mandates to foster a connection to a particular place. The ties between renewal and stability are also evident in a document that Kevin authored and circulated among VC members several years after his vow: "The Norwood Manifesto." The Manifesto's central feature is a list of ten statements of purpose, including:

We buy homes that are fixer-uppers on the "wrong side of the tracks" and beautify them, saying to our neighbors, "We're here for the long haul."

Kevin's identity as a new monastic begins with a vow and extends throughout his everyday life. For him, the thrice daily performance of fixed prayer, nightly communal meals, the crash of a hammer on a dented car door and the glide of a paintbrush on the side of a house are all moments in the same ongoing effort of change. This is precisely the kind of collapsing of experiential domains anticipated by a lived religion approach. Yet, as Kevin illustrates, this need not mean a total replacement of formal religious acts. The public vow is essential in the VC community memory, not a forgotten ritual.

Through his blog, "Unpimp and Remonk," Kevin has developed relationships with other Emerging Evangelicals. Glenn is one of those individuals. Their lives on the blogosphere initially intersected in 2001, and they have been close friends and ministry partners ever since. Glenn and his wife Cathy have also performed a public acceptance of the Benedictine stability vow. Like Kevin, they stress the importance of having done this formally with their house church members present. Consider two brief ethnographic moments that issue from Glenn's vow, mirroring the example of Kevin in Norwood and the lived religion quality of new monasticism.

August 7, 2008. After my first interview with Glenn we walked to a nearby public square. It was about 8:30 p.m., but still dusk because of the late summer daylight. He pointed out a few businesses along the way and remembered aloud a few forgettable facts about the town. A rock band was playing in the square, the finale to a weekly summer concert series. The scene was busy with people and their dogs, which Glenn observed as something that only happened when there are community-sponsored events.

Glenn spotted two familiar faces in the crowd, Jason and Andrea: a young married couple from their house church. They exchanged waves, he and I walked over, and introductions were made. The whole encounter lasted only a few minutes, but one of Jason's remarks has proved memorable. He described his job as a recreational director for a nearby YMCA, and explained that finding work had been difficult in the area. He added in closing, gesturing with a smile toward Glenn: "We were really ready to move, then we met this guy." They laughed meaningfully, but I was lost. It was only after several more interviews with Glenn that I realized how this brief interaction captured something of the effect of Glenn's avowed stability—the contagious nature of the desire to stay put. I would also learn later that Jason and Andrea's marriage was only the second one performed by Glenn in their house church. They had become cherished friends. Jason and Andrea bought a home less than half a mile from Glenn and Cathy, where they live communally with Jason's younger brother and sister. Describing their wedding day on his blog, Glenn returned to the value of simplicity:

And here in our living room, I was taken again by the presence of the Christ who so obviously takes delight in holy matrimony. Suffice it to say, I didn't even make it halfway through my reflection before I was teetering on the brink of blubbering outright for joy and for the immensity of the depth of our relationships that were being clarified in that kairotic moment. The beauty of it all was its simplicity. Everyone officiated in some way. Everyone contributed either in worship leadership, prayer, encouragement, laying on of hands, blessings or just merely being there. If we weren't all at some point a blubbering mess, we were pretty close. Especially when we surrounded Jason and Andrea in a circle of affirmation. That was simply powerful. What a wonderful community I have. I love my church.

March 1, 2010. On this night my girlfriend and I ate dinner with Glenn and Cathy at their house. It was our second time doing so (but would not be the last). We arrived shortly after 7 p.m. and stayed for nearly three hours. During dinner, Glenn asked my girlfriend what she liked least about the town. She answered easily, focusing on the small size and constant presence of undergraduates, then turned the question back to Glenn. He answered differently: transience. The trouble for Glenn, who moved to the town in 1999, was the instability inherent in a place reliant on a university and where the vast majority of graduates went elsewhere to start a career. College students move on. They interpret their existence in the town as temporary. The plan is always to be heading somewhere else. As a result, they tend to invest very little in this place. It is not home, and is not treated like home. This was endlessly frustrating for Glenn who, in direct contrast to this primary demographic, had vowed to stay. During his years as a city bus driver he had written an article for an Evangelical magazine that included a reflection on this problem:

As I look in their eyes, there is a vacuous hollow there. It seems to me that few of them are really "here." In other words, they are on the way to something else, somewhere else. I wonder how many are towing the line of gaining the collegiate experience and the sheepskin it's wrapped in and then off to the next experience. These moments in their lives seem like so many stones in a creek as they skip across them just to get to the other side, avoiding the stream of life altogether. We are told to acquire, amass, to "get" and we don't know how to just "be" because no one is in any one place for very long. They are on their way to the next big stage.

The closing sentence of the article posed a question animated by stability:

Where is our burden to live amongst a wayward and transient people as a prophetic roadblock to the slave syndrome under which our nowherely mobile peers live?

Stability, like simplicity, is a new monastic value fueled by cultural critique. In step with the broader Emerging movement, part of this critique is directed toward mainstream Evangelicals. Kevin and Glenn are both convinced that accepting vows enables longstanding Evangelical concerns (evangelism and building relationships, for example) in a way that traditional Evangelical practice cannot. As with simplicity, the critique they level against constant mobility is also a critique of capitalist aspiration. The disposition of being always on the move that Glenn abhors reflects the cultural conditions of post-Industrial life in late modernity (Harvey 1989). The equation that moving on equals success, improvement, and a general bettering of one's self and circumstance is challenged by new monastics. Still, they continue as inner-worldly ascetics. They vow to stay put, refusing seclusion or exclusion. While they create sites of communal living, they remain embedded in the world they wish to evangelize.

Predictions, Dumpsters, and Lived Monasticism

Lilly, as we saw earlier, is committed to the possibilities of a Christian identity grounded in being ancient-future, performed most explicitly through her maintenance of Thinplace. During my first interview with Lilly she made a prediction that aids our attempt to understand new monasticism as lived religion.

Her prediction began with an email remembered. It was sent in late May 2009 by The Emergent Village Network. The contents and title, "What, Exactly, Is Theology?" were excerpts from *The New Christians: Dispatches from the Emergent Frontier* (2008). The book's author, Tony Jones, cofounded Emergent Village and has been associated with the public personae of the Emerging movement since its origins in the mid-1990s. My first interview with Lilly took place the day after this email was sent. While she agreed with the email's premise ("virtually everything we do is inherently theological"), Lilly thought its institutional sponsorship indicative of a problem. For her, there was too much talk in Emerging public forums about the nature of theology and not enough reporting on what "inherently theological" lives looked like in practice. As we remembered this email together, Lilly narrated her history with the Emerging movement. In particular, she recalled an observation from leadership conferences she had attended in 2005. Most people at these conferences were in their late thirties and early forties, but very few in their early twenties, the supposed age demographic whose worldview and interests were represented by the Emerging movement. Lilly's prediction was that if public theological discourse continued in the spirit of Jones's email, then most young Evangelicals would be new monastics because of the overt emphasis placed on everyday, lived values like simplicity and stability.

I have no interest in affirming or challenging the accuracy of Lilly's prediction. But I do want to consider why her prediction is worth considering.

Steve is a twenty-one-year-old Evangelical. His father is a United Methodist pastor, and he "was always really involved with church" while growing up. When he began college he joined a local Evangelical Free Church as well as Campus Crusade for Christ (CCC). Through CCC he met Ryan, an eventual friend but initially an annoyance. At first, Ryan confused him. He didn't "fit the mold" Steve had of Evangelical piety. Ryan "cussed." Ryan was "not always happy." Yet Ryan "seemed more Spirit-led" than anyone else Steve had met in college. From this clash of expectations a friendship grew. Steve's confusion turned to affinity. During this period, Ryan gave him some books he had recently read. All were written by Emerging Evangelical authors: Brian McLaren, Donald Miller, Erwin McManus, and Shane Claiborne. When explaining his reaction to these books, Steve used a common Emerging Evangelical turn of phrase: these authors put words to thoughts he had had for most of his religious life. This reaction was especially strong after he read Claiborne's *The Irresistible Revolution*. In response to the book both Steve and Ryan did volunteer mission work in a nearby, economically depressed, postindustrial city. Steve compared this experience with his first fourteen mission trips, all organized by churches: every previous mission experience was about "fixing problems," whereas this one was about "just sitting and listening and being with people who were suffering."

Steve and his cohort of Evangelical friends have acted on the new monastic impulse advocated by Claiborne in less conventional ways. In 2008, Steve and seven close friends attended Ichthus, a popular Christian summer music festival held every June in central Kentucky. Claiborne was one of the event's featured speakers, and Steve remembers his message focusing on "the wastefulness of Americans." Steve and his friends observed an irony: Claiborne delivered this message of wastefulness to twelve thousand Christians who proceeded to leave a concert site littered with four days' accumulation of trash. Instead of leaving directly after the festival's end, as they had in years past, Steve and his friends stayed for several hours to "dumpster dive." They "rescued" a blue plastic tarp, which they used later in the summer for a church youth event. They rescued chairs and electronics, which they split between Goodwill and their home churches. The following summer at Ichthus, Steve dove again.

The image of this twenty-one-year-old, white, middle-class Evangelical, elbow-deep in the garbage of his Christian peers captures how Emerging Evangelicals have incorporated into their individual lives and into the institutional lives of their congregations values and practices attributed to monastic traditions. These new monastics take the details of their faith with them almost anywhere. As a form of lived religion, new monasticism is defined by its performance of everyday acts and the everyday exercise of meaning-making: modeling a portable definition of "church" for children, as Jamie did; replacing suburban stucco with agrarian straw bale, as Virgil aspires to do; publicly taking formal vows, as Kevin and Glenn did. Or, as with Steve, lived monasticism can take the form of a body submerged in refuse (at least momentarily, perhaps with breath intently held and legs desperately scissoring the air for balance).

We have illustrated that lived religion remains grounded in the broader cultural critique that circulates among Emerging Evangelicals. The simplicity of house churches for Jamie is made meaningful in part because it challenges her previous church experiences. A disinterest in conspicuous consumption, materialist accumulation, and commodity acquisition fuel Virgil's escape from suburbia. Kevin and Glenn's enactments of stability occur as self-conscious responses to a world in constant, dizzying motion. Compared to the remainder of my consultants, new monastics are especially suspicious of the worlds they inhabit. Their lived religion is an active response to this suspicion, and one that is applied to the most everyday, potentially banal affairs. Yet new monastics retain a characteristically Evangelical posture by remaining "within the realm of every day life and business" (Pals 2006: 173). Jaime still lives in the middle of exurbia and her husband still works for General Motors. Virgil still campaigns for public office. Kevin still lives and owns a business in Norwood. Glenn had still driven a public bus and still lives on a very ordinary residential street. They persist as inner-worldly ascetics. One phrase, unmistakably and venerably part of the American Evangelical lexicon, is still uttered by new monastics (uttered, it should be noted, without any qualifying or ironic contempt). I heard it numerous times, even amidst fervent critiques of conservative Evangelicalism: "Be in the world, but not of it."

Finally, this phenomenon of appropriating values and practices from monastic traditions should be read as a case of active, embodied remembering. The lived religion of new monastics is a matter of social memory. As a cultural process, social memory has been a topic of great interest among scholars from various disciplines. Anthropologists Cattell and Climo (2002: 3–36) identify four orientation points for the study and theorizing of memory: the meaning of pasts for individuals; the social sites and channels where pasts are renewed and reorganized; using pasts as a resource for constructing meaning; and representations of pasts through specific voices and texts. Each of these is prescient for understanding lived monasticism. The ethnographic examples we have just examined speak to individualized expressions (Kevin's translation of monastic principles to being an auto body shop owner); uses of body and place to recall values (Virgil's tattoo and agrarian home site); the making of meaning in everyday life (Steve's dumpster discovery of a monastic sensibility); and reference to specific historical moments (Kevin and Glenn's adaptation of St. Benedict's *Rule*). This lived, remembered monasticism is not an end in itself. With their Emerging brethren, new monastics couch their efforts as strides toward greater authenticity. For them, the problem is figured historically. If corruptions to authentic Christianity have proliferated in recent centuries, then one's memory must extend further back in time for solutions.

The new monastic acts of remembering we have explored were largely self-conscious responses to the cultural conditions of late modernity. However, we can also read the attraction to lived monasticism as an expression of late modern subjectivity. The anthropologist Kathleen Stewart (1988) argued that late modernity breeds nostalgia: "[I]n a world of loss and unreality, nostalgia rises to importance" (228), it is "the one point on the [social] landscape that gives hope of direction" (229). Relying on acts of remembering to achieve authenticity, in particular the remembering of better times long gone, is a disposition especially favored in late modernity. So long as we take nostalgia to mean a form of creative memory, and not lamented longing, this suits the social memory of new monastics. Awash in their cultural critique of conservative Evangelicalism, they are confronted with a decision: remain discontented in a faith they bemoan, change to an alternative faith tradition, create an altogether new expression of faith, or remember.

5

Missional I

Everyday Missionaries

As a worship consultant Lilly is, relatively speaking, a success. She travels regularly as a paid speaker at conferences, churches, and workshops to help Christian communities develop ancient-future worship events. She coauthored a manual about creating sacred spaces, published by a major Christian press. Since leaving professional ministry, her consultant work has been the primary expression of her religious vocation. But in her own backyard, in Cincinnati, Lilly maintains a worry.

Events like the journaling group are not uniformly appealing. Lilly recognized this fact, describing most Thinplace events as overly "cerebral," noting the bias toward well-educated, highly literate participants. Reading, reading aloud, journaling, sharing reflections on a text, sharing those reflections in mixed company: the cultural capital of these practices is not stable across social contexts. Lilly worried that Thinplace was too distant from the realities of Norwood, one of the urban neighborhoods she wants to "reach" and where the journaling group initially met at 1801 Mills. When it came to "serving the indigenous people of Norwood," she judged Thinplace as not particularly successful. Lilly characterized Norwood as a "working-class" community that "suffer[ed] from generational poverty," a description consistent with census and city demographic statistics. She had not been able to consistently involve neighborhood residents in Thinplace, and those who had participated "[found] it hard to adjust."

Lilly invoked a familiar Emerging Evangelical critique when thinking through the clash between her vocational passion and the context of Norwood. "Part of Christian culture," read: conservative Evangelicalism, "is to create some really cool thing and expect people to come. We need to go to where people are." And she did. She chose to host events at St. E and 1801, not closer to her home in an affluent neighborhood seven miles north of Norwood. Still, she struggled to make Thinplace a truly neighborhood group. "Right now, we're not very missional, yet we have missional hearts."

Why does Lilly use this word "missional" to explain her struggle to "[serve] the indigenous people of Norwood"? Of all the values and beliefs discussed with consultants, all the desires of faith reflected on, all the ideals imagined, none was more consistently or exhaustively reported on. No word was more widely asserted as being central to the pursuit of authentic faith. What do Emerging Evangelicals mean when they talk of being missional? What is at stake for them in having "missional hearts"?

Put succinctly, Emerging Evangelicals define missional as being a missionary to one's own society. Being missional is not, however, just an ideal. It encompasses ways of speaking, everyday acts of embodiment, the design of institutions, and desired aesthetics; or, as many consultants described it, "a mindset and a way of living." The analytical problem we confront here is how the cultural work surrounding being missional is a process of subject formation grounded in acts of learning.

Learning to Be Missional

Being missional upholds a definitive cultural feature of Evangelicalism because it is, ultimately, about evangelism. In the Introduction we identified this posture of being a missionary to your own society, influenced by theologians like Lesslie Newbigin, as a primary lineage for the Emerging movement. It is the lineage most explicitly concerned with "reaching the lost," and like the other genealogical sources it is firmly situated in the movement's broader cultural critique. My consultants were either unconvinced of the effectiveness, or at odds with the principles, of the evangelizing methods they associated with conservative Evangelicals. They included a host of familiar scenarios in this critique: preaching on a street corner; handing out pocket-sized tracts with tidy theological explanations; delivering well-rehearsed conversion narratives; using explanations derived from systematic theology to witness; inviting "spiritual seekers" to a weekly congregational event; distributing en masse a relatively inexpensive food commodity (a bottle of water, for example) in a public setting, accompanied by some brief theological literature; picketing Planned Parenthood offices or other highly politicized sites; and relying on training materials about how to effectively evangelize, often studied in weekly small groups.

Why are Emerging Evangelicals troubled by these techniques? Why is Lilly not content to institutionalize Thinplace closer to her home? Why is seven miles too far? The most direct shorthand accepted as an index for the problems of conservative-style evangelism is "relationships." Emerging Evangelicals treat as a taken-for-granted truth the idea that no successful evangelizing can occur without personalized, trusting, and lasting relational commitments. They are certainly not the first Evangelicals to talk about "relational evangelism" (Bielo 2009: 113–134), but in their view established efforts to cultivate relationships with "nonbelievers" suffer from two debilitating problems. First, those efforts maintain the expectation that the unconverted should "come to" Christians rather than Christians "going to" the unconverted. Second, those efforts attempt to foster relationships through programmatic church events rather than through "organic" friendships. For Emerging Evangelicals, the only way to create and sustain relationships with those they want to "reach" is to mimic the acculturating foreign missionary: settle into a locale and learn the intricacies of a place and its people.

Learning to be missional issues from a certain assumption about the spiritual condition of contemporary America. Recall Newbigin's description of "modern Western culture," quoted in the Introduction: "paganism . . . born out of the rejection of Christianity" (1986: 20). Emerging Evangelicals see America, from individual spiritualities to institutional structures, as by and large a post-Christian nation, not wholly secular but discernibly without a Christian canopy. For my consultants, their mission fields are not filled with people competent in Christian theology who simply need convincing. Following Newbigin, their missionized subject is a population that must be learned so that "the gospel" can be "contextualized" to "reach" them. Despite being an explicit critique of "modern Western culture," the cultural category of being missional carries forward a distinctly modern disposition. As Cannell (2006) noted when describing the relationship between missionaries and modernity: "Whatever their tolerance of local practices, they also believe that [Christian] Truth is communicable to all God's creatures" (36).

Following the travels of "missional" throughout the Evangelical world is a Britannica-like project quite beyond our scope. For a hint of its ubiquity, consider that as of August 2010 Internet searches for "missional" conjured about 450 results on Amazon, 1,200 in *Christianity Today*, 1,300 on YouTube, 18,000 on Google Books, 46,000 on Google Images, and 150,000 on Google Blogs. Like other Evangelical cultural categories, "missional" traffics widely through various institutions: local congregations, regional and national conferences, seminaries, and parachurch organizations. The Gospel and Our Culture Network (GOCN), a parachurch network roundly lauded by my consultants, is an example worth highlighting because of its age relative to the Emerging movement.

The GOCN was founded in 1987 as an "ecumenical" and "informal" network. The inaugural newsletter articulated three guiding purposes:

1. Link together people who share a sense of the missionary importance of the encounter of the Gospel and Western culture and are engaged in some way in cultivating that encounter.
2. Exchange information about where and how these issues are being raised and wrestled with so that we can mutually encourage each other.
3. Explore ways in which we might highlight and foster the encounter through joint action.

The GOCN now functions primarily through its website, which includes feature articles, a quarterly newsletter, a blog, and discussion boards. The "About the Network" page confidently asserts that there are "rapid changes taking place as we move from a 'modern' to 'postmodern' form of society," and that there is a "growing un-ease of the church as it experiences a dislocation from its prior places of importance." Emphases on modernity, postmodernity, and decreasing Christian hegemony all bear the direct impress of Newbigin's missiology. His influence also animates the GOCN's "What We Do" explanation:

> [We] exist to give careful attention to the interaction between culture, gospel and church. It arises from the conviction that genuine renewal in the life and witness of the church comes only with a fresh encounter of the gospel within our culture. The network focuses its activities, therefore, on the cultural research, theological reflection and church renewal necessary for the recovery of the church's missionary identity.

In 1997 the GOCN contracted with William B. Eerdmans, one of the largest Christian publishers in the United States, to produce what became a widely influential book series. Their second publication, *Missional Church: A Vision for the Sending of the Church in North America* (Guder and Barrett, eds. 1998), was an extremely common text cited and applauded by consultants when discussing their discovery and continued learning of "thinking missionally." Many of my consultants, including four pastors whose seminary mentors were GOCN founders, thought the GOCN functioned as an important mediator between highly academic theological debates and the messy, everyday dilemmas of pastoral ministry.

The undiscerning spread of "missional" highlights its pervasiveness among Evangelicals. Many consultants joked with me during interviews that "*everybody* wants to be missional," stressing and often exaggerating the opening pronoun. Their anecdotal analysis meshed with my ethnographic observations. Viewed collectively, my sample diverged on issues from the slightly nuanced to the extremely divisive: core doctrines and specific theological points, worship styles and methods, ecclesiological and denominational preferences, biblical hermeneutics, favorite Christian authors, seminary training, and the social contexts of their ministries. By contrast, the desire to be missional was shared without exception.

The discourse and enactment of being missional entails the construction of a missionized subject. This is not simply a matter of identifying a cultural Other. It is a case of imagining this Other as one that must be learned in order to be effectively evangelized. Because the missionized subject takes the form of a local population, the Emerging missional impulse becomes a process of religious learning. The anthropologist Tanya Luhrmann (2010), in her analysis of how charismatic Christians acquire prayer competencies, describes how ethnographies of religious learning "draw our attention to how hard religious practitioners work, how they labor to develop specific skills and ways of being, and how those skills deeply shape their experience of faith" (67).

The missionized subject imagined by Emerging Evangelicals differs from that constructed by their conservative counterparts. As a foil for the examples we examine below, consider Omri Elisha's (2008b) ethnographic work with megachurch Evangelicals who are socially engaged, suburban, and politically and theologically conservative. He describes those who evangelize in the inner city as "suburban churchgoers [who] interact with cultural strangers affected by conditions of poverty, distress and marginalization" (156). Elisha argues that the moral and emotional difficulties of these suburban evangelists derive from a "theology of exchange" where "evangelical acts of compassion and charitable gifts are conceived as graceful gestures with 'no strings attached,' [but] they invoke norms of reciprocity and indebtedness that are central to evangelical thought" (157). Elisha's depictions of "cultural strangers" and "indebtedness" are precisely what Emerging Evangelicals interested in being missional diagnose to be the problem. For them, the missionized subject must be learned, must cease to be a stranger, otherwise no trust can be generated. As they perform this learning of local mission fields, and create institutions based on what they learn, specific and generic cultural assumptions are activated and reproduced.

Missional Acts

How do Emerging Evangelicals translate their missional desires into practice? This is a crucial question if we are to examine how the project of being a missionary to your own society is a project of religious learning. The forms of action pursued in the name of being missional are windows into how the missionized subject is imagined. Innumerable responses were given when I asked how church communities were attempting to be missional. My consultants would likely understand this variety of responses through the missiologic that being attuned to the particularities of a setting are vital to properly "contextualize the Gospel." Still, there are distinct categories we can use to sort these innumerable responses. Worship—as a style, an aesthetic, and a space—is one possibility. Local activism is another. Some forms of activism entail joining existing efforts—for example, soup kitchens or food pantries organized by established congregations or institutions like the Salvation Army. Activism also took the form of creating new institutions. In some cases, strides toward being missional meant that individuals and communities had to make minor adjustments to existing practices. In other cases, being missional meant a severe rupture of personal and congregational circumstance. The three examples below highlight cases of new institution creation and represent actualizations of idea(l)s valorized by many of the individuals and communities in my fieldwork.

A Teenage Jerusalem

The sign in the window reads "Empowering Students to Impact the World." The window fronts the corner unit of a recently built, brick and concrete strip mall in a northern exurb of Cincinnati. Across the street is a tenth- to twelfth-grade high school that enrolls nineteen hundred students. Despite the cramped-looking strip mall, the inside extends back deeper and the ceiling is much taller than the outside lets on. Everything looks sleek. The hard concrete floors are shiny, polished, and painted black. All the lighting is dim. The furniture is a lightweight silver aluminum. The wall and ceiling paints are alternating shades of bright, arresting neon colors. The long, S-shaped welcome desk at the immediate front divides the unit. The room to the right is smaller, and has a series of moveable tables and chairs. The left opens up into several distinct spaces. The first has several Foosball and billiard tables, four computers, and multiple video gaming stations. The second has a stool-lined bar stocked with soda, smoothie, and coffee offerings. The third has a small stage with an open space and numerous chairs. The last, in the very back, is an enclosed room with cushy couches and a large-screen television. The Edge Teen Center was started by Wellspring Community Church, a midsize nondenominational congregation whose main building is a half-mile away. Carl initiated both these institutions, Edge in 2007 and Wellspring fifteen years earlier. He is the senior pastor at Wellspring and Edge is their primary missional outpost.

When I first interviewed Carl, he was consuming some juxtaposed products. For the meeting site he chose a local representative of a national restaurant chain. He was sitting on the outdoor patio when I arrived, overlooking the parking lot vista and surrounding big-box store sprawl. He has a slight build and tanned, olive skin. He was wearing khaki shorts, a short-sleeved black polo shirt, a sterling silver wristwatch, and closed toe sandals. His hair, dark and peppered with silver, was neatly trimmed and accompanied by a small soul patch above his chin. He sat with legs crossed, engrossed in a book. My initial thought was that he resembled a business executive on vacation, maybe in Hawaii or some Caribbean island. His reading material conjured a different impression. *The Divine Commodity: Discovering a Faith beyond Consumer Christianity* (2009) is Skye Jethani's first book and, along with his regular writings for mainstream Evangelical periodicals, his first major contribution to the Emerging Evangelical culture industry. Jethani is unrelentingly critical of American Christianity's reliance on the idioms, organizational structures, and assumptions of consumer capitalism. He writes in Chapter 1, "Our deficiency is not motivation or money, but imagination" (18). The clash between Jethani's message and the unapologetically commercial setting repeats a tension Carl lives daily: an exurban pastor committed to Emerging Evangelical critiques of conspicuous consumption.

Carl narrates his religious identity as a double deconversion. He grew up in a Pentecostal household and graduated from the global charismatic mecca of Kenneth Hagin's Bible College in Tulsa, Oklahoma (see Coleman 2000). Carl moved to Cincinnati in 1983 to be an assistant pastor at a small Pentecostal church. He helped the congregation grow from a hundred to eight hundred people in nine years, but could not ignore a "gnawing feeling" that Pentecostalism was incongruent with his "[spiritual] gift mix." His faith was more "grounded," less reliant on the high experientialism of charismatic Christianity. At a 1989 church growth conference Carl discovered the Seeker-Sensitive congregational model, where Sunday worship services are pitched as a primary site to evangelize and attract spiritual seekers. He said it was "unlike anything I had ever heard." This began his first deconversion, from Fundamentalist Pentecostalism to Seeker-Sensitive Evangelicalism. In response, he left his assistant pastor position and started Wellspring Community Church in 1992 with his wife and four friends. In 1996 they moved from a rented space in a storefront into their current building. By 2004 Wellspring had grown to three hundred members, but Carl had a "realization" that the congregation was doing nothing "missions-wise." True to the Seeker-Sensitive logic, their staff and volunteer energies were heavily directed toward the Sunday worship service. He was "convicted" one day reading the Parable of the Sheep and the Goats in Matthew 25 and its references to "whatever you did for the least." At the same time one of his congregants recommended a recently published book, *The Present Future: Six Tough Questions for the Church* (2003), which was "key" for Carl's "transitioning from thinking about missions to thinking missionally." (This book, it is worth observing, was one of a few texts cited repeatedly, across theological lines, as deeply influential in changing consultants' approach to evangelism.) This began his second deconversion from being a Seeker-Sensitive to an Emerging-missional Evangelical. In 2004 they did not have any outreach ministries and in 2005 they had eight. The trade-off was a de-emphasized Sunday morning worship service, which prompted several dozen members to leave the church.

Through Carl's direction, Wellspring started "Kingdomworks," an annual tithing effort designed as an enactment of Acts 1:8: "you will be my witnesses in Jerusalem, and in all Judea and Samaria, and to the ends of the earth." They interpret the three locations in this text to mean their immediate exurban locale, the nearby urban context of Cincinnati's racially and economically diverse neighborhoods, and the global population. Globally, they donate to the building of water wells in a Ugandan village. In Cincinnati, they restored and now rent out three homes in a lower-middle-class neighborhood three miles north of downtown and twenty-five miles south of their exurb. In 2007 they started planning their Jerusalem: The Edge Teen Center, a community space for high school kids. As of January 2010 they attracted nearly fifty teenagers to a daily after-school program and over a hundred to events on weekend nights.

The Edge Teen Center is their attempt to be exurban missionaries. It is an institution that reflects their understanding of the local population and, by extension, an enactment of the cultural assumptions used in imagining their missionized subject. As Carl explained it, they began by asking "how to serve upper-middle class suburbanites." He was confident that the answer was not "help with finances or personal issues," both of which he considered heavily guarded and kept out of public view due to preoccupations with privacy, reputation, and personal responsibility for self-improvement. The answer was children. Carl constructs a social-psychological image of exurban teenagers. He considers them to be severely "troubled" by the psycho-emotional stress of fulfilling the expectations of success that develop among two-income, economically advantaged households. The main consequence he assigns to this stress is a persistent loneliness that leads teens into legal and illegal substance abuse, addiction, and other destructive behaviors. This view of the missionized subject translates into a need for safe, positive places where teenagers can gather. The Edge Teen Center is Wellspring's response. In addition to the after-school program and weekend events, Carl wants to add a tutoring program, counseling, "life skills" classes, and opportunities for "community service." For the latter, he wants to address another problem endemic among suburban teenagers, being "sheltered" in an upper-middle class environment that is disconnected from the economic and personal dilemmas of living in poverty. He hopes to find volunteer opportunities for Edge Teen kids in the economically depressed, postindustrial city of Middletown, fifteen miles north. Carl wants them to "do something more than rake grandma's leaves." The creation of The Edge Teen Center and its ongoing programs are guided by this imagining of teenage suburbia.

A Necessary Bridge

Three large windows are framed, respectively, with the words "Coffee, Community, Creativity." They front a singular, three-story brick building on an urban street corner. Across the street in one direction is the University of Cincinnati, a 40,000-student public university two miles north of downtown. In the other direction is a low-income residential neighborhood. The exterior suggests an older building, an impression confirmed by the inside. The walls are a faded brick and the wood floors are well-worn. The outside's three-part, alliterative window framing is repeated on three side-by-side bulletin boards to the left of the entrance. The "Coffee" board posts information about the benefits and details of fair trade coffee, along with newsprint and glossy pictures of smiling, laboring Hispanic farmers. The "Community" board mixes information and announcements about the city with left-leaning political messages. There is a world map entitled "What does an Empire look like?" with the sites of U.S. military bases marked throughout the globe. There is a paper cutout in the shape of George Washington's head filled with red, white, and blue puzzle pieces containing egregious environmental policies from the George W. Bush presidency. The "Creativity" board posts upcoming events featuring local musicians and artists. The up and downstairs are littered generously with desks, tables, chairs, and couches. The brick walls showcase art collections by Cincinnati artists, which are changed each month. The Taza Coffee Shop was started by D'Vine, a Vineyard Fellowship church that was planted in 2006. Aaron was the planting pastor for D'Vine, opened Taza in 2008, and hoped it would be the church's primary missional outpost.

Aaron became a born-again Evangelical at age seventeen, but from high school through college and into his years in graduate school he felt like he had "just visited churches for a decade." He first committed himself to a congregation in 1999, a suburban Vineyard megachurch north of Cincinnati. Three years later, still an active member of the church, he "felt called to this part of the city." The megachurch wanted to be the sponsoring congregation for new church plants in the city and Aaron accepted a staff position overseeing the formation of small groups in different neighborhoods. After three years in that position, he felt ready to plant D'Vine with the goal of opening a missional coffee house. From 2006 until late 2009 D'Vine struggled to strike the balance of being a missional, self-sustaining church that concentrated on and equally served two populations: a mixed college student demographic and economically distressed black inner-city residents. Taza struggled to be a self-sustaining business that did not rely on financial giving from D'Vine members or the sponsoring megachurch. But D'Vine never grew above fifty members and never attracted more than a hundred and ten people for Sunday worship. Aaron considered his three years leading D'Vine "the hardest place [he'd] ever done ministry."

During one of our interviews, Aaron told a story that he felt captured the difficulties of being missional in this location. During their first years as a church, D'Vine members collected leftover bread once a week from the nearest Panera (a national chain sandwich restaurant) and distributed it to local residents. On one Easter Sunday, a characteristically large attendance week, "the neighborhood drunk" came into the worship service at Taza looking for the man who delivered her bread. The deliverer happened to be the bass guitarist for the worship band and was on stage performing when she entered. The neighborhood woman "made a beeline" for the stage and stayed there hugging the bassist and crying for "what seemed like a half hour." A week later, following a particularly rough period of attempted sobriety, she returned, requesting to be baptized. She remained a part of the D'Vine community for the next eighteen months—sometimes drunk, sometimes sober— and relied heavily on members' help for food, clothing, transportation, and a listening ear. She died unexpectedly in late 2008. Reflecting on her death a year later, Aaron asked, "How would the last year and a half of her life have been different had she not been part of our community?" For Aaron, this story—characterized by tenuousness, unpredictability, and exhaustion—was the story of trying to be missional in this neighborhood.

In late 2009, Aaron, his wife, and other founding members of D'Vine made the decision to stop doing weekly worship services and other organized church meetings. Aaron asked several members to find a new church home because they were involved only in Sunday worship, and did no ministry work in the neighborhood. For all practical purposes, D'vine, as a congregation, folded after three years. However, Taza remained open as a missional outpost. Aaron and his wife took over the rights to the business and it now functions as a self-sustaining coffee house. Taza is a regular and impromptu host for various Emerging Evangelical events: for example, Doug Pagitt's promotional book tour and Lilly's MapRoom. Aaron failed as a church planter, but he is not particularly disappointed. During a brief interview in late March 2010, Aaron explained his missional work as a process: "[F]inally, after four years, what we've wanted is happening; we're meeting students and we're a presence in the community. It's amazing what can happen when you're not hung up on putting on the weekly production."

Taza has remained Aaron's focus because it represents the possibility of a necessary bridge between college students and neighborhood residents. But why *this* kind of institution? Why a coffee shop? Aaron is convinced that coffee shops provide an experience that ignites aspects of a shared God-given humanity: the need to gather and the need to express creativity. Unfortunately, their success thus far has only been with half of their desired mission field. Ninety percent of Taza's business derives from students, 10 percent from business professionals who live and work elsewhere in the city, and none from residents in the adjoining neighborhood. On all my visits to Taza, widely varied by time of day and day of week, I never once saw a customer who matched the desired demographic of poor blacks. Still, Aaron remains encouraged that the needs Taza promises to serve—community and creativity—will ultimately succeed despite the neighborhood's inherited, structural problems. He does not think that providing a public space for community and creativity will relieve residents' economic difficulties. He does think that serving the needs of community and creativity enriches life and is an embodied way to "share the Gospel." As part of his learning and imagining a missionized subject, Aaron believes that these values are missing from residents' lives. The story he chose to share about the woman who interrupted Easter worship serves this logic. The narrative focus of Aaron's telling was not how her death could have been prevented, or how she inspired a brand new program for confronting addiction. Rather, the narrative focus was the woman's last year and a half and the difference the church made in her quality of life during that period. Unlike Carl, whose religious learning focused on a single demographic, Aaron concentrates on cultivating values that he considers part of being human.

A New City

Mason, Ohio is a new-growth residential outpost fixed halfway between two Interstate highways. It is twenty-six miles northeast of downtown Cincinnati and thirty-five miles south of downtown Dayton. In 1970 it was home to less than 6,000 people, quadrupling in size by the 2000 Census. The county Mason is in has the fifth highest median housing value and the fourth highest median household income in the state. The 3,000-student high school in Mason is 84 percent white. Demographically, historically, and structurally it is an iconic representation of American exurbia.

North Cincinnati Community Church (NCCC) is a midsize Evangelical (Presbyterian Church of America, PCA) congregation near the geographic center of Mason. It is well-positioned to continue the process of suburban megachurch growth perfected by late twentieth century Evangelicals (Luhr 2009). But they are resisting that process. The membership of NCCC hovers around six hundred, and they are determined to maintain that size. Rather than grow exponentially, their ministry plan is to be a sponsoring congregation for new church plants throughout Cincinnati's urban neighborhoods. The first stride in this direction started in 2008 when NCCC's youth pastor, Josh, gathered a "launch team" for a new church.

Whenever I interacted with Josh, irrespective of the situation's formality or context, he always struck me (recalling my first field note description of him) as tidy. His shirts, often pressed, were usually tucked into his pants, often khaki. His hair and beard were always trimmed neatly to a short length. Everything had the impression of being cared for. Such meticulous attention to appearance can be off-putting, but Josh allays this danger with an easygoing, yet enthusiastic demeanor. He joined the staff of NCCC in 2003 as their youth pastor, but always with the intention of being their first urban church planter.

Josh's born-again conversion occurred in junior high school, and his faith matured in college through Campus Crusade for Christ. Through CCC he went on two mission trips, the first in 1996 to Japan and the second in 1997 to South Carolina. These were the "first seeds" of his missionary sensibilities. He graduated with a degree in Mass Communication, joined the ministry staff at CCC, and made his first attempt at full-time missionary work when he started a campus ministry at the University of Leiden in the Netherlands. The ministry was marginally successful, and Josh left the position early to complete a master's degree in Comparative Religion. He exercised his missionary interests in this setting as well, writing a thesis on "why and how" the early Evangelical revivalist George Whitefield was able to "adapt himself to different social contexts" in Scotland, Britain, and the United States. From 1999 to 2002 Josh attended Princeton Theological Seminary to pursue a second master's in Divinity. Josh joined the PCA denomination while at Princeton. At this time he also began listening to online sermons and reading books from two major voices in the Evangelical, church planting world of Reformed Calvinism: Tim Keller and Mark Driscoll, pastors in New York City and Seattle, respectively. They spoke the language of "being missional," which aligned with his formal education at Princeton, including classes with Darrel Guder, coeditor of *Missional Church* (1998).

Josh's church planting aspirations materialized in late 2008. With the guidance of NCCC's senior pastor and his wife Paige, he invited twenty-one people to join the new church launch team. Although three married couples were not able to accept, the remaining fifteen people began meeting weekly in January 2009 to "cast the vision" for their church. Along with Josh and Paige, the launch team consisted of seven married couples, two single men, and one single woman. Two couples were in their fifties, and the rest were in their late twenties and early thirties. All were white, and most were living and working in the exurban land of Mason.

Their church would be in Oakley, a middle-class urban neighborhood six miles northeast of downtown Cincinnati. Why this neighborhood? Josh's official Church Plant Proposal announces on the opening page, "approximately 60,000 people live within seven minutes of Oakley Square," a fact Josh and other launch team members committed to memory. Josh "strongly encouraged" the entire launch team to leave their current residence and move to or near Oakley. The model of evangelism and social engagement typical of Evangelical megachurches, represented ethnographically by Elisha (2008b), is to return to suburbia following a day's labor in the city. Following his training at Princeton and his consumption of missional resources, this model was flawed and the move from Mason to Oakley was not just a good idea; it was necessary.

As of May 2010 all but four launch team members had relocated. Those who had not, the two older couples, had their houses on the market and searched actively, often daily, for a new home. Josh and Paige bought a home in Oakley, several months prior to the first worship service in October 2009. Mike and Becky began renting a condo in Mt. Lookout in 2004, an upwardly mobile, young professional neighborhood, two miles south of Josh and Paige. They had been commuting every Sunday to NCCC and remained active members on the promise that the urban church plant was immanent. Mark bought a condo in Hyde Park in mid-2009, a largely upper-middle-class, family-oriented neighborhood and a ten-minute walk from Josh and Paige. Tim and Claire bought a home in Madisonville in late 2008, a working- and lower-middle-class, primarily black neighborhood, two miles east of Josh and Paige. Matt and Katie began renting an apartment in Oakley in late 2009, just over a mile from Josh and Paige. And Peter moved from a rented apartment in Mt. Lookout to a purchased home (with his new wife) in Hyde Park in early 2010. They all, following the language and logic of being missional, see themselves as missionaries to Oakley and have intentionally placed themselves close to the center of Oakley and close to each other.

The name they chose for their church, "New City," is intended to echo St. Augustine's fifth-century canonical work, *City of God*. Connecting their missional logic to this historic resource is a theological-rhetorical move that Josh wanted as part of their public personae, featuring it in the "Our Story" segment of their website. Note the ancient-future tinged opening clause:

> A long time ago, St. Augustine said that there is a city of God within every city of man. His meaning was that God was at work in every human city by planting and establishing an alternate city within that city, whose purpose was to renew and restore the human city. This city of God, the church, is meant to act as a preview society, demonstrating and declaring what life can be like under the reign of Christ.

The language of renewal, redemption, and reconciliation that Josh assigns to Augustine repeated throughout 2009 as the New City launch team met weekly to plot their plan and purpose. In late July they held their first public "information meeting" at a coffee house/art gallery in downtown Oakley. A portion of their eventual worship band played a few songs, but the event was mainly social. Early in the evening Josh gave a brief, fifteen-minute advertisement for their new church. He included an Augustine-inspired explanation of their chosen name:

> We call ourselves "New City" because we want to be a light for the city of Cincinnati. We want to model for people what the kingdom of heaven will be like by showing them the love of Christ. How would our relationships be different? How would marriages and families be different? How would

friendships be different? What would race relations be like? How would it change the way we live in community with our neighbors?

The meaningfulness of their chosen name was also highlighted in their first worship service. The sermon, "All Things New," was the first in a six-week series of the same title. The chorus of the service's introductory praise song, "In Your Name," continued this theme of urban redemption:

> And Oh that this city would know your love
> And Oh that this city would feel your touch
> And Oh that this city would live with hope
> Give us hands to touch, give us hearts of love

The iconicity of newness is central to their imagining of a missionized subject. They do not begin as Carl and Wellspring do, in thinking about a demographic, or as Aaron and Taza do, in thinking about a base human need. Josh and New City begin with an imagined place, one in need of renewal. Their intentional relocation to Oakley is part of this imagined change. In late 2009 and early 2010, I completed a round of interviews with New City launch team members. One question I asked each of them was, "How would you describe Oakley to someone not from Cincinnati?" Their answers emphasized one quality over any other: Oakley as an urban crossroads. They consider it a mixed place, though not necessarily a place of mixing. They see class diversity, mirrored by its location between neighborhoods that are affluent (Hyde Park to the south, Mariemont to the southeast) and less affluent (Norwood to the west, Madisonville to the northeast). They see increasing age diversity, with an established contingent of middle-aged and older adults and a recent influx of young professionals attracted to Oakley's comparatively cheaper real estate. They see both transient and settled groups in these demographics. However, they see this as a segregated diversity. They do not see these distinct groups coming together in any meaningful way. They see an opportunity in their missionized subject: bringing unity to a divided city.

Missionaries or Colonialists?

These three examples—Carl and The Edge Teen Center, Aaron and Taza, Josh and New City—speak to the lived experience of Emerging Evangelicals acting on the logic of being missional. Their missional acts entail the imagining of a missionized subject, and in doing so they reproduce specific cultural assumptions. Carl envisions an ideal type for the American suburban teenager, Aaron posits an innate human need that goes unmet in economically difficult circumstances, and Josh sees a city in need of renewal. Thus far, we have resisted a critical reading of the Emerging missional impulse: an analysis of how middle-class whites speak for and position racialized and classed Others. Such an analysis seems prescient for the numerous church planters in my fieldwork who are indeed middle-class whites exercising their missional impulse in race-class contexts different from those they matured in. An ethnographic moment from October 2009 allows us to reflect on this tension.

In the same week that New City had their first worship service, the Christian Community Development Association (CCDA) held their annual three-day conference in downtown Cincinnati. CCDA is an ecumenical organization that began in 1989 and whose stated mission is "to inspire, train, and connect Christians who seek to bear witness to the Kingdom of God by reclaiming and restoring under-resourced communities." I arrived at the conference center thirty minutes before the scheduled opening plenary, which was held in a 40,000-square foot ballroom. There were at least two thousand chairs set up, and by the end of the night the overflow pushed people to line up along every available wall. It was multigenerational and multiethnic; in fact, the percentage of blacks was over-represented. An anecdotal glancing of name tags revealed a well-traveled audience, with every region of the United States represented as well as British, Scottish, and other transnational Anglophone attendees. There were five large projection screens at the front, and two elevated camera crews in the middle of the room. The size and setting made for an impersonal feel, which clashed with the constant reunionesque ("I-have-not-seen-you-since-last-year's-CCDA!") hugs.

The plenary speaker was Dr. Soong-Chan Rah, Associate Professor of Church Growth and Evangelism at North Park Theological Seminary in Chicago, and author of *The Next Evangelicalism: Freeing the Church from Western Cultural Captivity* (2009). Rah was assigned to address one of the conference themes, "Subversion: New Approaches to Activism," and spoke about doing urban ministry in the context of changing national and global racial demographics. Much of his talk was a criticism of mono-ethnic Christianity and how white Evangelicals conduct urban ministry. Midway through his talk he boldly asserted, "*If you, as a white person, want to move into an urban setting and do ministry, and you don't have any nonwhite mentors, you're not a missionary, you're a colonialist.*" This was promptly followed by a surprised round of "oohs" and "whoas" from the audience.

TABLE 5.1

Respondents to Soong-Chan Rah's Missionary-Colonialist
Comment at 2009 CCDA Conference

Name	Age	Denomination	Place of Ministry	Year Current Ministry Began
Aaron	31-35	Vineyard	Cincinnati, Ohio	2006
Josh	31-35	Presbyterian Church of America	Cincinnati, Ohio	2009
Bart	41-45	Non-denominational	Cincinnati, Ohio	2005
Michael	31-35	Southern Baptist Convention	Cincinnati, Ohio	2009
Tim	31-35	Southern Baptist Convention	Cincinnati, Ohio	2008
Kevin	26-30	Non-denominational	Middletown, Ohio	2006
Jeremy	31-35	Reformed Church of America	Lansing, Michigan	2005
Aaron	31-35	Southern Baptist Convention	Phoenix, Arizona	2000
Bobby	41-45	Non-denominational	Phoenix, Arizona	2006
Scott	41-45	Presbyterian Church of America	Phoenix, Arizona	2003

Rah's assertion reminded me of Lilly. His condemnation seemed to echo the worry Lilly levied at herself about not being missional enough in Norwood. She spoke across class lines, not race lines, but the idea was much the same. Driving home from the CCDA conference that night I was distracted by a single thought: how would my consultants respond to Rah's missionary-colonialist comment? Several days later I emailed his quote, along with an explanation of the context it occurred in, to eighteen of the white missional Evangelicals who fit Rah's profile. Ten responded, including Aaron and Josh from above. I posed an open-ended question, asking them to respond to Rah's criticism in any way they wanted. Table 5.1 offers a brief portrait of these respondents.

Six themes characterized their responses, informing our understanding of the religious learning entailed in Emerging Evangelical imaginings and practices of being missional.

Respondents appreciated Rah's sentiment and accepted a general truth in his critique. Kevin highlighted the habitual nature of white privilege: "I think many white pastors seem to think they have the answers to the problems of their city/context. White people are arrogant towards other races most of the time. It is usually subtle and often they are unaware of their arrogance, but it is there." Bart placed the onus of avoiding a colonialist posture on the hopeful missionary: "Becoming culturally bilingual, I think, is a primary responsibility of the white guys." Respondents accepted, in a theoretical sense, the missionary/colonialist distinction and its racial underpinnings.

Respondents assigned a rhetorical, hyperbolic quality to Rah's statement. Bart called it "an unrealistic guilt trip on a practical level." Michael, "needlessly provocative;" Jeremy, "inflammatory;" and Josh thought "colonialist" was used for "shock value." Aaron (from Phoenix) invoked the familiar Emerging Evangelical critique of commodification: "good quote to sell books and book speaking engagements." Respondents recognized the performative opportunity of an opening plenary speech at a large, national conference.

Respondents problematized Rah's critique on what they consider historical-biblical grounds. Bobby listed several examples: "The first Christians were all Jewish and were each mentored by a Jewish rabbi: Jesus. They of course were given the message of taking the gospel to the entire world. Historically, I don't believe St. Patrick (Ireland) nor Hudson Taylor (China) had the privilege of being mentored by a representative of the cultures they were called to evangelize and disciple (nor did William Booth or Mother Teresa). If Patrick, Taylor, Booth, and Mother Teresa were Colonialists, so be it." Tim did the same: "Israel was called by God out of Egypt to a pagan land, Jonah was called to Nineveh, Jesus was called to humanity, many of Christ's 12 went to different cultures, and Paul was called to the Gentiles. God has shown he will call 'strangers' unto a land that is not known to them." Respondents who took this stance used one logic (the historical continuity of Christians acting missionally) to trump another (the problematics of contemporary U.S. race relations).

Respondents thought Rah needed greater nuance with respect to race-class relations. Aaron (from Cincinnati) was most explicit on this point: "I assume he is using the word 'urban' to equal 'nonwhite.' That's a big leap for me especially in my 'urban' context where white is still the majority. I also think this is old thinking, to classify and group by race rather than get more specific. I am interacting with more and more biracial 20-somethings. On my leadership team right now I have people who are half Vietnamese, half African American, and half Mexican as well as an African American woman who is far more 'suburban upper-middle class' in upbringing than most of the 'whites' on my team." Respondents were not content with singular racial categories or with any explanation that tried to disentangle race from class.

Respondents criticized Rah for removing all agency from urban missional Evangelicals. Kevin said, "If a white man is going to pastor/plant a church in a racially diverse area, he needs to listen often and speak seldom when meeting people throughout the city." Michael echoed this conviction: "My suspicion is that white people working in an urban context will soon enough develop meaningful relationships with nonwhites and they can learn from one another. If that is what is meant by 'mentor,' then this will happen if the white person is open and teachable." And Josh, who planted in Oakley, which is 88 percent white, agreed: "I have been conscious of seeking out a partnership with a nonwhite church, largely because of our proximity to Madisonville, which is 75 percent black. And I have made it clear that we are entering into this relationship as 'learners,' meaning that we are looking for them to teach us about the needs of the community and some of the things God is doing there." Just as they imagine a missionized Other, respondents imagine an idealized missionizing Self that is first and foremost a "learner."

Finally, respondents reveal themselves as reflective, self-conscious religious subjects. They do not dismiss Rah outright, nor do they accept his critique uncritically. Rather, they interact with my elicitation dialogically, not defensively. In doing so they renew a core value that has animated the Emerging movement since its inception: the desire for ongoing dialogue when it comes to matters of faith. This interactive posture reflects an important assumption about their religious learning: while they may desire to be learners, their learning is never complete. Being a missionary to your own society means submitting to the fact that the job you have set for yourself will never be accomplished. You will never know the people you want to missionize as exhaustively as you would like. Yet this same assumption fuels the ongoing desire to be missional. If the learning is never complete, then there is a lot of learning left to do.

Being missional is, fundamentally, about two actions: evangelism and learning. As Emerging Evangelicals seek to "have missional hearts" they construct an imagined missionized Other, the details of which are used to create institutions for fostering evangelistic efforts. By accepting the posture of being missionaries they take on a modern subject position, which will likely continue to receive Rah-like critiques in late modern cultural conditions of racial and class inequality. In the next chapter we will continue our analysis of what it means to be missional by examining a cultural category that has appeared several times already: the kingdom of God.

6

Missional II

Kingdom Theologies

I reviewed the diagram once more before holding it up to show everyone. For several minutes I had been sketching it in my field notebook. In the middle of the page was one word, in capital letters, "KINGDOM." Curved and straight lines extended in all directions from this centerpiece. Capping the lines was a series of words: "Identity," "Worship," "Missional," "Theology," "Environment," "Place," "Politics." I wanted to convey (however inartistically) the idea that so much of Evangelical thought and practice is connected to, if not derived from, kingdom theology: understandings about the nature—the what, when, where, why, how, and who—of "God's kingdom."

This diagram was sketched during the plenary session of the May 2009 Subversion/Truthvoice conference organized by Virgil (whose story of simplicity we heard earlier). Because of my research with Emerging Evangelicals, Virgil asked me to participate in a ninety-minute public question and answer session to close the opening day of the conference. This plenary session, "The Church, Emergent Christianity, and Its Future," featured Virgil asking questions and facilitating audience inquiries about the Emerging Church to myself and Fred, a pastor and real estate agent from Atlanta, Georgia. The conference was in a suburban Holiday Inn east of Dayton. Our session was in a lecture-style room with slanted seating and an open front stage where we sat in three side-by-side chairs.

Midway through the session I was ready to share my sketch with Virgil, Fred, and the roughly sixty-person audience. Virgil had asked what kinds of observations I was making in my research. In response, I held up the diagram and explained its intent: the kingdom theology one advocates can impact virtually every element of religious life. It was a very brief moment altogether, and the remainder of the session continued uneventfully. Afterwards, Virgil thanked me for participating and asked to see the diagram again. He assessed it briefly, smiled, and exclaimed that it was strikingly similar to a diagram he planned to use for his conference presentation the next

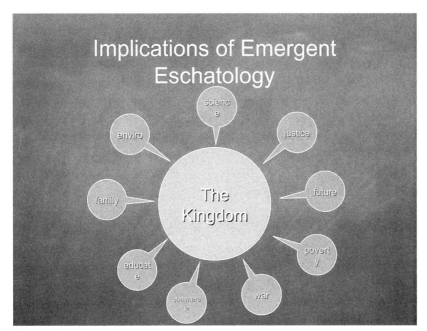

Figure 6.1. Closing PowerPoint slide from Virgil's May 2009 conference presentation.

day. Honestly, I thought he was being polite, trying to express some appreciation for my agreeing to be on the panel. I was wrong. When Virgil sent me a copy of his presentation PowerPoint the last slide more than resembled my ad hoc creation (Figure 6.1).

Virgil, thinking as a theologian, and I, thinking as an ethnographer, were convinced of the same conclusion: kingdom theology is central to Emerging Evangelical processes of identity construction, everyday interpretations, and institution making. We will consider several questions here. Where do kingdom theologies fit in the cultural logic of being missional? How do kingdom theologies offer adherents models of temporality, religious subjectivity, and agency? Why should we distinguish between different kingdom theologies? And how might the cultural work performed through kingdom theology capture a tension that confronts all Christianities?

Kingdom, Time, Action

The anthropologist Jon Bialecki (2009) provides a helpful framework for understanding how kingdom theology operates in Christians' social and religious lives. Writing from the vantage of his ethnographic work with Vineyard neo-charismatics in southern California, Bialecki argues that kingdom theology provides a clear view of the sociopolitical motivations and mobilizations of his consultants: theologically conservative, politically left-leaning Progressive Evangelicals. He explains that kingdom theologies address issues of temporality, "the phenomenological and cultural sense of and models for time's immediate passing" (35), and eschatology, models for understanding God's interventions in humanity's future. The eschatological event of Christ's Second Coming—much like other major events in Christian theology (creation, incarnation, resurrection, conversion) —reveals Christianity as a religion of rupture and discontinuity (Robbins 2007). In turn, the attention devoted to "God's Kingdom" by Evangelicals reveals them as religious subjects preoccupied with ontological change, and the interplay of pasts, presents, and futures.

The kingdom theology promoted by Vineyard charismatics is traced to George Eldon Ladd, an Evangelical professor at Fuller Theological Seminary (Pasadena, California) who wrote during the 1950s, '60s, and '70s. Vineyard members believe that "'the kingdom of God' is suspended in its existence, as 'already' and 'not yet' at the same time" (Bialecki 2009: 116). This now, not yet view of the kingdom reckons that:

> Although Jesus' death on the cross—and the advent of the Holy Spirit— has opened up an interstitial moment in which divine justice is imaginable and supernatural healing is possible, justice and healing are conceived of not as consistent with the present order but as moments out of time, part of an alien future whose only relationship with the present is that of pure incommensurability. (ibid.: 116)

The now, not yet kingdom theology structures the possibilities for social action that are imaginable among Vineyard adherents, namely, the "inability to think through short-term political projects" (ibid.: 112). The intersection of kingdom, time, and action is ultimately a problem of hope: "a fundamental reorientation of knowledge, as it enables one to think through problems prospectively rather than retrospectively" (111). Kingdom theologies are foundational in Christian culture because they offer models of time and subjectivity, and because they promote forms of thought and action that reflect the relative presence or absence of hope. Emerging Evangelicals make kingdom theology a central part of the cultural logic of being missional. My consultants constantly talked about their desire to "show people the kingdom," the base intention of which is to convert the unconverted. Being a missionary to your own society includes bringing your understanding of the nature of God's kingdom to the local mission field.

We should not, however, assume that all Evangelicals mean the same thing when they talk about "the Kingdom," "God's Kingdom," "the Kingdom of Heaven," or "the Kingdom of God." As Bialecki's work suggests, the differences are meaningful for understanding how Christians organize their sociopolitical efforts. Three kingdom theologies are operative in American Evangelicalism, two of which are advocated among Emerging Evangelicals. Policing the boundaries of these two views of God's Kingdom—the now, not yet version and a theological system called Preterism that claims the kingdom has been fully present since 70 C.E.—is yet another means of Evangelical identity distinction. That is, to accept one kingdom theology over another is one way to position yourself in the religious field of contemporary Evangelicalism.

The Kingdom as Coming

We begin with the kingdom theology that dominated conservative Evangelical thought during the twentieth century (Frykholm 2004). It is still pervasive among American Fundamentalists, and Emerging Evangelicals use it as a reliable foil. More dramatic in its plotline than the kingdom theologies promoted by Emerging Evangelicals, it epitomizes the claim that Christianity is a religion of radical discontinuities (Robbins 2007). This kingdom theology is the basis for the hugely popular *Left Behind* book series. Beginning in 1995 with a book of the same title and culminating in a sixteenth volume, *Kingdom Come: The Final Victory*, in 2007, *Left Behind* is the highest grossing series in Evangelical print history and the progenitor of a multimedia industry (Monahan 2008). The plot is organized as a fictional retelling of the Book of Revelation set in contemporary times. Among the more recognizable events structuring *Left Behind* is the rapture: the global, sudden, instantaneous, unpredictable ascension of all born-again Christians into the skies above. The rapture is particular to the eschatological system called pretribulational dispensational premillennialism. Pretribulational refers to the promise that Christians will not have to endure a lengthy period of harrowing trials that will torture the globe. Dispensational puts the rapture in a historical scheme: God has divided the time of eternity into discrete periods (dispensations), each marked by events prophesied in scripture. The rapture marks the beginning of the final dispensation. Premillennialism means that the literal Second Coming of Jesus will occur prior to, not after, a thousand-year period that precedes God's final eternal judgment of humanity. In this scenario the Kingdom of God is a physical place—currently separate from the earth—called heaven, which will eventually replace the insufferable conditions of Earth.

As of 2005, the *Left Behind* series had sold 63 million copies in 37 countries, was translated into 33 languages, and had earned $650 million (Monahan 2008). Pulitzers have done less. The genealogy of pretribulational dispensational premillennialism extends through Fundamentalist Hal Lindsay's 1970 single-volume rapture fiction success *The Late Great Planet Earth*, the 1909 Scofield Study Bible which upheld the doctrine of the rapture in footnotes, and the Fundamentalist writings of John Nelson Darby in the late nineteenth century. It dates to 1830, when a Scottish woman reported a prophetic vision of this end times narrative.

The history and political economy of *Left Behind* are less prescient here than its kingdom theology. *Left Behind* communicates to its readers a series of assumptions about the nature of God's Kingdom: heaven and hell are literal places that physically exist somewhere; the earth will endure severe destruction before eventually being evacuated by Christ and His followers; the Second Coming is a literal event, unknown in occurrence but imminent; the warfare between Good and Evil depicted in the Book of Revelation is literal and unavoidable; Christians are unable to demonstrably improve any societal conditions because of the plague that is human sinfulness; and awaiting the apocalypse is an activity replete with interpreting signs of prophecy fulfillment.

Knowing that kingdom theologies exercise a structuring power in Evangelical life, what real world impacts has *Left Behind* had? Susan Harding's historical ethnography of born-again Christians, *The Book of Jerry Falwell: Fundamentalist Language and Politics* (2000), provides an answer. Two prominent examples include American governmental support for Israel and a narrative frame for everyday interpretations. Because the establishment of the nation of Israel is a necessary condition for the Second Coming in *Left Behind's* eschatology, adherents typically favor the fate of Jewish Israel over Islamic Palestine. For American congressional members and presidents, this translates into various iterations of pro-Israeli policy. Harding also describes how "apocalypticism [is] not just a set of beliefs, conscious or unconscious. It [is] a specific narrative mode of reading history; Christians for whom Bible prophecy is true do not inhabit the same historical landscape as nonbelievers" (ibid.: 232). Fundamentalists marshal interpretive strategies to discern what events are signs of the end times, and use them in their consumption of news media, evaluation of popular culture, and reactions to minor and major happenings at home and abroad. Robbins (2001), arguing from the different ethnographic vantage point of recently missionized Pentecostals in Papua New Guinea, demonstrates how this eschatology results in an everyday millenarianism where adherents live with a constant sense of time's potential ending and eternity's promised beginning.

This kingdom theology continues to inspire thoughts, actions, and institution making for millions of Fundamentalists, Pentecostals, and other conservative Evangelicals. The Herculean success of *Left Behind* is but one sign of its ubiquity. However, in three years of fieldwork with Emerging Evangelicals I never once heard this kingdom theology advocated. That is not to say it was absent. My consultants, when explaining their views of God's Kingdom, constantly used *Left Behind* and its eschatology as a foil. For some, creating distance from the rapture and the assumptions it travels with was part of their deconversion narrative. Prior to internalizing the Emerging cultural critique, they had eagerly read *Left Behind* alongside their conservative brethren. For others, it was a readily identifiable source against which they formulated and articulated their own kingdom theology. As with *Left Behind* supporters, kingdom theologies provide a temporality that informs their religious subjectivity.

The Kingdom as Now, Not Yet

The kingdom theology advocated by most of my consultants was that described by Bialecki (2009): the kingdom is already, but not yet. This theology suggests that the perfections of heaven were introduced by the birth, life, crucifixion, resurrection, return, and ascension of Jesus and the advent of the Holy Spirit, but that reality cannot be fully realized until the Second Coming. Unlike *Left Behind*, the now, not yet standpoint does not travel with any definite end times scenario. This prompts a shift in temporality: "[R]ather than look for an eschatological tomorrow . . . attention is turned to incommensurable inbreakings of the future in the present" (Bialecki 2009: 116). This introduced, but only partially fulfilled, kingdom is evidenced by the experiential domain of healing and the political domain of justice (ibid.). Now, not yet theology accepts that acts of miraculous physical healing are possible, but does not expect them for every need. The New Testament era introduced healing into the hands of Christians, but because we still live in a sinful world healing cannot always happen. Likewise, Jesus revealed what was morally just, but because we still live in a sinful world justice can only be glimpsed and glanced. The biblical call is to transform the world, but it is accepted that full transformation cannot happen this side of heaven. Living in the now, not yet kingdom creates a space for human agency, but it is a low-ceilinged agency: "Theirs is always a demand for a course of action for which there can be no discernible course of action" (Bialecki 2009: 116).

This limited political imagination is the primary outcome Bialecki identified for now, not yet adherents. Although I certainly saw evidence of this, my consultants were much more committed to organizing acts of social engagement intended to "reveal" the nature of God's kingdom to Christians and non-Christians in their mission field. The language of revealing is important for them because it reflects their now, not yet view: visible, partially achievable, and representative of heaven's unrealizable glories. We encountered an example of this earlier with Josh and New City. Now, not yet references were front and center throughout the launch team's year of planning. Recall Josh's brief presentation during their first public information meeting: "We want to model for people what the kingdom will be like by showing them the love of Christ." This logic of revealing and modeling was the primary outcome I observed among now, not yet adherents. However, modeling is as far as their hope stretches, a crucial point of distinction with our third kingdom theology. Kevin's case offers an extended example of an Emerging Evangelical attempting to reveal the Kingdom of God.

"Linking arms, changing lives"

Kevin is extremely affable. Actually, it is not so much geniality or sociability that is so disarming about him, but gentleness. He maintains this affability in spite of a tall, brawny frame and a full brownish-red beard that conjures up Viking images. Perhaps it is his voice and speech that tempers his physicality: soft, measured, reflective, articulate, but not overly intellectualized. I first interviewed him in January 2009; he was twenty-eight and days away from being a first-time father.

Kevin grew up "nominally Christian" in a mainline Presbyterian church, experienced a born-again conversion with the neo-charismatic Vineyard Fellowship in the mid-1990s, and began volunteering with Young Life in 1999. Young Life is a conservative, nondenominational, Reformed Protestant parachurch organization that ministers exclusively to high school students. In 2005, Kevin reached a turning point. Two years earlier he had graduated from college with a history degree, and had been working as a regional director for Young Life. As the director he trained roughly thirty volunteers a year and organized Young Life ministries for five high schools in the Dayton-Cincinnati corridor. Working for Young Life was satisfying, but not the same as being a pastor for his own congregation, an aspiration he had had since the age of sixteen. This desire made it all the more tempting when he was offered a job as senior pastor with a suburban church in Florida. It was the kind of offer he had longed for. But he declined. He had the strong impression that this congregation—located next to an affluent, residential subdivision—was comprised of wealthy, white individuals accustomed to paying for anything they wanted. He considered them benefactors of comparatively enormous economic privilege and did not want to be complicit in extending this advantage to their religious life.

In May 2006, along with his wife and three married couples, Kevin decided it was time to start his own church. For several months they prayed for "direction" and in August they started a weekly Bible study in his brother's home with six married couples. This quickly grew to thirty people and Kevin was convinced the decision to plant a new church was the right one. In September 2007 The Oaks Community Church was officially launched. As of September 2010 "The Oaks" attracted between two hundred and fifty to three hundred people for Sunday morning worship, and maintained twelve weekly small groups, each with fifteen to twenty participants.

Middletown, Ohio is the home of The Oaks. This city will probably never be a tourist mecca. Aside from not possessing any wonders of natural beauty or historic landmarks, Middletown is iconic of a failing industrial America. In December 2008 *Forbes* published a special real estate issue on "America's Fastest-Dying Towns: Ten Spots Where Jobs Are Vanishing, Incomes Are Dropping and Poverty Levels Are Rising" (Woolsey 2008). Based on the U.S. Census Bureau's 2005–2007 American Community Survey, Middletown ranked with the lowest of the low. A city of 50,000 people, it epitomizes "economic decline." Among other disparaging statistics, "the seven-year poverty rate jumped from 12% to 22%," only "12% of residents possess a bachelor's degree or better," and "the town's median household income is $37,000." Much of Middletown's distress—in statistical and popular imaginations—results from declining production by A. K. Steel, a gargantuan steel factory that snakes along the city's southern and eastern edges. A. K. Steel is also largely responsible for the city's demographics. The 1940s and '50s brought nearly 2 million Appalachian migrants to America's industrial Rust Belt cities in search of work after losing coal mining jobs due to increased mechanization (Conn 1994: 86; Miller and Tucker 1998: 62). These migrants were overwhelmingly white, and Middletown's current racial composition reflects this history: 90 percent white, 10 percent black. There are very few racially mixed residential neighborhoods, which Kevin considers emblematic of Middletown's social ills: high racial prejudice, segregation, and livelihood disparities.

Middletown's race relations are inconsistent with Kevin's understanding of God's kingdom. For him, the ideal and perfection promised by God does not allow for divisions. There will only be unity. Living in the now, not yet kingdom means modeling that unity, not reproducing the sin of de facto segregation. This incongruence was especially troubling for Kevin because almost all his congregants were white. Every time The Oaks met on Sunday morning they violated kingdom ideals.

The Oaks had been using a second-story rented space located on Middletown's downtown main street for worship services and other collective church events. The space was far from perfect. It is surrounded mostly by empty storefronts and struggling retailers, not a generous scattering of dining options for Sunday, lunch-hungry churchgoers. The stage for the worship band is cramped. The acoustics are mediocre at best. There is no open, communal area for congregating after worship services. The nursery and Sunday school rooms are small and crammed close together. The temperature is not centrally controlled. Two large vents in the worship area pump plenty of cool air, along with a distractingly loud *HUMMM*. This noise is relieved in winter, but gives way to a different dilemma: a single small vent near the ceiling that must be turned on on Saturday night to make the space warm enough by Sunday morning. But Kevin was intent on staying downtown. He believes it is extremely important that The Oaks not do what so many Middletown churches have done in recent years: relocate to more prosperous new growth residential areas in the nearby exurbs.

Kevin met Pastor Michael Bailey in the fall of 2008. Bailey is in his mid-sixties and has been the senior pastor at Faith United, a nondenominational black church, since 2000. Kevin knew Bailey's daughter through her work with Middletown's city revitalization team. She introduced them at Kevin's request, and the two pastors began meeting sporadically. In June 2009 Kevin and Bailey attended the same "Diversity Dialogue," a series of three three-hour workshops focusing on "racial reconciliation" hosted by the city council. Following this collaboration, they agreed to initiate a three-phase plan. In the first phase The Oaks would begin sharing Faith United's ample building. In the second phase the two congregations would begin doing weekly worship and small groups together on a regular basis. Then, the two churches would become one.

The Faith United building is a short walk further down main street from The Oaks's previous location. It is a large, brick building divided into three parts: a series of small rooms, a large gymnasium, and an equally large sanctuary. The small rooms were built in the first quarter of the twentieth century and the other sections were added later. Faith United worships in the main sanctuary, a carpeted, stained-glass-windowed sanctuary with pews. Their weekly worship attendance is less than a hundred people, most of them aged between forty-five and sixty-five. In January 2010 The Oaks began worshiping in the gymnasium. Kevin describes the move as a "no-brainer" from the perspective of price and space. The rent is $500 cheaper at Faith United and the spaces for worship, children's nursery, and Sunday school are all much larger. Kevin recognized that the spatial segregation for worship reinforced the same racial divide their move hoped to challenge, "but you have to start somewhere." And because the Sunday morning church nurseries were combined, the initial integration was not purely theoretical.

In March 2010, after three months of sharing the building, Kevin listed several tensions that had surfaced. The nursery, a positive symbol of integration, also provided a moment of conflict. Kevin understood the disagreement in "cultural" terms. "Black churches" maintain a family-oriented environment of trust, which meant they did not do any record keeping for nursery workers. The Oaks, coming from a "white, suburban," documentation oriented environment, required background checks for anyone working in the nursery. They resolved this discrepancy, but it was an early sign of diverging expectations. Faith United operated a small-scale food pantry that served Middletown's low-income and homeless populations. Members of The Oaks had asked Kevin if they could get involved and increase the volume of the pantry, but Kevin was hesitant: "I don't want us to be the young white people coming in and taking over." During The Oaks's first Sunday worship service, Faith United members objected to coffee being served in the worship space and to books being displayed for sale. The two congregations held two joint worship services in their first six months together. These were considered a success by most involved, but arranging the music was not easy. Not only do they have very different music styles, but there was a distinct communication breakdown about who was responsible for which songs. The challenge that Kevin stressed as most difficult was the difference in authority structure. Again, he appealed to the idiom of "cultural differences between black and white churches." For Faith United, Pastor Bailey is the sole authoritative voice. But at The Oaks, they maintain a "plurality of elders" where leadership decisions are shared. When Kevin first explained this difference we were sitting in a meeting room at Faith United. I pointed to a banner hanging on one of the walls. It was a collage of pictures featuring Bailey and his congregants, titled at the top with "Thank you Pastor Bailey for being our shepherd!" Kevin confirmed that a banner like this would never be found in a church like The Oaks.

Despite these challenges, Kevin is optimistic about the second and third phases. He showed me two signs that fueled his optimism. The front placard of the Faith United building, the kind Fundamentalist churches often use to display pithy and rather obvious theological wordplays, names both men as "Pastors." (During our March 2010 interview a Faith United deacon stopped by the building with his son to pick up a table and chair set. When he saw us talking, he addressed Kevin as "Pastor.") Along with this publicly visible announcement, there is a logo the two churches designed together: a circle with an oak leaf inside overlaps with a heart that has a cross inside. Underneath, the intersecting symbol reads, "Linking Arms, Changing Lives." The logo is etched onto the glass doors of the building's main entrance, on two side doors, and on a bulletin board that hangs in the shared hallway between the two sanctuaries. Kevin recalled a story he thought captured the spirit of this logo. The two churches practice communion differently. The Oaks invites adherents to the front of the worship space where they tear a piece of bread from a common loaf and dip it into a common cup. Faith United distributes small, plastic cups and crackers to individuals seated in the pews. During their joint worship services the two pastors have served communion to one another using the other's method. Serving Pastor Bailey communion, and being served by him, was among the most powerful moments of the initial phase for Kevin, and for many others in both congregations.

The limits of hope?

By combining The Oaks with Faith United, Kevin is enacting his now, not yet kingdom theology. Middletown's racial divide conflicts with the kingdom-inspired reconciliation he wants to model. We do not see in this example the kind of limited political imagination Bialecki (2009) describes for his Vineyard consultants. Instead, we see kingdom theology as a motivation for direct action. However, we do see a similar orientation toward "hope" (ibid.: 119). For the Vineyard charismatics, there is no expectation that the perfections of the kingdom will be fully realized. Like them, Kevin is also convinced that Middletown's racial problems will likely persist, irrespective of what happens with The Oaks and Faith United. Kingdom realities can be modeled, but that is all. However, because modeling is deemed achievable, the now, not yet kingdom theology offers a distinct sense of hope. Kevin is equally convinced that if The Oaks and Faith United can become one church, then Middletown will be compelled by the promise of the kingdom. It would be wrong, though, to conclude that hope is an inevitable traveling companion of the now, not yet kingdom. For some, this kingdom theology is unsettling, confusing, and even potentially dangerous.

Nathan was unlike any of my other consultants. I first met him in the early summer of 2009 at an informational meeting hosted by New City as part of their launch process. He had known Josh since 2005, seemed well-versed in Emerging Church writings, and we met for our first interview a few weeks later. We sat on the outdoor patio of a coffee shop. It was mid-morning and very sunny, the kind of day that heats up rapidly as noon approaches. Nathan was dressed in a Green Bay Packers T-shirt with khaki cargo shorts and leather sandals (the exact outfit he had worn weeks earlier when we first met). He keeps his hair shaven close to bald and wears patently unstylish glasses. He is short and stoutly, powerfully built. His face is large and round, fair-skinned, and pimply. Nathan has an awkward presence, uncomfortable in almost every situation that involves other people. His most remarkable physical feature is his voice. It is booming, clear-toned, and carries effortlessly across rooms and open spaces. His laugh erupts volcanically and frequently, receding as quickly as it arrives. He is forthcoming, articulate, bookish, and intelligent, though there is something unrefined about each quality.

Nathan was born-again at age five while watching a televangelist program. His parents were conservative Evangelicals, but they had no denominational loyalty, which meant that Nathan experienced a variety of Protestant styles and theologies while growing up. His father was a career military officer, and they moved numerous times before settling in the upper-middle-class exurb of West Chester, twenty miles north of downtown Cincinnati. As he entered high school Nathan went from "being socially awkward" to struggling with "major depression," "violence issues," and "hating authority." He contemplated suicide, beat up other students, and threatened to kill some of his classmates. His parents homeschooled him through the remainder of high school and he performed well academically, receiving full tuition waivers from several Christian universities. He opted for Kansas State instead because it had a strong military history program, his primary intellectual interest, and because he wanted to escape the "Christian bubble" in which he had matured, as well as his troubled past in the Cincinnati area.

But his social struggles continued in college: "I dressed like the Unabomber. I didn't shave. I stopped showering. I just didn't take care of myself." He did not experience a loss of faith, but he did experience a sort of here-and-now nihilism: "I thought Jesus was the ideal, but not of this world. I read Machiavelli's *The Prince* in a freshman philosophy course and figured that must be the reality of this world." By his junior year his GPA had slipped to 1.9 and he was forced to move back to Cincinnati.

Nathan's father asked him to consult a family friend about his problems. Nathan did, but thought "he sounded just like dad." This friend suggested that Nathan talk with Josh. They met in September 2005, a date Nathan marks as a social and religious turning point. During their first meeting Josh recommended that Nathan read *Blue Like Jazz* (2003). The book, an episodic story of the author's spiritual journey and eventual distrust of establishment Christianity, is very popular among Emerging Evangelicals and is cited by many of my consultants as part of their deconversion. Nathan ordered the book immediately following his meeting with Josh: "It blew me away." Like others we have met thus far, Nathan experienced the book as putting "words to the feelings [he had] had for a long time about the church." The author, Donald Miller, articulated several sources of Nathan's disenchantment with conservative Evangelicalism: too much focus on academic-style learning, too much focus on political issues, too much focus on money, and too little focus on "authentic community." He read *Blue Like Jazz* in two days and reread it the following week. Since then, he has read it four more times along with "everything else" Miller has published.

Soon after their meeting Nathan joined a small group Bible study Josh led for twenty-year-olds at North Cincinnati Community Church in the neighboring exurb of Mason. Nathan remained an active member of North Cincinnati until October 2008 when Josh ended the Bible study to concentrate his energies on planting New City. The dissolution of the group was difficult for Nathan, but he accepted the advice of peers and sought out the nearby suburban Vineyard megachurch for their many and varied small group opportunities. Beginning in November 2008 he joined several groups at this Vineyard; some were disappointing, but others approximated his experience at North Cincinnati.

Between Josh and the Vineyard, Nathan was exposed to the now, not yet kingdom theology for the first time. While growing up he had "always thought of the kingdom as heaven, not the here and now." Given his social and psychological difficulties, he was convinced that "you suffer until death then you get the reward of heaven." He came to accept the now, not yet theology, but it has been a difficult acceptance. Nathan has struggled to square his ongoing depression and always threatening suicidal and violent tendencies with the idea that the kingdom is even partially in existence. If the perfection of heaven has been introduced, if the reward of heaven is not altogether unavailable before death, then why is life so challenging? If healing is possible, why hasn't he been healed? The hope described by Bialecki (2009), and that is evident with Kevin, does not map easily onto a life like Nathan's.

The Kingdom as Come

The Subversion/Truthvoice conference presented earlier is one Virgil has organized every year since 2003. For the 2009 version he hoped to bring together two audiences that, in his estimation, did not communicate with each other enough but ought to. The first group was made up of the cohort affiliated with the Dayton area Emergent Village, which Virgil also facilitated. The second consisted of advocates of a kingdom theology called Preterism (a.k.a "Kingdom Now," "historical eschatology," or "fulfilled eschatology"). Roughly a hundred people attended the two-day conference, most of whom were there as part of the latter audience. Virgil's motivation for attempting a joint conference was his assessment that many popular Emerging Church authors articulated Preterist ideas about the kingdom but did not appear conversant with the history of Preterist writings—most notably, Max King's *The Cross and the Parousia of Christ* (1987). Preterism was far less visible in my fieldwork than the now, not yet kingdom theology; only eight consultants accepted Preterist theology. Yet Preterism is part of the Evangelical religious field and offers a different relationship between kingdom, time, and action.

Quite unlike *Left Behind* and now, not yet advocates, Preterists do not believe that the Second Coming of Jesus is a future event. Preterism is based on the understanding that prophecies in the Book of Revelation were fulfilled in the first century C.E. The destruction of the Jewish temple in Jerusalem in 70 C.E. was the Second Coming of Jesus. New Testament references to "the kingdom of God," particularly in the four Gospels' reported speech of Jesus, do not refer to a future place, time, event, or sphere of existence separate from the earth. The kingdom is here, now, complete. The kingdom, in all its fullness, began with the ministry of Jesus and continues today. As a result, there are no end time events yet to unfold, no apocalypse, no rapture, no literal return of Jesus to await, and no eschatological signs in need of discerning.

The hermeneutic details of Preterism are many, but here we are more interested in how Preterism offers a distinct temporality that informs religious subjectivity. There are two major consequences for Emerging Evangelicals, like Virgil, who accept the Preterist view that the kingdom is here and now. First, quoting Virgil, Preterists see themselves as "partners with God" and "active agents" in making the kingdom known to all. Second, they prioritize the need for immediate action in that partnership. The limited agency and deferred political action described by Bialecki (2009) for the now, not yet kingdom theology do not hold for Preterists. These two kingdom theologies are further differentiated along the axis of hope. Unlike now, not yet proponents, who ultimately concede that their efforts will fall short of the kingdom this side of heaven, Preterists have no "incommensurability" (ibid.: 116) between future promise and present change. Because the kingdom is here and now, its perfections are fully realizable. Heaven on earth is not a cliché; it is a commandment.

Recall Virgil's new monastic-influenced decision making from chapter 4. He considers all those actions—selling an extravagant suburban home, building a straw bale house, living minimally, rejecting opulent materialism, growing as much of his own food as possible—as acts that help make the kingdom visible. He considers the domestic and economic life he wants to cultivate with his wife and children more akin to the nature of God's kingdom than the life they want to transition out of. He does not see himself as merely modeling what the kingdom will be like. Rather, he sees himself playing whatever role he can, however small, in making that kingdom known to all. Kevin, the house church pastor in Norwood who also appeared in chapter 4, is a Preterist and sees his everyday life as a response to the kingdom's immediate presence and the need for immediate action. In explaining his kingdom theology to me, Kevin contrasted his orientation to daily action with *Left Behind*-style assumptions. He described how dispensationalists ultimately believe that the earth, as a physical place, will "go up in flames" and are therefore generally uninterested in the long-term effects of their decisions. To Kevin, dispensationalists' time is running out and hope is only ever a future, forestalled possibility. This is not his temporality: "God has a long agenda for this earth." As a result, "every tree, every car, every person, and the environment are valued." He gave an example from his auto body repair business to illustrate: they only use water-based paints, not solvent-based ones, because of the positive accumulated environmental impact. Kevin, Virgil, and the other Preterists I encountered during my fieldwork emphasized this ethic of responsibility for their surrounding social and environmental conditions. The absence of a future event promising to usher in perfection means that the present is the only basis on which they can mobilize for action.

Kevin's explanation of kingdom theology—juxtaposing it with *Left Behind*—indexes the dialogical nature of American Evangelicalism. This dialogism occurs in all directions and Preterism is a known target for dispensationalists. Two weeks prior to my participation at the Subversion/Truthvoice conference I received an email. It was sent by a theological opponent of Preterism who devoted time to tracking Virgil's activities online, and had made it a regular practice to contact every participant in the conferences Virgil organized. His email was a call to boycott the conference, the introductory portion of which read as follows:

> As Christians, we can and do allow for variance within doctrine BUT there comes a point where a variance separates groups claiming to be "Christian" from actual, historic Christianity—such as Mormonism and Jws [Jehova's Witnesses] which though they claim to be Christian, they are not accepted by historic Christianity as such. Hyper-preterism is NOT Christian.

As this concerned emailer suggested, debates about kingdom theology matter very much to Evangelicals and the ontological stakes are high. The divergent views of time and human agency that travel with different kingdom theologies become the means by which Evangelicals distinguish between varieties of Christianity and, for some, between who is and is not a Christian. This example recalls Garriott and O'Neill's (2008) invitation for the ethnographic study of Christianity: "[A]nthropologists should turn their eye towards the kinds of problems Christian communities themselves seem to be preoccupied with . . . [including those] between different kinds of Christianity" (394). Mapping Evangelical debates about the who, when, where, how, and why of God's kingdom creates access not simply to theological divisions, but to identity distinctions and organizing cultural logics. The three kingdom theologies presented here reveal three different temporalities, three different relationships between belief, time, and action.

Kingdom, Time, Utopia

As modes of temporality, kingdom theologies inform Evangelical subjectivity, conceptions of human agency, and the potential for social engagement (cf. Bialecki 2009). Virgil, for example, does not assign an end point to time, understands the kingdom as fully present, and therefore asserts that he is responsible for immediately improving his surrounding social conditions. Virgil's Preterism diverges from the now, not yet view of the kingdom with respect to the extent to which real change is possible. Kevin in Middletown, for example, is certain that while he may be able to model racial reconciliation, a widespread social shift is never fully realizable this side of heaven. We can also situate the dynamics of kingdom theology as representative of a tension that confronts all Christianities.

The idea that Christians continually deal with a particular set of cultural tensions is well-established. In his ethnography of Fijian Methodists, Matt Tomlinson (2009) names "three key facts" (12) unearthed in the comparative study of Christianities:

> (1) Christianity generates particular tensions that confound simple distinctions between local and global, traditional and modern, and individual and collective; (2) It often fails to resolve the tensions it generates, and the tensions are, in fact, often irresolvable; (3) Such failures are not end points but drive people's ongoing efforts in ritual, doctrinal, theological, and other realms (ibid.).

Thomas Kirsch (2008), in his ethnographic work with multiple denominations in Zambia, views these tensions as dichotomies: body/spirit, immanence/transcendence, materiality/immateriality, visibility/invisibility, presence/absence, this-worldly/other-worldly, immediacy/eternity, and letter/spirit. An exemplary case of an anthropologist using these tensions as a launching pad for cultural analysis is Matthew Engelke's *A Problem of Presence: Beyond Scripture in an African Church* (2007). Engelke begins with a seemingly odd incarnation of Christian culture—Zimbabwean Apostolics who self-identify as "the Christians who don't read the Bible" (2). Texts, they say, are impediments to religious experience and so they reject them, favoring a "live and direct" (3) relationship with the Holy Spirit. Engelke understands these convictions as the Apostolics' attempt to work through two related tensions: materiality/immateriality and presence/absence. Unlike Christianities that use material objects to communicate with God, these Apostolics rid their religious lives as exhaustively as possible of the physical: scriptures, hymnals, jewelry, buildings, excessive adornment, and even ethnographers' notebooks. Removing materiality is their way of mediating a relationship with the divine.

Much like Engelke, Tomlinson's third point is most relevant here: these tensions are actively used to fuel social and religious action. Kingdom theologies suggest an as-yet unobserved tension, that of utopia/dystopia. All Christianities confront questions of temporality. For American Evangelicals these questions are addressed through the register of God's kingdom. Whether it is present, visible, deferred, or awaiting, the kingdom signifies perfection. Whatever is deemed outside of, or inconsistent with, God's kingdom signifies a failure toward that perfection. When Evangelicals imagine the kingdom they imagine a utopic version of human-human and human-divine relations. That utopia is always at odds with a sinful world that is forever leaning toward social dystopia. Living between the constant reality of these two poles is a phenomenological condition that helps structure Christians' socio-religious lives. We can observe this utopia/dystopia tension in some recent anthropological work.

Francio Guadeloupe (2009) explores the culture of Christianity on the Caribbean Island of Saint Martin/Sint Marteen (SXM). He focuses on the everyday lives of these Christians as well as the media performance of Christian radio disc jockeys. Central to his analysis is how DJs promote hope, optimism, and tolerance, encouraging SXM Christians to envision themselves as co-creators of a unified nation. Their imagined and achievable utopia is constantly weighed against perceived threats to that utopia, and how to combat those threats. This same dynamic of Christians using their Christianity to imagine and address social utopias and dystopias is evident in Kevin Lewis O'Neill's *City of God: Christian Citizenship in Postwar Guatemala* (2010). O'Neill argues that in the demonstrably dangerous conditions of Guatemala following a decade-long civil war, neo-Pentecostals are grounding their sense of national citizenship in the religious resources offered by their local mega-church (for example, prayer, fasting, and spiritual warfare). Envisioning a positive future for Guatemala, and the responsibility of each individual in bringing about that vision, are central to this neo-Pentecostal culture. These are both very rich ethnographies, and a cursory review hardly does them justice. They are relevant here for the single purpose of suggesting that the tension of utopia/dystopia is a consistent one across Christian cultures. How this tension is reasoned through and acted on relates directly to the theological, political, and economic contexts in which Christians operate. Utopic and dystopic conditions—real or imagined, present or promised—work to structure Christian thought and practice.

The tension of utopia/dystopia is a helpful way to understand the role of kingdom theologies in Emerging Evangelicalism. Recall Kevin in Middletown. He is working to combine his white, youthful Evangelical congregation with an older, black church. While his efforts at racial reconciliation might be hailed as civicly positive, he is convinced that a glimpse of harmony is the best to be hoped for. He does not think the combining of their churches can fix the racial dystopia of Middletown, but he does think it can offer Middletowners an example of what the kingdom of heaven is like. Recall Nathan. His personal dystopia of violence and depression has been difficult to square with the possibility that the utopia of the kingdom is not confined to a deferred place and existence. Recall Virgil. The kingdom of God is not a future reality for him; it is fully present. All the perfections of heaven promised by scripture should not simply be hoped for, they should be made visible in the here and now. Virgil would be the first to tell you that contemporary America is not a utopia, but he would also tell you that it could be. His efforts to sever as many ties as possible with the institutional structures of late capitalist consumption are directed toward that utopic vision.

We have observed how Evangelical debates about God's kingdom involve specific models of time and entail distinct consequences for social action. The constant attention Emerging Evangelicals invest in these debates can be read as a response to the utopic/dystopic tension present across Christianities. Indeed, these orientations are mutually informing. Utopias and dystopias are not imagined apart from a placement in time, and temporalities are normatively judged models of time's passing and one's relationship with the unfolding of time. Emerging Evangelicals live in a religious landscape defined by dialogue. Individuals and congregations are faced with multiple theologies of the kingdom, and thus multiple possibilities for situating themselves in relation to the perfections of heaven. My consultants categorically dismiss the dystopic view of society and the always deferred utopia posited by *Left Behind* eschatology. The kingdom theologies they do accept—now, not yet and Preterism—differently orient individual agency with respect to the visibility and achievability of heavenly ideals.

7

Church Planting I

A New Work

From the audience of about fifty people, a young man who looked to be in his late twenties asked, "When you have a team ready to plant, how do you find a church willing to mentor you?" Three of the four panelists answered him. Dustin, "lead pastor" for a 2005 church plant in the eastern suburbs of Louisville, Kentucky, assured the questioner that if he had the flexibility to move anywhere he and his team would be "snapped up in a second." Following some advice from others in the audience, Rick, lead pastor for a 2006 church plant joked that Lexington, the city of his church, might be nice. As proof, he proudly announced that Lexington was recently named by *Forbes* magazine as "one of the most influential cities in America." This evoked an appreciative but modest round of laughter. Before the laughs had fully subsided, Kevin, lead pastor for The Oaks whom we met earlier, suggested in the calmest of tones that they consider Middletown: "We were in *Forbes* too. They named us one of America's ten fastest dying cities." The amused uproar jolted the room. Kevin's tongue-in-cheek rejoinder to Rick's class-infused quip was a lighter moment in an otherwise serious day.

The panel was the featured event of a seminar, "Church Planting for the Rest of Us," held at Sojourn Community Church in Louisville, Kentucky. I spent nearly three hours there on a cold morning in late January 2010. Founded in 2000, Sojourn was an early member of Acts 29, an Evangelical church planting network with two hundred and ten churches in forty-two states (as of October 2010). Everyone at the seminar was a current or hopeful Acts 29 church pastor. Because of its tenure with the network, Sojourn regularly hosts training events like this seminar and is well-known among Acts 29 leaders. Kevin described Sojourn as "the intellectuals" of the network, particularly influential for "innovation and the arts."

The seminar was held in Sojourn's main building near downtown Louisville: a late nineteenth century, 57,000-square foot converted elementary school. The dominating element inside the building is an engulfing presentation of art. Most of the walls are lined with professionally displayed pieces of various media: black/white and color photography, paintings, drawings, etchings, collages. The seminar room is on the ground floor and adjoins an art gallery that is open to the public. The Sojourn staff change the exhibits in this gallery every four to six weeks, and accept bids from local and national artists. That morning, a University of Missouri art professor's work was on display: a photographic tour of American megachurches.

"Church Planting for the Rest of Us" had two halves. In the first half the four panelists listed "three or five things every church planter should know," followed by a question-and-answer session with the audience. A cumulative list from the four men ranged from the practical to the spiritual: read widely in the church planting literature; build a launch team unlike yourself; be mentored by a successful church planter for six months; be yourself; count on more spiritual attack than you expect; remember that you cannot please everyone; concentrate on doing a few things well as a church; do not ground your identity in what you are against; be humble; emphasize service to your city. The second half, followed by another round of questions, addressed "three or five mistakes to avoid when planting a church": do not launch too early; do not try to mediate every problem; pray; create specific blocks of time for rest; try not to over- or underestimate problems; pastor your family first.

The panelists and audience were all in their twenties and thirties; all (save one exception) were white, and all were men. These demographics are nationally representative for Acts 29 pastors. Age and race are sociological, structural reflections of the network's history and the New Calvinist movement more generally (Hansen 2008). The absence of women is theological. Acts 29 pastors describe themselves as "complementarians": they interpret certain biblical texts (for example, 1Timothy 2:11–13, Titus 1:5–9) to mean that males and females have been designed and assigned by God to serve different, complementary functions within the local congregation. Only men can be "elders." This theological conviction does prompt some social conventions. For example, a sense of hyper-masculinity pervaded the Louisville seminar. Performances of the interpersonal greeting were standardized: bump fists together; execute an intensely firm handshake concluded with a decisive pump of the wrist; a quick hug punctuated by loud, thudding open-handed pats on the back. Deep voices made frequent use of "dude" and "man." The fashion aesthetic repeated: flannel shirts, worn blue jeans, thick beards, closely trimmed or fully-shaven hair styles, and large, Christian-themed tattoos conspicuously displayed on muscular arms. The hyper-masculinity associated with Acts 29 does not go unnoticed, and at times becomes a resource for reflexive, self-deprecating humor. When talking about the need for church planters to be "adopted into Christ," Kevin suggested that the theological value of submission is often missed in favor of more active calls to evangelism because "as dudes we get mission, going out and doing something."

More than this performed masculinity, more than Sojourn's artistic proclivities, more than the singular demographic, the defining element that morning was the tone of seriousness. Throughout the seminar everyone, especially the four panelists, maintained an emphatic sobriety regarding the role of being a church planter. When listing what all church planters should know, Rick invited everyone to ask themselves a question: "Are you really called to plant?" He stressed that there is a large gulf separating two identities, "[J]ust because you are a pastor *does not* mean you are a planter." Dustin opened his list of recommendations with a certainty that was repeated verbatim at various times throughout the seminar, "Planting a church is the hardest thing you will ever do."

"A new work" is a shorthand consultants often used for planting a church. The work referenced is intended as a "work of God," a congregational ministry that hopes to be, echoing the New Testament metaphor, the hands and feet of Jesus in the world. Founded in 2000 as an interdenominational network devoted to planting new churches, Acts 29 testifies to the recent surge of Evangelical interest in church planting. It is not necessarily a representative institution because of its staunchly Calvinist theological commitments. But attention to theology is a point to be made: church planting is promoted across theological lines, often for the same reasons (for example, the conviction that church planting is the best method of evangelism). When I initiated my ethnography of Emerging Evangelicals in the fall of 2007, church planting was not on my mind. But my consultants quickly taught me that church planting was a vital part of their identity, ethos, and institution making. By the time my fieldwork ended I had spent as much time and energy examining church planting as any other aspect of the Emerging movement. My sample of consultants included twenty-seven men who identified as "church planters," not "pastors." My fieldwork also included planters' wives, and we will explore some of the gendered dynamics involved with church planting.

In the Introduction we noted two observations worth repeating here. First, church planting is not a new phenomenon among American Evangelicals. What is new is the way that Emerging Evangelicals have made church planting a craft to be mastered, and how being a church planter has become an organizing identity. Second, church planting figures centrally in the Emerging cultural critique of conservative Evangelicalism, most notably as an indictment of the suburban megachurch. Both these observations appear several times in this chapter, although our analytical focus will be elsewhere. As an issue of individual subjectivity and collective institutionalizing, church planting exemplifies a central argument of this book: Emerging Evangelicals are at once modern and late modern religious actors, relying on dispositions from both eras. We examine four expressions of this dual identity below, and in doing so reveal several cultural tensions that result from an Evangelical movement that is simultaneously modern and late modern.

Church Planting and the Discourse of Measurement

In his marvelous ethnography, *Angels' Town: Chero Ways, Gang Life, and Rhetorics of the Everyday* (1997), Ralph Cintron observes a defining condition of modernity: the discourse of measurement. Cintron disentangles the contentious community relations between a dominant white population and a subaltern population of Mexican immigrants. Their social conflicts frequently take shape around the expectations and consequences of a discourse that unceasingly promotes the Enlightenment values of rationality, precision, order, control, manageability, and coherence. The modernist institutions that operate according to, and require competency in, these values sometimes upend and are sometimes cleverly manipulated by the Mexican Americans. This discourse of measurement hinges on an impulse: all phenomena, human and natural, even the most unwieldy and excessive, can and should be measured, mapped, and mastered.

Cintron guides us through multiple examples to demonstrate how the discourse of measurement animates everyday life. For example, the city's use of a street grid system is a "symbol of rationality" (18). Cintron quotes a 1924 public official to illustrate the venerability of this idolization: "The curve is ruinous, difficult and dangerous; it is a paralyzing thing. The straight line enters into all of human history, into all human aim, into every human act" (18). Government documents use numbers and words to manage people, "objectifications that reduce to manageable proportions the excess of what it means to be an individual" (56). Subaltern actors like Don Angel, one of Cintron's key consultants, manipulate these strides toward that which confers official status and legitimacy by repeatedly manufacturing false identities. Educational systems devise medically couched diagnoses to classify students who struggle to perform on par with their peers. Valerio, a consultant Cintron observed from adolescence through young adulthood, was labeled learning disabled: "'word retrieval' and 'latency time' [were] mystifying terms . . . that reconfigured a simple problem of not knowing a second language as a kind of miswiring" (103). Then, there was Ramon. Cintron describes him as "a kind of buzzing confusion of entrepreneurial ambition, failure, disorganization, laziness, and cleverness" (200). Ramon exploited the discourse of measurement by creating "an image of competency and professionalism by adopting certain distinguishing details" (202). He used a clipboard, estimated job costs on graph paper, and wore tidily kept work overalls complete with a laminated name tag. "Through such details, he created what he wasn't (a reliable blacktopper) and covered up his very real struggle with impending chaos" (202).

Cintron understands the discourse of measurement as an index of modernity. The Enlightenment and Industrial Revolution—as creators of intellectual, social, economic, and political conditions—made measurement values essential for legitimacy and success. When we access this discourse—when we pursue tidy definitions, when we manage excess through categorization, when we insist on delimiting, when we satisfy the desire for precise documentation—we reproduce a distinctly modern set of dispositions. Church planters use the discourse of measurement when they imagine, design, and execute the planting of a new work. We can observe this accessing of measurement values empirically through an artifact most church plants begin with: the Church Plant Proposal (CPP).

Every church planter in my fieldwork researched and authored a proposal for the church he hoped to start. CPPs are used for several purposes: to solicit funding from individuals and institutions; as part of an application to a denomination or parachurch; to recruit potential staff members; and as a way to solicit interested individuals prior to the church's launch. It is a document intended for both official and popular audiences. I collected ten CPPs, which were 4, 5, 8, 9, 10, 13, 56, and 108 pages long, respectively. They had several common elements: statements of "vision," "mission," and/or "purpose"; a list of core values; a resume and personal profile of the church planter; and a projection of financial needs. Some planters included information that the others omitted: two detailed the location of worship services and two provided their initial promotional materials (for example, web pages and post-card flyers). However, one element appeared prominently in all ten CPPs and most decisively reveals church planters' reliance on the discourse of measurement. It was always placed in the opening pages, often on the very first page and often prior to any other substantive information. Literally and narratively, my consultants mapped their proposed mission fields.

In *Angels' Town* (1997) Ralph Cintron explains that maps are persistent artifacts of modernity, human attempts to conquer that which cannot be conquered: "We transform real space onto a 'surface that can be dealt with," thereby "reduc[ing] overwhelming space" (37). The map is a premier example of the discourse of measurement because "by converting enormous forces into objects under control of the hand and eye" (37) the map "sounds again one of [the discourse's] central metaphors . . . the making of a shape where before there was a different shape" (36). By mapping we make claims on space: that we comprehend that space, that we can manage it, navigate it, and ultimately, exercise a degree of control over it.

The CPP maps are geographic, atlas-style road maps with one defining imposition: a shaded area indicating a ten-square mile radius surrounding the location of the church plant. This shaded area is the targeted "mission field." Each of the shaded road maps is accompanied by several elements: a list of communities or neighborhoods within the bounded mission field (in several cases these were also starred on the map); population figures for the area, including various demographic divisions; a narrative portrayal of the mission field, with attention to history and community reputation; and demographic statistics for faith traditions in the region, often with the underrepresentation of Evangelical churches made explicit compared to other Christianities in the local religious marketplace. In one case, a Southern Baptist church plant in downtown Cincinnati, the shaded area took the form of three numbered boxes: the location of the plant's initial three weekly "city groups." Extending from each box is an arrow, explained by the following text:

> City Groups will be planted in a southerly direction toward the river, covering the entire downtown basin. The three initial City Groups will form a unified front of Christian witness and ministry in the target neighborhoods, which will multiply into more surrounding neighborhoods. Each City Group will be led by a resident of that area, and each area is racially and economically diverse.

This particular map conjures up the image of a missionizing wave that promises to cover the targeted area. The direction and scope of evangelism appears full of design and certainty, lacking in disorder, ambiguity, or immeasurability. The maps, lists, figures, and text of the CPPs remind the planter and inform potential funders and members where the boundaries of evangelistic focus will be.

The narrative depictions of mission fields blend secular and Evangelical voices to reinforce the message that this particular locale, as opposed to some other, has been strategically selected. Consider Kevin's CPP for The Oaks in Middletown. In one corner, below a map of the region with the standard imposed, shaded ten-mile mission radius and population "quick facts," he cites an economic promise from the county's Executive Director of Transportation:

> What we are doing is really thinking about what the whole I-75 corridor between the two beltways [of Dayton and Cincinnati] looks like and its impact on job growth in southwest Ohio. Long range, that corridor—that handful of exits—will be the center of the universe.

Next to these official, authorizing words are Kevin's, describing his missional logic for planting in Middletown:

> Middletown is a very diverse region in many ways, and it currently sits under a cloud of depression—both economically and socially. While surrounding cities are seeing steady growth, Middletown has seen little positive growth or development. The vast financial and social needs of the city provide very real opportunities to serve the area, and to be a catalyst of growth, development, and change for a hurting city. If we can help enact a healthy change within the city of Middletown, we will most certainly have a positive impact on the surrounding communities.

Through the discourse of measurement, Kevin reduces the "overwhelming space" (Cintron 1997: 37) that is Middletown. He creates a straight line that connects the documented mission field, governmental assurances of vitality, and the Christian metaphor of being a beacon of hope and light ("If we can help . . ."). The message is one of intentionality and opportunity: it is no accident they chose this place over other potential sites, and the conditions of this place offer a distinct chance to model the kingdom of God.

Through these mapping efforts church planters envision the mission field as a managed socio-geographic space. Mapping becomes a crucial prelude to the work ahead; before a church can be planted, its soil must be defined. The values Cintron (1997) identifies—rationality, precision, order, and coherence—all structure the CPP. As authors of this artifact, church planters reproduce the modern dispositions that travel with the discourse of measurement. Of course, the impulse guiding the discourse of measurement, namely, the promise of control, is a fiction. The unmanageable cannot be managed. Overwhelming space cannot actually be reduced. For church planters, knowledge of the mission field cannot be exhausted. My consultants were well aware of this, often calling attention to the limitations of demographics for knowing a place, the inherent inability of statistics to capture the missional experience of "being there." Yet they still insist on the necessity of measurement values for church planting success. The CPP is lauded as a crucial part of the planting process, an important step in figuring out the church's "vision" and "mission." Many regularly redraw their maps and recommission statistics in the hope that they can maintain an up-to-date portrait of their mission field. Several consultants have purchased products from the Percept Group, an ecumenical Christian institution that specializes in generating regional demographic profiles for churches. This is their cultural tension: abiding by the discourse of measurement while fully aware of its distorting promises.

Church Planting and Entrepreneurialism

The cultural era of late modernity has developed in step with neoliberal economics (Harvey 1989). Anthropologists have devoted significant attention to the characteristics and consequences of being a neoliberal subject. For example, Freeman (2007) identified "the embodiment of an entrepreneurial esprit" (254) as a distinctive neoliberal impulse. Neoliberal economies—due to flexible labor forces, heightened competition, specialized consumption niches, the idealization of personal responsibility, and economic creativity— value the self-starting economic subject. Freeman goes so far as to call the entrepreneur "neoliberalism's quintessential actor" (252). Entrepreneurs are favored in neoliberal contexts because they prize ingenuity, self-invention, adaptation, dispensing with establishment hierarchies, and self-mastery (252–261). Church planting can be read as a religious incarnation of late modernity's entrepreneurial disposition.

The seriousness animating this chapter's opening vignette reminds us that being a church planter is quite meaningful for Emerging Evangelicals. It is considered a distinct identity: "Just because you are a pastor does not mean you are a planter." When narrating their experiences and reflecting on the nature of this role, my church planter consultants referenced a hard-to-locate interior state. They spoke of an "instinct," "calling," "passion," "bug," and "heaviness" that they often harbored for the better part of their adult lives. They also identified themselves as people who "like to start things" and "like to be in on the ground floor." Eight of these twenty-seven church planters were either successful economic entrepreneurs who then "felt called" to plant a church, or bivocational pastors who owned and operated successful businesses. One of these men, Tim, who planted a Vineyard church in 2005 in urban Cincinnati, went a step further. At one point in our first interview he translated the role of the economic self-starter into theological terms: "[T]he Church would call an entrepreneur an apostle."

An integral part of entrepreneurialism is the creation of an expert niche comprised of skills that must be mastered (Freeman 2007). Seminars like the one in Louisville are common in parachurch institutions like Acts 29 as well as in established denominations. They position church planting as an art, and promise to hone skills for cultivating that art. Church planters talk frequently about "what it takes" to be a successful planter. (For them, success refers minimally to maintaining a church over time in the same locale that has been able to plant other churches.) Acts 29 authored an official list of ten qualities essential for church planters: "strong marriage and family life, theological clarity, missional lifestyle, emotional health, entrepreneurial aptitude, disciple-making skills, leadership abilities, clarity and strength of calling, and relationship building." This list foregrounds core cultural features in Acts 29: strictly defined gender ideology, premium on theological competence, evangelism, states of interiority (emotion, being a leader, receiving a divine calling), and a highly intersubjective faith. My church planter consultants affirmed a similar set of qualities and, moreover, considered them extremely difficult to master. Church planting is not for everyone, they insisted, reiterating the specializing impulse that feeds "the entrepreneurial esprit" (Freeman 2007: 254).

Just as the expertise required for church planting is not taken lightly, so goes the process by which planters are confirmed. Denominations and parachurches both require their planters to successfully complete an "assessment." The Nehemiah Project, the primary church planting institution of the Southern Baptist Convention, sponsored two of my consultants and they assess applicants in five categories: "calling to ministry, spiritual formation, interpersonal relationship skills, ability to gather and make disciples, skill competency in church planting." The Presbyterian Church of America's Mission to North America also sponsored two of my consultants, and they require a four-day assessment that focuses on seven "competencies": "vital spiritual life, strong prayer life, personal integrity, family life, evangelism, visionary leadership, and preaching." Acts 29's assessment process, which nine of my consultants completed, was described as especially "intense" (or, in the words of one consultant, "a killer"). It starts with an online application. This requires that the potential planter affirm the Apostle's and Nicene Creeds, twenty-two statements of "Evangelical," "missional," and "Reformed" belief, eighteen statements of what is not believed, and a covenant with eight points of agreement. This is followed by a questionnaire regarding personal information and further questions about theology. One Acts 29 pastor, who planted in urban Cincinnati in 2008, remembered needing three hours to complete the portion relating to questions about theology. If all this is approved, then the applicant and his wife are required to attend a weekend-long Acts 29 event, one day of which is devoted to their assessment. Two or three existing Acts 29 pastors (usually from different geographical regions) lead the interview, which prioritizes the planters' quality of marriage and family life, ministry strategy, timetable for starting the church, and an extensive series of theology questions. The latter continue the emphasis on Reformed (read: Calvinist) Protestant doctrine. The applicant and his wife are interviewed together and then separately about their marriage. Stephanie, whose husband Kevin planted The Oaks in Middletown in 2007, remembered the assessors asking her nothing about theology. All the questions were about their life as a young married couple: did they plan to have kids, when, how many kids, how does he care for her, what is their home life like, were they "still dating" after several years of marriage, what would be the nature of her involvement in the church plant. Based on this interview, the applicant is either approved, approved with conditions, approved with major conditions, or declined. Several consultants reported that roughly half of all Acts 29 applicants are declined after this interview. If the applicant is approved with conditions, he has twelve to eighteen months to satisfy the named requirements.

The details of the Acts 29 process are both unique and representative. Every church planting assessment application I collected emphasized theology and family, but the attention and degree of importance assigned to them by Acts 29 is exaggerated. Still, Acts 29 is quite standard in that it treats church planting as a highly specialized, nuanced, and difficult endeavor. In describing the neoliberal, entrepreneurial spirit Freeman writes: "Entrepreneurial pursuits are motivated frequently by the goal of creative self-invention, dispensing with hierarchy, bosses, and the 'establishment'" (257). While Acts 29 and other assessment institutions make clear that plenty of "hierarchy" exists for church planters, Freeman's observation about the nature of late modern entrepreneurialism does coincide closely with the Emerging

Evangelical penchant for cultural critique. By nature, as religious subjects inspired by discontents, Emerging Evangelicals value "creative self-invention" over reproducing "establishment" norms. As religious entrepreneurs, church planters embody this observation: rather than enter into existing job placement channels for pastors, they seek to start a new work.

The late modern disposition of entrepreneurialism has its share of tensions. Most explicitly, my church planter consultants said that the entrepreneurial quality of planting—with its specialization and self-mastery—can come dangerously close to being a commodified experience, of which they are, at least ideologically, suspicious. On numerous occasions they would reflect on and warn against treating church planting as an expert occupation to be perfected via a formal, portable, repeatable training process. As we have seen numerous times already, commodification figures centrally in the broader Emerging cultural critique and informs the aversion to megachurch life. Yet while this danger is self-consciously recognized, church planters still fully support the church planting industry. They encourage and mentor new applicants who want to be assessed, and they serve as assessors for sponsoring institutions. They contribute to church planting blogs and write articles about church planting for Evangelical media outlets. They are late modern religious subjects who are both committed to and weary of the process of entrepreneurial formation.

Church Planting and Urban Restructuring

Population movement is one index of the shift to late modernity in the United States. Consider a brief synopsis of America's residential restructuring. In the mid-twentieth century, following World War II and accompanying successes in the manufacturing industry and expansions of the middle class, Americans began suburbanizing by the carload (Teaford 1986). Urban centers throughout the United States witnessed an exodus of large numbers to their nearby, residentially oriented outposts. The suburbanization of America was not equally experienced: it was a process executed mainly by whites, families, the middle class and upwardly mobile. As suburbia became overcrowded, and the American economy underwent rapid deindustrialization, new residential-commercial blocs arose beyond the suburbs and further from urban centers. Edge cities (Garreau 1992), gated communities (Low 2001), and exurbs (Eiesland 2000) exploded across the American landscape as the 1970s drew to an end—collapsing rural-urban gaps, exacerbating class and racial segregation, and mirroring a consumption-hungry economy. Capitalizing on long-standing, but scattered attempts, the close of the twentieth and entrance of the twenty-first century saw organized efforts toward urban revitalization and the return of citizens to the city (Smith 1996). Positive and negative responses to gentrification abound. Some are quick to argue that individuals and families living in poverty are unduly displaced, while others point to various city improvements from environmental quality to decreases in violent crime. Ethnographic work with gentrified neighborhoods consistently shows local residents awash in divergent opinions that are optimistic, pessimistic, and all points in between (Brown-Saracino 2009). Whatever one's normative evaluation of gentrification, late modern America seems marked by a widening interest in urban restructuring. What would it look like to read Emerging Evangelical church planting alongside this interest?

The church planters in my fieldwork, and those involved with new church plants, were overwhelmingly part of an exodus back to the city. This is consistent with an urban-centric public discourse of Acts 29 and other church planting institutions. Indeed, we have already seen evidence of this restructuring: Jeff's deconversion narrative; Aaron's decision to start the Taza coffee house; the exchange between Soong-Chan Rah and my urban missionary consultants; Josh and New City's sense of self, from the launch team's relocation to their opening sermon series; the discourse of redemption in now, not yet and Preterist kingdom theologies; and part of the silent subtext for why Kevin's *Forbes* reference provoked so much laughter. Much like entrepreneurialism, late modernity's urban restructuring resonates with the broader Emerging Evangelical cultural critique. In particular, returning to the city coincides with the desire for distance from suburban megachurches.

The relationship between conservative Evangelicals and suburbia solidified in the late 1960s. The historian Eileen Luhr (2009) argues forcefully that Evangelical suburbanization was closely coupled with youth culture, consumerism, and conservative politics. Tropes of home and family defined this relationship: "The suburban home came to be viewed both as the sentimental repository of established [family] values and economic success" (6). By 1990 half the U.S. population called the land of cul-de-sacs home (8), and the evangelistic impulses of conservative Christians produced an organizational invention: the megachurch. The formula seems simple enough. Find an area of new residential growth and economic boom, provide a convenient, ample building and watch the pews overflow. Roughly speaking, that is what happened. The presence of megachurches soared during the late twentieth century, and suburbia became a born-again promised land.

TABLE 7.1

*Population Demographics for Corryville, Mt. Auburn, and
Over-the-Rhine (U.S. Census, 2000)*

	Total Pop.	Black	White	Black < 18 years	White < 18 years
Corryville	3830	49.71%	42.03%	25.52%	5.46%
Mt. Auburn	6516	72.97%	23.80%	33.14%	10.96%
Over-The-Rhine	7638	76.93%	19.40%	34.44%	8.77%

Elisha (2008b) offers an ethnographic analysis of how the Evangelical exodus to suburbia fostered a certain approach to social engagement. He describes the faith-based activism of white, middle-class, suburban Christian conservatives in Knoxville, Tennessee and argues that they refigure the condition of "compassion fatigue" to mean "the gaps between one's moral ambitions and the conditions of existence that reinforce and simultaneously threaten to undermine them at every turn" (155). Their activist efforts are directed toward economically distressed inner-city residents. Elisha shares one ethnographic scene especially relevant to our analysis here. It was the first ever meeting of the Samaritans of Knoxville, a faith-based organization founded by a former pastor. During the meeting a man named Howard, the only African American in a room of eighteen people, stood up. Howard proceeded to criticize what he was hearing: "I'm the one who has to clean up the blood of the messes you make when your churches just drop in, drop off, and leave the community behind" (161). The suburban Evangelicals had little comfort to offer Howard in response, and the meeting continued with the critique more or less unaddressed. Voices like Howard's are precisely what Emerging Evangelical church planters want to avoid.

Christ the King Church (CKC), like New City, places the values of redeeming and reconciling the city at the center of its congregational vision. Unlike New City, CKC is an Acts 29 church plant focused on a very different area of Cincinnati than the predominantly white, middle-class neighborhood of Oakley. CKC concentrates on three adjoining inner-city neighborhoods: Corryville, Mt. Auburn, and Over-the-Rhine (OTR). Corryville, where CKC holds their weekly worship services in a community recreation center, is two miles due north of the downtown business district. Table 7.1 provides some population statistics for these three neighborhoods.

Two observations about these numbers are most glaring. CKC is a (predominantly white) church plant in a predominantly black area of the city. Second, the percentage of children is much higher for blacks, indicating a disproportionate number of settled black families compared to transient whites. The three neighborhoods have similar socioeconomic profiles: largely working poor, underemployed, and unemployed individuals and families. While Corryville and Mt. Auburn are mostly nondescript residential neighborhoods, Over-the-Rhine is a different story. Because of its unique German history, large collection of Italianate architecture, and neighboring proximity to the downtown business district, OTR has been the primary target of urban revitalization in Cincinnati (Miller and Tucker 1998). The largest investor, Center City Development Corporation (3CDC), has spent $96 million on OTR since 2004. The neighborhood has also been the city's primary target of gentrification criticism, namely, that revitalization efforts actively displace poor people. In the city's public discourse OTR has the persona of a neighborhood plagued with high rates of violent crime and racial tension. Many Cincinnatians index this by a series of tumultuous riots that occurred in 2001. The riots were sparked by repeated shootings of black youth by white police officers. The neighborhood still bears the impress of the riots, with caged and boarded up storefronts, and decade-old bullet holes next to broken windows.

Michael, whom we met earlier as a respondent to Soong Chan-Rah's missionary-colonialist critique, planted Christ the King Church. After completing his Masters of Divinity at Southern Seminary in Louisville (a main seminary for the Southern Baptist Convention) Michael and his wife Laura wanted to plant a church. Their criteria were few: to be in a major city, to minister to a mixed demographic, to make racial reconciliation a centerpiece of their identity, and to be within reasonable driving distance from his family in West Virginia and her family in northern Ohio. Cincinnati fit the geographic profile, though they knew little about the city except that they loved the skyline view when descending onto the city driving from the southwest. The de facto segregation and the lingering presence of the 2001 riots in the city's collective memory suited their theological platform of racial reconciliation. And they were encouraged by the denomination's Director of Missions, who wanted the relative absence of SBC churches in Cincinnati's inner city to change.

Michael, Laura, and their three young children moved in the summer of 2008. They bought a two-story, 120-year-old townhouse in Mt. Auburn: one mile south of Corryville and one mile northeast of Over-the-Rhine. The house was one of eight lined side-by-side, converted from Section Eight several years earlier. While they recognized that they were beneficiaries of gentrification, Michael and Laura both had stories to share. Soon after the church launched in January 2010 Laura witnessed a shooting in the convenience store parking lot three hundred feet from their front door. A year earlier Michael had found a small, unidentifiable hole in the window shade of his youngest child's room. Several weeks after discovering this hole, when arranging the crib in the room, he found the cause of the hole behind his daughter's teddy bear: a bullet lodged in the wall just above where she sits, plays, and sleeps. This forced a difficult moment of reevaluation for both himself and Laura, but he responded with a return to the Emerging cultural critique: "I don't want my kids living in a perfect suburban shell. I want them to be realistic about the brokenness in the world."

For my first interview with Michael he suggested we meet at a recently opened coffee shop on Over-the-Rhine's Main Street (an epicenter of the 2001 riots). From the second I walked in, it screamed of white, middle-class public space. Light, elevatoresque jazz played through overhead speakers. Almost every patron was young, white, and quiet. I paid $11 for a soup and half-sandwich with Continental herbs and flavorings. During the interview, when discussing Michael's mappings of OTR as a church planter, he said that people rarely mix across class and race lines, especially in public. He immediately drew attention to the space we were in. "Where are all the poor black people? They are walking past the front window." He was right. They were. Several months later I asked Michael to evaluate a glossy flyer that I picked up from a downtown hotel, produced by 3CDC and promoting the revitalization of OTR. He assessed it briefly, then quickly pointed out the selective nature of the flyer's main photograph. The focus of the picture was the Cincinnati Music Hall, a late-nineteenth-century architectural marvel that was named a National Historic Landmark in 1974. He described the taking of the picture as "convenient" and placed his index finger on a space just outside the frame. To the left is an equally well-known entity in the city, a public park "notorious for drugs and crime," which Michael suspected was intentionally left out of the photo. I asked if new church plants should be part of the city's gentrification work. "Absolutely," but he continued with a caution: "[T]he problem with gentrification is that it never addresses the spiritual side of things, which is the origin of all the problems."

Michael, like most of my consultants involved in planting new churches, is a white, middle-class Evangelical who left the suburbs for the city. In the process of doing so, and as a necessary part of his responsibilities as a planter, he cultivates a heightened consciousness about the structural issues involved with urban restructuring. His evaluations of the coffee shop and the promotional flyer are small moments in a larger phenomenon: a different standpoint toward social engagement than that performed by conservative Evangelicals. Rather than grounding his urban experiences in the tangled idioms of "compassion and accountability" (Elisha 2008b), with which he is no doubt familiar, he appeals to a discourse of reconciliation. But, as evidenced by his final assessment of the city's gentrification work as nonspiritual, this reconciliation should not be confused as a twin of state-sponsored urban revitalization.

The tension accompanying participation in urban restructuring is one of measured sacrifice. My consultants recounted a variety of costs associated with leaving their suburban lives: losing money on houses sold and bought, losing spacious backyards, leaving established friend and job networks, changing jobs, entering children into lower-funded schools, and troubling (if not alienating) friends and family by relocating to urban contexts. These very pragmatic, potentially preventative, concerns were deemed secondary to their desire for reconciliation. Moreover, they are not forgotten concerns. They remain as symbols of encouragement; secular values devalued.

Church Planting and "Traditional" Gender Roles

The heteronormative nuclear family is a key institution of Evangelical modernity (Luhr 2009: 6). Ingersoll (2003) rightly observes that if we view Evangelicalism as a cultural system, then "gender is a central organizing principle and a core symbolic system" that structures meaning and action (16). The family is one social location where roles and ideologies for masculinity and femininity are mapped onto everyday life. The twentieth-century conservative Christian subculture is characterized by definitive patriarchy. Qualitative inquiry by social scientists, while generally finding support for this description, has sought to complicate simplified representations of how Evangelicals live out gender and family. Bartkowski (1997), after analyzing "over 30 popular Evangelical family manuals" (394), concluded that issues of household authority and decision making are contested territory among Evangelical leaders. Dominant notions of wifely submission and male headship are actively challenged by a "counter-hegemonic discourse of mutual submission" (399) promoted by Evangelical/biblical feminists. These divergent standpoints are grounded in differing scriptural hermeneutics and gender ideologies (traditionalists assuming that males and females are inherently different, feminists assuming an essential sameness across genders).

Gallagher and Smith (1999) argued that Evangelicals have experienced increasing gender equality at home due to the external pressures of American economic restructuring. Ideals such as men being the primary decision maker exist symbolically, "a card never played" (221) in the day-to-day affairs of family life. Yet other taken-for-granted ideas persist, such as men being the spiritual authority in the home and the domestic sphere being a female space. Ingersoll (2003) responded to the widespread understanding that Evangelical women locate forms of empowerment through their submission (Griffith 1997) by tracking the stories of Evangelical feminists and conservative women "who have chafed under patriarchy—those who have been sometimes nearly destroyed by it" (5). This body of work nuances a base social fact: Evangelicals are modern subjects insofar as they perform patriarchal-leaning gender separations. Emerging Evangelical church planters, by and large, continue this tradition of modernity. To illustrate, we look to the voices of church planters' wives.

Just as the church planter is construed to be a distinct identity, different from a pastor, the planter's wife is considered a role with its own unique responsibilities, challenges, frustrations, and rewards. Like the planter, the wife has available to her an expanse of specialized resources. For example, in 2005 the PCA's Mission to North America founded *Parakaleo* (literally, coming alongside), a network of church planters' wives that produces and distributes literature, maintains regional clubs, and holds gatherings at denominational and MNA conferences. My sample of consultants included five women whose husbands were church planters: Cathy (whose deconversion narrative we heard earlier), Niki (married to Chris, whose deconversion narrative we heard earlier), Paige (married to Josh of New City in Oakley), Laura (whom we met briefly in the previous section), and Stephanie (married to Kevin of The Oaks in Middletown). This sample of women is diverse in several ways: theologically they diverge on numerous points of doctrine; Cathy and Niki are part of house churches and the other three are not; they represent small town, urban, and exurban church plants; Cathy and Niki are nearly two decades older than the other three; almost all have kids but their kids differ in number and age; some are self-described "introverts" while others are "extroverts;" and, using a common piece of Evangelical language, they identify as possessing a variety of "spiritual gifts." Still, my ethnographic work with them revealed a great deal of continuity in their experiences of helping to plant a new church. These experiences align closely with what scholars have documented for the gender and family life of modern, conservative Evangelicals.

When I asked what their primary role was in planting the church, two answers dominated. First, they assumed responsibility for "hospitality." Their answers paid precise attention to the details of everyday domesticity. Niki and Paige offer useful side-by-side illustrations because of the distance in time between their church plants, Niki's in 2001 and Paige's in 2009. Niki recalled that "in the beginning everything was in our home," and stressed how necessary it was "to be open to your home being used. People need to know they can go wherever they want. They don't have to ask for everything they use, they just help themselves." Food was equally important. "Everything starts with a meal, and it's my job to have everything available for people." She emphasized "basics," like coffee creamer, and how having them ready helped make everyone feel at home. Paige's discussion sounded the same chords, describing the need to "see the home as a place of ministry." During the launch team's year of preparation, almost every event was hosted at her and Josh's home. Just prior to the first public worship service, they started hosting a weekly small group. Paige talked about her role in "preparing the home" for these events: cleaning the bathrooms, vacuuming and sweeping, making sure there was something to eat, and making sure there was always coffee and creamer. Paige named two considerations she thinks are important to remember: "not overcommitting to other things so I have time to maintain our home" and "a willingness to do things last minute."

The second answer was to "support" the planter/husband. Again, these women attended closely to the minutia of everyday acts. Stephanie was among the most elaborate on this point. She recalled a moment from a "women's session" at an Acts 29 church planting retreat just before The Oaks launched. She asked the other women, whose churches had already been planted, "what they all wish they had known before they started" and the unanimous response was to "not feel obligated to stretch yourself. Your number one job is to support your husband. Let others step up and serve." Almost three years after launching, Stephanie had a decisive list for how she supports Kevin: make things as easy as possible around the house, from doing laundry to making sure there is coffee ready in the morning; keep their daughter busy when he works from home; not talk about church business when they go on dates; be at the sermon each week and debrief with him afterwards; and be tolerant of people in the church (and ethnographers) desiring constant access to him, many wanting a "special relationship" with him, and most thinking "they're the exception" to informal rules like not telephoning Kevin on his rest day.

The biggest danger these women articulated about being the wife of a church planter was the possibility of "loneliness" and "isolation." Cathy, when remembering the first years of their church plant, felt "emotionally disconnected" from Glenn because so much of her time was spent mentoring the college-aged women their ministry attracted. Paige confirmed that this danger is the one most often stressed in *Parakaleo* literature and meetings, but she did not wrestle with this psychological-emotional difficulty. She immediately recognized herself as an anomaly because she is a native of the city they planted in, allowing her to begin the planting process with an extensive support network. Laura, however, was troubled by loneliness and isolation. Recall from above that she and Michael moved to Cincinnati to plant their inner-city church, a half-day's drive from either of their families. Speaking in a somber and straightforward tone, Laura identified several other complicating factors. She felt there were not a lot of people "like [her]" where they lived, including very few stay-at-home moms. She enrolled two of her children in a preschool program at the University of Cincinnati, but the other moms there were "either really rich or really poor, or didn't speak English very well." Six months after their church plant launched they had attracted few families or young children. All this, of course, overlapped with their decision to plant and live in a neighborhood where she witnessed a shooting and Michael dislodged a bullet from the wall just above their baby's crib.

My purpose in pulling these women's voices together is to illustrate some of the gender dynamics involved with church planting. These women focus their responsibilities on the domestic sphere and on supporting their husbands' duties as planters. Overwhelmingly, these performances parallel the gender work said to characterize modern Evangelicalism (Bartkowski 1997). While many planters' wives may have left suburbia, they have brought with them to the city the cultural models for family that typifiy suburban Evangelicalism.

The tension here is that while loneliness and isolation were voiced, these women also spoke about the positive consequences of seeing themselves as coplanters. As Paige phrased it, "You are a we." She contrasted the experience of planting New City with being married to Josh when he was a suburban youth pastor: "We are really doing ministry together now. I feel like more of a partner than I ever did before. Our job is to get to know people and we do that together, rather than always doing separate guys' and girls' stuff like we did with youth ministry." All five women offered some version of this partnership sentiment, often juxtaposing church planting with previous experiences where they felt disconnected from their husbands because of the latters' pastoral responsibilities.

Church Planting and Emerging Evangelicalism

Church planting—as much as deconversion, ancient-future, or missional—is an integral part of Emerging Evangelicalism. Institutionally, the significance of starting new churches in a movement defined by cultural critique makes a great deal of sense. If these religious subjects were perfectly content or mildly unhappy with their culture of faith, then there would be little impetus to begin "a new work." In particular, church planting can be read as part of the Emerging Evangelical aversion to the megachurch movement. House church and cell-church models, as discussed in the Introduction, are intended as alternatives to the boundless increase of a single congregation. Apart from figuring in their cultural critique, how does church planting help us understand Emerging Evangelical subjectivity and institution making?

The process of church planting, and the identity of being a church planter, capture a dynamic that defines the Emerging movement: Emerging Evangelicals are religious subjects informed by two eras, modernity and late modernity. The examples above illustrate this dual identity by showing how dispositions created by the cultural conditions of both eras help explain the dynamics of church planting. Modernity is enacted via the discourse of measurement and performance of traditional gender roles. Late modernity is enacted via the entrepreneurial impulse and patterns of urban restructuring. In each case, modern and late modern dispositions lead to defined cultural tensions. Measurement values are unrealizable, entrepreneurial efforts are constantly in danger of commodification, relocating to the city from suburbia entails practical sacrifices, and feelings of empowerment exist alongside the patriarchal aspects of church planting. Emerging Evangelicals remain aware of these tensions, though they do not attempt to resolve them. The dual identity of being modern and late modern does not mean that church planters live some kind of schizophrenic existence. Rather, the simultaneous presence of both sets of dispositions results in a religious subjectivity with multiple roots, all relied on as resources for forms of action, decision making, and institution creation.

While the various institutions of Evangelical life remain interconnected, it is also helpful to disentangle them. For example, observing that their gender work remains distinctly modern is not a license to assume that Emerging Evangelicals are not late modern in other, equally significant ways. And despite a highly self-conscious cultural critique of conservative Christianity, Emerging Evangelicals remain inheritors of a particular religious culture, and those ties do not evaporate as quickly as objections materialize. Emerging Evangelicals wish to see themselves as distanced from their conservative counterparts, and in some ways they have certainly achieved that distance. But their everyday practice belies a complete break with their past.

In the final ethnographic chapter, we will consider an expression of Emerging Evangelical culture that reveals these religious subjects as actively responding to their cultural critique and the conditions of late modernity: sense of place.

———————————————————————————— 8 ——

Church Planting II

Sense of Place

————————————————————————————————————

Doing ethnography with missional church planters in Cincinnati proved to be fortuitous. Neighborhoods are the reason. Cincinnati—much like New York or Chicago—is a city defined by its collection of distinct neighborhood enclaves. When you ask Cincinnatians where they live—or for driving directions, or where an address is located, or where they would like to buy a house, or where the best place to (insert desired activity) is—they begin with a neighborhood. Rhoda Halperin, an economic anthropologist and former professor at the University of Cincinnati, used this social fact as an ethnographic starting point in her book, *Practicing Community: Class, Culture, and Power in an Urban Neighborhood* (1998). Halperin focuses on the East End, a working-class neighborhood where residents have mobilized for political capital, urban planning, and the creation of inclusive community institutions. To understand how the East End fits into Cincinnati's socio-political life, Halperin situates it as one of fifty-two neighborhoods (in an area of roughly eighty square miles). Halperin's ethnographic eye for neighborhood distinctions is, to grossly understate the case, not lost on church planters.

Tim, who planted a nondenominational church near the University of Cincinnati in 2008, recast the congregation's ministry plans in late 2009. In their first year they focused solely on Clifton and Clifton Heights as missional locales, the neighborhoods most closely associated with the daily and yearly rhythms of the university. Their new "vision" was for a "city-wide church" based on "contextual ministry" in "local communities." This reorientation included a revised Church Plant Proposal that foregrounded the city's borough-like character: "Cincinnati has 137 close-knit neighborhoods within a 10 to 15 mile radius of the city. Renewal must begin with strategic neighborhood churches that network together for the common good and renewal of the city" (emphasis in original). The next page of the proposal lists these

137 neighborhoods in alphabetical order. Tim's parameter was slightly larger than Halperin's, including older and new suburbs, but their conception of the city is grounded in the same logic: the local particularities of place matter greatly to Cincinnatians, and any attempt (ethnographic or evangelistic) to understand the city and its people must recognize this. We have already encountered several examples of Emerging Evangelicals responding to Cincinnati's cityscape, such as Michael's racial reconciliation efforts in Corryville, Mt. Auburn, and Over-the-Rhine. Consider a further example.

The small college town where I teach is about thirty-five miles northwest of downtown Cincinnati. Consequently, a large number of students have close ties with the city. In late March 2010 a male student was walking down the town's main street and wearing a T-shirt with "Oakley Is Not Hyde Park" emblazoned on the front. I instantly thought of Josh, New City, and their missional focus on Oakley. The shirt, produced by a Cincinnati-based company founded by a comedian native to the city, is both ironic and serious. Its irony derives from the two neighborhoods' similarities. They are roughly the same size and share a lengthy east-west border. They are both largely residential with small commercial districts. And racially, they are both overwhelmingly white: Hyde Park at 93 percent and Oakley at 88 percent (U.S. Census Bureau, 2000). Its seriousness derives from Cincinnatians' insistence on neighborhood distinctions. For Oakley and Hyde Park, the difference is sketched as a matter of social class. Hyde Park is said to be more exclusive, geared toward the upper-middle class, while Oakley is considered patently middle class. Housing values, for example, are significantly different despite the very close proximity of the two neighborhoods. According to local real estate listings, the mean selling price for Hyde Park homes in 2009 was nearly $330,000, which was $130,000 more than Oakley. Seeing this T-shirt prompted some anecdotal, wireless ethnography; I informed Josh via text message of the sighting. Within minutes he replied, "Sounds like a good kid, buy him a beer for me!" I did not, but I did joke back, "Is New City manufacturing those?" He whimsically concluded the exchange: "No, wish we'd thought of it, though."

Cincinnati's neighborhood-driven social geography resonates with the missional logic of church planters. In a city that emphasizes the differences among neighborhoods, the missional impulse to "contextualize the Gospel" adapts easily. This intersection also indexes an important observation about Emerging Evangelicals: mission field locales are highly valued and, as a result, a defined sense of place is cultivated. Because this observation is grounded in the widespread cultural logic of being missional, this argument is not confined to Cincinnatians or church planters—although planting pastors, more so than their congregants, were especially apt to make their sense of place explicit and to intentionally find ways to nurture it. We will illustrate below that integrating a sense of place into everyday religious subjectivity is crucial for Emerging Evangelicalism writ large, and provides further evidence of the movement's ties to the conditions of late modernity.

Place and Late Modernity

"Sense of place," the cultural work people do to create and maintain attachments to their socio-geographic setting, is an established research tradition among anthropologists. Rodman (1992) was among the first to urge ethnographers to reorient their theorizing of place from "locale, the setting for action, the stage on which things happen" (643) to "the physical, emotional, and experiential realities places hold for their inhabitants at particular times" (641). Steven Feld and Keith Basso poignantly responded to this call with their volume, *Senses of Place* (1996). They conclude their Introduction to this collection of essays with a question: "What could be truer of placed experience— secure or fragile, pleasurable or repugnant, comforting or unsettling—than the taken-for-granted quality of intense particularity?" (11)? Their question rests on the fundamental difference between physical space and inhabited place. We humans, as members of social collectives, can be counted on to invest spaces with meaningfulness that our fellow place-makers would not predict. "Sense of place" promises that through careful ethnography anthropologists can trace, unpack, and convey "local theories of dwelling . . . ways of fusing setting to situation, locality to life-world" (ibid.: 8). Or, as Basso (1996) says in his contribution to the volume: "dwelling [consists] in the multiple, 'lived relationships' that people maintain with places, for it is solely by virtue of these relationships that space acquires meaning" (54).

At stake, then, is not simply how humans become attached to places and the meanings they assign to those places, but how place becomes a primary vehicle for understanding and asserting a sense of self. Place is a means of learning, creating, and performing identity, a social fact that Emerging Evangelicals work out in their own manner. Sense of place should not be confused with the analytic of "sacred space," which captures social actors separating a certain locality from its physical surroundings in an ontologically significant way. As Chidester and Linenthal (1995) put it: "set apart from or carved out of an 'ordinary' environment to provide an arena for the performance of controlled, 'extraordinary' patterns of action" (9). The idea that some spaces are sacred and others are not invokes the kind of sacred-profane logic that my consultants consistently rejected because of its connotations with "modern, traditional" Christian thinking. Rather than look for rituals that are mapped onto physical space, "sense of place" looks, to echo Basso, for the relationships people create and live vis-a-vis particular spaces. Sense of place is about dwelling, not sacralizing. Rodman (1992) suspected this phenomenological quality, writing, "[P]laces come into being through praxis, not just through narratives" (642), and recognized that senses of place are not simply discursive constructions: they are embodied, felt, remembered, and otherwise internalized.

The importance that Emerging Evangelicals assign to place figures into their broader cultural critique. They insist that one problem with conservative Evangelicals is their inattention to the particularities of place. This critique figured into the group interview with Aaron, Larry, Becky, and D.G., the roundtable scene that opened this book. Toward the end of the interview I asked them to comment on the potential connections between place, everyday ministry, and religious identity. Aaron, a member of the new monastic house church community in Norwood and campus pastor at Northern Kentucky University, began the exchange:

> AARON: A lot of that Evangelical sort of tradition has no, to use a pun, has no place for place. It's a-contextual. Fuller's Gospel Hour. Didn't matter if you were living in rural Minnesota or if you were in urban L.A., you got the same Gospel message beamed to you through your radio.
> BECKY: Mhmm.
> AARON: And the presenters, in a sense, could care less.
> D.G.: Yeah.
> AARON: And that's true of course with other forms of mass media.
> LARRY: Well, it's like preaching.
> D.G.: It's the reason why conferences need to be regional and not national.
> LARRY: It's like the Gospel is proclaimed. There is no conversation. Once you start having a conversation—discourse, dialogue—like I think Jesus really had.

Along with their Emerging brethren, these four believe that conservative Evangelicals maintain a regrettable disposition: a one-size-fits-all ministry mentality. This clashes with their missional understanding of contextually distinct, culturally different mission fields. The Emerging Evangelical sense of place—as an everyday, embodied subjectivity—meshes with the value of being missional, as it does the monastic value of stability. Alongside these cultural logics, we can also read the Emerging attraction to place as a response to the cultural conditions of late modernity.

Losing, forgetting, and otherwise being disconnected from a sense of place is an experience commentators have consistently attributed to the late modern era. Said (1979) called it a "generalized condition of homelessness" (18), Gupta and Ferguson (1992) described it as the "profound sense of a loss of territorial roots, of an erosion of the cultural distinctiveness of places" (9), and Appadurai (1996) termed it "deterritorialization" (49). Regardless of the preferred signifier, the idea is the same: staying rooted in one locale and forming a meaningful relationship to that locale became an increasingly unfamiliar phenomenon as the twentieth century waned. The state of constant mobility that fuels this rootlessness has several major sources. There is an economic impetus stemming from the realities of post-Fordism: highly flexible labor forces and increased forms of labor not reliant on a geographic location. There is also the growing number of diasporic and transnational communities: changes in transportation technology and political policy make the global flow of people drastically easier. The conclusion, irrespective of the sources stressed, is the same: late moderns are on the move like never before, resulting in a general, collective detachment from place.

As a cultural condition, the anxiety of this homelessness, loss, and erosion has incited a variety of discontents. People are increasingly mobilizing in an attempt to restore a relation to place in an era that works against such attachment. Some work out this desire through consumption practices; the Slow Food movement and related strategies for creating a relation to place via agriculture, food, and eating is one commonly cited example (Wilk, ed. 2006). The anthropologist Peter Benson (2005) describes this late modern response for a Connecticut community seeking urban revitalization through minor league baseball. "Deindustrialization [in this city] has run together with white flight, residential segregation, and advanced economic and social marginalization" (97). The city created the baseball team as a symbol of community, an attempt to ignite nostalgia for the authentically local and to "make dwelling a power" (95). Cases like this abound. Social actors from different communities of practice, with differing motivations, do not simply internalize the condition of deterritorialization; rather, they respond to it by actively cultivating senses of place. For Emerging Evangelicals, forming attachments to local mission fields becomes yet another exercise in desiring authenticity. To illustrate we follow two urban church planters, Kevin and Bart, through their missional locales and listen for how they use place in their constructions of "real" faith.

Two Places

Between June and August 2009 I was led on two neighborhood tours: by Kevin in Middletown, and by Bart in urban Cincinnati's West Walnut Hills. As these tours unfolded, the sense of place cultivated by these two pastors became impossibly clear. Kevin and Bart offer an excellent side-by-side illustration because their stories diverge more than they converge. Both are white, well-educated, middle-class, family men who voluntarily moved into a setting unlike the ones in which they grew up and unlike those to which secular logics of upward mobility might expect them to aspire. Both are former suburbanites who felt "convicted" to begin a life as an urban missionary. Their similarities mostly end there. Theologically, they are far from identical. Both maintain a Jesus-centric faith and understand the Bible as God's most direct and complete revelation to humanity. But, as an Acts 29 planter, Kevin is committed to a Calvinistic Reformed theology that stresses human depravity and the exclusivity of the doctrine of Jesus' substitutionary atonement on the cross as the means for eternal salvation. Bart is far more ecumenical. He identifies as a "post-Christian," affirming love and grace as the signifying attributes of God, but questions doctrinally centered soteriologies. During my fieldwork, Kevin was in his late twenties and Bart was in his mid forties. Their chosen cities are dissimilar. Middletown is a primarily working poor white city, whereas Walnut Hills is a largely un(der)employed black neighborhood (84 percent in 2000). From the beginning of the church planting process, Kevin intended to affiliate with Acts 29. Bart wanted a ministry with no institutional affiliations. The Oaks maintains a rather typical congregational structure, and Bart's ministry is far more grassroots with little in the way of organized gatherings. Kevin is a paid clergyman. Bart is not. Still, and this is the crucial observation for this chapter, despite their personal, contextual, and institutional differences Kevin and Bart have formed strikingly similar senses of place.

"My job is not to fix Middletown"

On June 25 Kevin led me on a three-hour, winding, but ultimately circular driving tour of Middletown. The weather was staggering: over 90 degree-heat, high humidity, little cloud cover, and no breeze. It was perfect for afternoon swimming.

The previous week, along with thirteen other pastors and community leaders, Kevin had attended three three-hour workshops on "racial reconciliation" hosted by the City Council. Those details were fresh in his mind and clearly occupied his attention, as he frequently connected them to our roaming conversation. As a matter of church planting course Kevin already knew the racial demographics of Middletown (~10 percent black, a very small constituency of Hispanics, and the rest white). Much of the Council's discussion had turned "political," which Kevin intentionally avoided. He is not, he continually found occasion to tell me, very interested in political commitments, including the hot button "culture war" issues of conservative Evangelicalism (for example, abortion or homosexuality). The main lesson Kevin took from the workshops was that of "white privilege." He felt this was what he and his congregation most needed to hear about, what they were most unaware of.

Toward the end of our drive Kevin turned on Minnesota Street ("the Sota"), which runs directly through the city's largest and densest black residential section. "This is the worst street in Middletown," by which he meant various forms of known and undiscovered criminality. Kevin parked the car briefly at Douglass Park: a modest, partly grassy affair with a jungle gym and a dozen or so water streams that shot up from the ground. It was busy, but not diverse. Everyone milling around, from adults carrying picnic baskets to children splashing and laughing in the water, was black. We paused for a moment and Kevin reminded me that fifteen minutes earlier we had passed Sunset Park—a much larger complex, quite verdant, with a large community pool (large enough for two lifeguards), and a nearly all-white populace. He explained that the city used to fund two community pools until a massive state budget cut forced one to close several years ago. The recompense for Douglass Park was the series of spouting shoots sporadically rising through half-dollar-sized holes drilled in concrete. He offered this as a case in point for the Council's focus on racial privilege, and precisely the kind of dynamic to which his congregants needed to pay more attention. Soon after we left, proceeding down the Sota, Kevin pointed to a large football stadium on the left. The hosts of the racial reconciliation meeting claimed that high school football games are the only consistent occasion when whites and blacks occupy the same social space in Middletown. Kevin, who tries to attend every home game as part of his missional work, affirmed this and went further to say that seating is not segregated. "Everybody's mixed up together. It's great."

Central Avenue—downtown's main drag—is two miles from the Sota. From December 2007 until their move to integrate with Faith United in January 2010, a two-story unit on this strip was the rented home of The Oaks' collective gatherings. The wide, steep, wooden stairwell ascending to the second floor worship space was lined on the right wall with artfully composed black and white photos. The first featured a sign reading "Middletown," one of several that mark entry points into the city's corporate limits. The final picture, aligned with the final staircase step, featured the high school football stadium, lit brightly for a night game.

Earlier in the tour, when we first pulled on to Central Avenue, Kevin described the strip as "like a bomb went off downtown, the further away you get the nicer things get." This became evident on our way to eat lunch, further down Central, past the rented worship space. Kevin wanted me to eat at his favorite restaurant, a locally owned Italian-themed diner. "When you hear people talk about being missional," he reflected, "one thing you'll hear is finding places to be a regular." Kevin eats there about eight times a month, brings out-of-towners (visiting pastors, friends, family, and hungry ethnographers) there, and has church events catered from there. He recalled with no small amount of fondness the first day he was greeted by name. The owner—who spoke familiarly and in detail with Kevin on our visit—has worked hard to improve the building and its surroundings, one reason Kevin likes supporting the business. The one exception is an adjacent, bedraggled house the owner has tried unsuccessfully to purchase. Kevin described it as a "crack house or something, lots of drug deals moving through," using the ostensibly illicit epicenter as an example of a pervasive problem in Middletown—drug abuse. "Marijuana is huge here. Even middle-class folks are pretty big pot smokers; it's just part of the culture."

Lunch was $20 for two sandwiches and two drinks. We ate inside, separate from the midday heat. Most of our talk was a rumination on how Kevin's coming to know "the culture of Middletown" has impacted what he does as a pastor. Two examples excited him most. First, Kevin has become much more self-conscious about his sermon writing. Acts 29 pastors, and others tied to the revival of Reformed Calvinism in America, are well-known in the Emerging movement to be expository preachers (Hansen 2008). Rather than organize their preaching topically, they prefer to explain scriptural texts week-to-week with incredible deliberateness (critics might say tediousness). Kevin once spent five months teaching 1 Peter, a considerably slight New Testament epistle of only 105 verses. On an average Sunday he aims for forty minutes of preaching, which distills fifteen to twenty hours of weekly preparation. But the longer he preaches in Middletown, the more he worries this style is "too linear, too academic." Tim Keller is a church planter in Manhattan, and an extremely influential author and public speaker among Acts 29 pastors. However, Keller has proven to be an inexact model for Kevin's preaching. Keller's Manhattan audience does well with *New Yorker* and *Econ-*

omist references. *Time*, Kevin suspects, is a stretch in Middletown. He also haggles over words in a new way. "Things like 'glory' and 'gospel' have all this meaning for Christians that other people are missing." His solution has been to recruit a proof reader who will not be stingy with criticisms—his wife Stephanie. She diligently scans each sermon text for words, phrases, and references that might exhaust the knowledge and patience of poorly educated Middletowners.

Kevin's second example frets about class and race more than education. When he first planted The Oaks Kevin drove a baby blue Honda Accord. The longer he drove in Middletown the more he worried about looking like "too much of a yuppie." After consulting with his wife, they made a change: a black Chevy pick-up truck. It was our mode of transport that afternoon and was no small-bed, comfort-first, low-sitting model. It is a bulky, metal, step-up-to-get-in, grumbling-engine, move-it-or-lose-it kind of truck. Kevin's anxiety later shifted to appearing "too redneck" to African Americans. This is precisely the kind of missional dilemma he presents to his congregants. "How would we feel if we pulled up and the church parking lot was filled with BMWs? If you were going to be a missionary in Africa you'd pay attention to these things."

When we left the restaurant in the black Chevy we headed to a house he hoped to purchase. Kevin, Stephanie, and their two young children live only six miles from Central Avenue, but outside the Middletown city limits. He is anxious to change this, but cannot afford to buy a new home until their current one sells. Two mortgages are too much for their annual income. Most pastors in the city, he reported with a tone of deep regret, commute nearly twenty miles from West Chester or Mason: largely affluent exurbs of Cincinnati. Kevin intentionally avoided these communities when planting The Oaks, despite their relative proximity and likely abundant tithers. The house of interest was further down Central, further away from "the bomb," and further into where "average, everyday, working people live." The neighborhood did indeed have an "average" quality to it. It was no "Sota"—less than ten minutes away—with its rusty, broken fences and crooked, crumbling gutters. But there was nothing flashy or extravagant about it either. The house he showed me was a two-story brick home with a small veranda upstairs. The front yard boasted a large, canopied oak tree. The backyard was bigger, including an ample kitchen garden and covered back porch. The asking price was $130,000, a considerable bargain so long as structural concerns like electrical wiring and plumbing did not violate building codes and require maintenance. Kevin used the house as an opportunity to explain the Middletown housing market. Steep economic decline directly tied to A.K. Steel's labor and production downsizing had sparked a sizeable emigration, and an even larger dip in housing costs. One result had been an influx of young, first-home-buying families. This is good news for The Oaks. Kevin consistently encourages congregants to buy homes in the city and, as of May 2010, about half of the Oaks' members had done so. Throughout our drive he identified houses where church staff and lay members lived.

As we toured Middletown Kevin made two comments that serve as book-ends for his sense of place. Driving past the A.K. Steel plant, on our way to "the Sota," Kevin said after a moment's silence: "To be a church planter, you have to be an economist, you know? You have to be a sociologist and a demographer and an urban planner." I asked in response: "Did you get more than you bargained for?" He replied: "Absolutely. I wasn't really prepared for this." Indeed, Kevin's intimacy with Middletown has formed through a process of learning local social, economic, and historical details. Not only did he seam-lessly rehearse housing fluctuations, crime, racial residential patterns, and employment trends, but he also talked about voting patterns, homelessness, urban-suburban trends, and union culture. As the tour ended and we headed back to where my car was parked, Kevin explained with focused intensity: "My job is not to fix Middletown. As much as I would like that, that's not what I'm here for. My job is to find out what these people's deepest fears are. And my job is to find out what their greatest hopes are. And then I need to show them why Christ is *more* than either one of those. That's my job." Kevin's sense of place is mediated by a clear sense of evangelistic purpose.

"If you are going to care for people, you have to care about what they do"

On August 7 Bart led me on a two-hour, winding, but ultimately circular walking tour of West Walnut Hills. The weather was pleasant, nothing like the oppressive heat six weeks earlier in Middletown. I arrived at Bart's office around noon and waited as he concluded a prior appointment. When we left a few minutes later Bart turned to me: "We're just gonna take a walk. Okay?"

We had gone just a few hundred feet when Bart paused on the sidewalk next to a one-way, three-lane road. He traced with his finger in the air the boundaries of the neighborhood—major street arteries going east and west, freeways going north and south. The streets, houses, businesses, services, people, and lives in this area provided the everyday context for the Walnut Hills Fellowship (WHF).

After walking for several minutes we turned north on a quarter-mile resi-dential street. This is where Bart lives with his wife and two teenage children. The house directly north of theirs belongs to a WHF member, as do two others on the street. Numerous houses are abandoned; a fact reflected by grossly overgrown grass, shrubs, and trees. A retired couple who have been in the neighborhood most of their lives live toward the end of the street. Bart and his wife know them well and have invited them to join WHF's weekly dinner. But the couple remember the neighborhood's earlier prosperity and want nothing to do with its current disarray. Bart, in what would become a familiar conversational routine, had a ready explanation: "When you get involved in [residents'] lives their chaos gets all over you. That's why middle-class black families are so hard to get involved." The suggestion is that racial obstacles are hard enough to overcome in a segregated city without inviting others' burdens.

We turned the corner and Bart immediately pointed to a nearby apartment complex. "That's the worst building in the whole neighborhood," an assertion he propped up with reports of crack-cocaine dealings, brutal violence, and the species of traveling mayhem that follows such behavior like a magnet. It was there, two years earlier, that two ministry interns working for WHF got caught in the middle of nighttime gunfire on their way home. Luckily the souvenir bullet holes were restricted to car doors.

We turned south, heading back in the direction of his office. After a hundred yards or so there was the first instance of what would prove to be an afternoon refrain—Bart encountered a familiar face. This time it was an older black man in a motorized wheel chair, accompanied by a small dog. They greeted each other warmly and shared a brief informational exchange. Walking away Bart explained that he is "a good guy," a reputable landlord for several neighborhood houses. He had barely finished when we paused again. Bart pointed to a sardine line of six two-story townhouses, all built within the last three years. They were painted a floral tone that was in sharp contrast with the nondescript, beige, white, and gray surroundings. They seemed an untainted eyesore. All but one was unoccupied. Bart, again, sensed my confusion. He explained that the city used a government subsidy to build them, then placed economic restrictions on residency—one could not earn too much or too little money each month to live there. The asking price has already decreased by $20,000, which Bart suspected would continue to decline along with their vacancy. He reckoned the whole thing to be a parade of governmental stumbling.

A few hundred yards further we reached the main street artery that travels east. On every visit I have made to West Walnut Hills, irrespective of the time of day or day of week, there has been a steady congregation of young black men lining this street one block west: milling about, talking, and rarely laughing. Before I could pause and ask, Bart said knowingly, "We need to keep moving." (Later, he would add to his verbal mapping of this corner: "I don't walk that direction with people I don't know. The place is drug central, anything you could want.")

We continued for a half-mile, encountering a series of businesses and a flurry of sidewalk socializing. Everyone was black. It was intergenerational, and appeared evenly composed of males and females. The businesses, Bart informed me, "are not real businesses," pointing out wig shops, a dollar store, and a check cashing service. I saw a CVS drug store one block east and, intending a bit of irony on the ubiquity of chain retailers, quipped: "I see CVS found their way in." Before I could attempt a laugh Bart responded, "Thank God for it," describing the stability offered by incorporated entities. He gestured toward a Kroger grocery store a further block east, assigning it the same significance. He explained how the Cincinnati-based Kroger Corporation tries every year to shut this store down, but community response keeps it open. (At lunch Bart would compare the abundance of the store's alcohol aisle to its miniscule vegetable section.) The sidewalk bordering the Kroger parking lot was the busiest scene of the day: small huddles of people talking, solitary smokers, and a man selling jewelry behind a wooden stand. Thick inside this crowd Bart greeted a middle-aged black man and exchanged a few quick words about finding a place to live. Mixing regret and hope, Bart informed the man that one-bedroom apartments were hard to find, but if he could secure a roommate a two-bedroom would be immediately available. As we departed Bart reminded him of the weekly dinners that WHF hosts. The man said he would be there (though his tone and manner suggested he had made this promise before).

The downtown corridor of West Walnut Hills begins two blocks east of the Kroger. The condition of the buildings appeared no better than those we had just passed, but the architecture was markedly different: older, larger, and more aesthetically creative. Bart explained that in the 1920s and '30s this was a thriving neighborhood in Cincinnati. Eighty years later it is vacant and decrepit. Bart pointed to a massive building across the street, which stretched the length of the whole block: a gigantic brick monument of neglect. It was owned by a local man who repeatedly turned down buyers and refused to fund renovations. Just as he said this, a middle-aged black woman walked by and affirmed his description: "That man is crazy!" She informed us that he had recently been hospitalized and was expected to die soon. She added, walking away with her head slanted halfway back toward us, that he also hoarded all manner of things, the back door was never locked, and we could help ourselves anytime. Everyone else did.

We walked further east, then south, then east, then back north. We stood on the sidewalk of the major east-traveling artery and Bart pointed to a collection of buildings just over a not-too-distant hill: East Walnut Hills. Bart carefully distinguishes "East" from "West" when talking to local Cincinnatians, so as not to be confused with the "rich, white" populace that resides over the hill. He turned his indexing finger to a closer object, a high-rise brick building across the street from where we stood. Formerly a nationally known hotel, it had been shut down for several decades. A private company recently used federal funding from the Department of Housing and Urban Development to buy it and turn it into Section Eight. Rent is income-based, and the unemployed can get a room for $25-a-month. Several WHF members live there. "When their life falls apart, we find a place for them there." He described the everyday happenings in and around the building as "not all that violent, but still terrible."

Our walking resumed, now heading west. We passed a brand-new elementary school to the north. Bart identified it as another governmental blunder. The multimillion dollar project occurred in lieu of increasing teacher pay, broadening the number of faculty, or improving pedagogical resources. "It's the same crappy school, it just looks pretty now." A few hundred feet later we turned south to a public library. Built as part of Andrew Carnegie's national library program in 1906, the entrance is framed by two ornate pillars. Directly inside there was an armed, black police officer. The building is not large, but it is part of the city's forty-branch public library system and almost any book can arrive within a day. In a reading room Bart saw a black woman he knew who looked to be in her early thirties. She was reading books by Joyce Meyer and Suze Orman. Bart greeted her, assessed the small pile, and smiled: "Prayer and financial freedom, I need both of those." She laughed appreciatively. Much like the CVS and the Kroger, Bart considers the library a "positive space," a crucial sliver of infrastructural hope.

Southeast of the library is a local diner, the only one in the neighborhood. We dined on a sandwich and salad bar for $12 combined. Bart is a regular there, and was immediately recognized by the waitress—a slightly overweight, beaming black woman in her early twenties. Most of the customers are not local residents, but all the staff is. Our lunch conversation heaped more details and stories onto an already dizzying afternoon. We traversed local employment rates; residents' heavy reliance on government aid; family and gender dynamics; sexual and familial expectations for adolescent females; the cyclical nature of urban poverty; and the psychological trauma of need, neglect, and fear. As lunch came to a close, Bart spoke explicitly about the idea of place. He knows people who really care about locations, about architecture, green spaces, community development, and so on. That is not him. Place is "a means to an end of building relationships." But he believes those relationships will never happen without a knowledge of place. It contextualizes those he wants to reach. "They could bulldoze the whole thing and it wouldn't really make that much difference to me, but it would matter a lot for the people I work with every day. If you are going to care for people, you have to care about what they do."

We left the diner and headed west, back toward the office. On the way Bart returned to themes of place and stability. He recalled how, when he and his family first moved to the neighborhood, they lived in a bare apartment, cooked off a hot plate and slept on the floor. It threatened the intimacy of their relationships and he realized for the first time that "if you've always had stable housing you can never understand this." We turned the final corner, onto the street where my car was parked outside Bart's office. We were almost back when he greeted a group of three people sitting outside a dilapidated house in rickety lawn chairs. An older black man introduced Bart to a black man and woman in their twenties, both drinking 24-ounce cans of Budweiser. After a small amount of small talk we continued to our last stop, his office's front stoop. Before shaking hands good-bye we rested for a few minutes, trading reflections on the barrage of images and stories he had just presented.

The neighborhood tours led by Kevin and Bart illustrate the sense of place that is cultivated by Emerging Evangelicals, in particular those who plant new churches. Three characteristics define the contours of this sense of place.

First, it is comprised of a diverse body of knowledge that stresses intricate, nuanced details. Kevin and Bart demonstrate a competency in a wide range of affairs: racial privilege and disenfranchisement, local government, high school sports, restaurants, class performances, businesses, drugs, violence, literacy, automobiles, residential patterns, housing markets, employment, long-time residents, retail and commercial activity, building history, infrastructure, masculine and feminine expectations, and governmental assistance. Their sense of place does not allow them to be uninformed about the details of local affairs.

Second, it is an integrated, multifaceted consciousness. Kevin and Bart demonstrate an attentiveness to multiple histories, social dynamics, social structures, and social semiotics, including race, class, economics, education, geography, gender, language, residency, criminality, and stability. Place, critical awareness, and religious subjectivity intersect to create a lived experience of space that does not disentangle the performance of faith, community improvement, social consciousness, and local memory. Feld and Basso's "intense particularity" (1996:11) appears here in the unique familiarities Kevin and Bart foster toward Middletown and West Walnut Hills.

Third, it is a mediated sense of place. In Bart's terms, it is "a means to an end." Sense of place is not the goal, nor is it the conditions of the game. It is a tool for reaching people. For Emerging Evangelicals place is only significantly useful when it helps strengthen a community of faith. Unlike the essays in Basso and Feld's volume, the sense of place evident here is not a form of cultural context that the ethnographer strains to piece together. This sense of place is not, in Basso's terms, "vaguely realized most of the time, and rarely brought forth for conscious scrutiny" (1996:83). Rather, it is a strategic, and strategically made, lived reality in the ongoing attempt, as Kevin would have it, "to show them why Christ is *more*," or as Bart would have it, to "be in relationship with people."

Place and Emerging Evangelicals

This chapter springs from a repeated ethnographic observation: Emerging Evangelicals care a great deal about place. Church planters, especially, cultivate an intricate, nuanced sense of place in their missional locales. Indeed, learning the intricacies of a place is integral to their training and responsibilities. As we outlined earlier, the significance of place in the Emerging movement can be understood in terms of a response: the valuation of place is an expression of their status as late modern subjects discontented with deterritorialization and the social conditions that accompany economic restructuring. As Meyer and Geschiere (1999) predict: "[P]eople's awareness of being involved in open-ended global flows seems to trigger a search for fixed orientation points and action frames" (2). In short, the late modern norm of detachment from place does not suffice for some. To further understand how place fits into the Emerging Evangelical imagination we can consider a different, though still place-oriented religious practice: pilgrimage.

Coleman and Eade (2004) view pilgrimage as an ethnoscape, a phenomenon "in continuum with other practices of mobility in late modernity" (Feldman 2007: 353). This interpretation of pilgrimage marks a departure from earlier analyses, which concentrated on the pilgrim as a liminal subject in which the pilgrims' search for place was primarily a means of separation (Turner and Turner 1978). This earlier tradition upheld the notion that pilgrimage sites were fundamentally sacred sites, "places where miracles once happened, still happen, and may happen again" (ibid.: 6). More recent work, not altogether ready to dismiss the ways in which pilgrims sacralize specific spaces, casts the pilgrim's place as a destination (Bajc, Coleman, and Eade 2007: 323): a physical site where religious subjects perform the cultural work of place making (Bajc 2007; Feldman 2007). Sites of religious destination are (not wholly blank) canvasses upon which pilgrims narrate and embody their faith. Combining these orientations toward mobility and emplacement, recent anthropological interpreters read late modern pilgrims as religious subjects who use particular places to inform, enliven, texturize, and otherwise internalize their faith. Place becomes a religious resource, a way to enhance belonging and experience. How does this explanation satisfy Emerging Evangelicals' relation to place?

Not well. The sense of place cultivated by my consultants was not a resource; it was an everyday condition of lived religion. Place, as a meaningful site in their faith, was not somewhere they went to, it was somewhere they stayed in. Place is not a destination for them, it is a home. The earlier example of Lilly is instructive here. In particular, recall her interest in Thinplaces, sites where the presence of God are said to be most easily experienced. Hers was a reworking of a Celtic tradition. Rather than seek out established Thinplaces—that is, go on pilgrimage—Lilly sought to create Thinplaces wherever she was. Her decision to do this in public spaces, such as the Taza coffee shop, follows the kingdom theology logic of redemption. The public scenes of our everyday existence are seen as being in need of reclamation and reconciliation. Lilly's sense of place, much like Kevin's and Bart's, insists on dwelling in a single locale, in the hope that they can change the others who are there. Analytical models regarding the ties between religion and place that derive from pilgrimage studies, much like those deriving from sacred space, are not best suited for understanding cases like Emerging Evangelical attachments to missional locales. Sense of place, with its phenomenological grounding, is far more useful.

To conclude, we should note that the Emerging sense of place is not cultivated without its own uneasy tensions. Consider a different Kevin, the house church pastor in Norwood whom we met earlier. Given his monastic-inspired emphasis on stability, I expected Kevin to uphold this theme of place in a relatively unqualified manner. But he surprised me in his discussion of St. E, the late-nineteenth-century Catholic church purchased by his house church network. Kevin talked for some time about the church's relationship with "the old lady," as they had come to call St. E. Their job, as Kevin explained it, was to "steward" the building for the next generation. They saw it as a tangible way to "give back to the neighborhood." All this was so congruent with Emerging attitudes toward place that by the time he reached "giving back to the neighborhood" I was certain I could predict the rest to follow. I was wrong. Kevin articulated a tension. He described how their self-ascribed role of stewarding St. E conflicted with their house church ethos, which disconnected the meaning of "church" from the presence or absence of owning a "building." They were adamant that their identity as a church community should not be equated with a physical site where they sometimes gathered. Kevin worries about "dumping money" into a building that will always need more repairs. Recalling their most recent expenditure in early 2010, $30,000 to fix St. E's rain gutters, he wondered aloud what kinds of mission work that money might have been used for instead. He cited Paul's first epistle to Corinth where the apostle "speaks of being unencumbered." The sense of place that is so valued by Emerging Evangelicals prompted a question for Kevin. How can they be good stewards and remain unencumbered? How do they continue investing in a place when the place may not be a good investment? He is not likely to find a resolution. Like other Emerging Evangelicals whose commitment to a missional locale collides with practical concerns, Kevin will continue to live in the middle of this tension.

Conclusion

Dialogic Evangelicalism

On Saturday, October 2, 2010, at 9 p.m. I was standing in the scene that opened this book, the neighborhood street corner in Norwood between 1801 and St. E. Looking in three directions the view repeated: silent streets, empty sidewalks, half-lit by dim street lights. Looking west, the view was much the same, save one difference: one porch, bright with candles and lighting, voices and laughter ringing, echoing against the otherwise sleepy backdrop.

The porch was that of the Vineyard Central communal house, where Kevin, who had vowed stability in this neighborhood, lives with his wife and other residents. I had been at the house since 5 p.m., and the last hour was spent porch-sitting. There were nine of us: Kevin and his wife, Aaron (the owner of Taza) and his wife, Aaron (the Northern Kentucky campus pastor), Chris (house church pastor in exurban West Chester), and two of his house church members. Most of us had spent the morning and afternoon at the same event: an Emerging Church author from Lexington spoke at Taza about the vow of "simplicity."

The event was part of a creation that Kevin, the two Aarons, and two others had been building: a twelve-month spiritual formation program designed for house churches and new monastic communities. They called it "FORMED," signifying the ideal of being spiritually molded by the biblical model of Christ. The initial idea was Kevin's: it would be a product to satisfy the final requirement for a doctoral degree in ministry. Aaron, the campus pastor, provided a jumpstart to a process that had proved frustratingly slow for Kevin: he outlined the program as part of a six-week seminary course.

FORMED consists of four elements. 1) Each month of the program addresses a vow: soul-keeping, simplicity, community, prayer, study, work, service, hospitality, justice, holiness, sabbath, and celebration. 2) Each month has a prayer book that guides fixed-hour prayers in the morning and evening. Each day's prayers, to be performed among families or community members, follow a repeating structure: call to morning prayer, restatement of monthly vow, reading of vow-related scripture, reading of vow-related quote from past or present Christian author, a fixed prewritten vow prayer, reading of Gospel text, reading of Lord's Prayer, reading of Psalm text, an open period of intercession to address specific prayer requests, a fixed concluding prayer, midday restatement of vow and vow prayer, call to evening prayer, and finally a repetition of the morning structure, except with a different Christian author quote, Gospel text, and Psalm text. 3) On the first Saturday of each month they arranged to bring a speaker to Cincinnati to present a public talk introducing and elaborating the month's theme. 4) A FORMED website provided participants with further devotional exercises and vow explanations.

Beginning in mid-2010, the five FORMED creators met every Friday to plan this program. They considered the months of September 2010 to August 2011 the "beta year" of FORMED, a trial run to "work out the kinks." Kevin had always thought of the program as "a curriculum for Christlikeness," a phrase he borrowed from Dallas Willard. *The Divine Conspiracy: Rediscovering Our Hidden Life in God* (1998) is Willard's best-known work among Evangelicals, and was an important influence for all five men (sparking or coinciding with their deconversions). As a program of spiritual formation, or "discipleship," FORMED joins a longstanding dialogue among American Christians: how to be a disciple of God. Kevin's initial desire to create the program, and the other four's desire to help develop it, began as a discontent. They were not satisfied with any of the discipleship resources available in the Christian marketplace. Reliably, their discussions during weekly planning meetings would make reference to existing discipleship products and their shortcomings: for example, the immensely popular *40 Days of Purpose*, based on Rick Warren's mega-selling *The Purpose Driven Life* (2003). In particular, they objected to the way existing products were short-term and not based on a twelve-month effort; were not based on daily fixed-hour prayers; did not emphasize monastic vows; and did not combine the wisdom of "ancient" and contemporary Christian thinkers.

On that October night in 2010 the porch was filled with cigar and pipe smoke. (Chris showed me that his pipe was handmade in England, and that Kevin's was a gift he bought for him in the Ukraine several years ago.) Aaron and Kevin sat on a hanging porch swing, the rest of us in chairs. The most raucous moment occurred just before my leaving at 9 p.m., and centered on a megachurch in suburban Atlanta. The name they initially chose for FORMED was "12 Stone Path"; stones symbolizing vows. (Part of the porch revelry was directed at the unintended impropriety of "six guys and 12 stones.") In May 2010 they purchased a web domain for the program, and the following day they received a "cease and desist" email from the Chief Financial Officer of the Atlanta megachurch. Similarly named, this church owned all rights to domains that included "12 stones." The laughter began when they told this story to Chris and his house church members. Aaron, the campus pastor, had saved the email on his Iphone and read it aloud. Every time the registered trademark symbol was used in the email, Aaron would signal it with a mocking "®" drawn in the air with his index finger. The joke escalated when they referenced a recent issue of a popular Evangelical magazine. This exurban Atlanta megachurch was featured as one of the fastest growing in the United States, and the same CFO was quoted, attributing the church's success to "establishing a brand identity." Amusement erupted into hilarity when they explained to Chris the irony of the man's first name: Norwood.

Their retelling was interspersed with familiar themes in the Emerging cultural critique: out-of-whack megachurch priorities, tribalism in the Evangelical subculture, and consumerism's polluting effects on authentic faith. As with their impetus for creating FORMED and their discontented references to dissatisfying spiritual formation programs, this porch performance never strayed too far from the ties that bind and unwind in American Evangelicalism, and the discourses that organize and result from their intertwining.

Evangelicals: Definitions and Dialogues

FORMED thrives on cultural critique, following in step with much that circulates in the Emerging movement. It was born out of opposition. Throughout this book we have stressed the continuing importance of this critique for Emerging Evangelical subjectivity and institution making. Emerging Evangelicalism is a movement defined by a deeply felt disenchantment toward America's conservative Christian subculture. My consultants assigned a wide range of problems to their Evangelical brethren: suburban largesse, faulty biblical exegesis, poor theologies of worship, misguided evangelistic practices, and the kind of megachurch consumerism that fueled the humor of "12 Stones," to name just a few. However, their cultural critique did not result in a loss of faith, nor did it produce religious subjects content to be discontent. Emerging Evangelicalism is about redressing the perceived problems of the conservative Christian establishment. At stake is a sense of lost authenticity. In the eyes of my consultants the conservative Christian subculture has lost touch with "real Christianity." Their desire to recapture an "authentic faith" drives their ongoing efforts, as individuals and as community members. Even for those like Kevin, whose deconversion is more than a decade old, cultural critique remains potent.

There is an important lesson that comes with Kevin. Cultural critique is not just relevant for the beginnings of movements and identities. It might be reasonable to suspect that disenchantment fades quickly as alternative values become fixed. Then again, why should it? As we established at this book's outset, the history of American Evangelicalism is in many ways the history of cultural critiques. Even though they became recognized as distinct identities in the early twentieth century, Fundamentalists continue to understand their sense of self through their separations from Pentecostals, Catholics, and "liberal" Protestants. To conclude, let us position cultural critique as not simply a defining condition of the Emerging movement, but also a foundational condition in the study of Christian culture, history, and identity.

The approach I am advocating here was outlined by Garriott and O'Neill (2008) as a "dialogic" understanding of Christianity. Following the work of Mikhail Bakhtin (1934 [1981]), Garriott and O'Neill presume that "competing claims to truth and authority" (382) are inherent to the "conditions of knowledge and practical activity" (ibid.) that define human social life. Anthropologists of Christianity should, in turn, shift their focus to "the kinds of problems Christian communities themselves seem to be preoccupied with" (388); in other words, to the struggles over claims to truth and authority. In doing so, we will gain access to "what is at stake in the lives of Christians" (383). We must attend to the long-standing debates and everyday concerns that Christians invest their energies in resolving. This echoes a central theoretical goal that anthropologists of Christianity have identified, resetting our thinking from "Christianity" to "Christianities." Not only does this affirm the cultural differences among Orthodox, Catholic, and Protestant Christians, but it also opens up a conceptual space to seriously consider the intracultural differences of Christians. As Cannell (2006) rightly observed: "It is not impossible to speak meaningfully about Christianity, but it *is* important to be as specific as possible about what kind of Christianity one means" (7, emphasis in original).

To recognize Christianities as dialogic is to recognize how local Selves are formed and performed via a series of relationships with various Christian and non-Christian Others. New Christian identities are always born into a world of existing and competing Christian traditions, and develop in dynamic interaction with them. This invites a comparative question:

what happens when Christianities interact? Emerging Evangelicalism is an extraordinary case study in this regard. Our analysis of who Emerging Evangelicals are has very much been about the existing Christian resources they invoke and challenge. Throughout this book we saw individuals and communities accepting and rejecting the categories, narratives, and vocabulary of Evangelicalism. As with the example of FORMED, Kevin and the rest of the group rely on categories such as discipleship and spiritual formation, but they believe themselves to be addressing these concerns differently than their conservative brethren (for example, by emphasizing monastic-inspired practices and values, like fixed-hour prayer and simplicity).

In calling for a dialogic understanding of Christian cultures, at least three conceptual mistakes should be avoided. First, this approach is not restricted to formal debates among Christian elites (though it certainly should include them). Focusing only on those individuals and institutions who have the power to produce authorized knowledge marginalizes those not able or interested in joining the public channels of circulation. Examining the problems that Christians themselves are preoccupied with entails going to a front porch in Norwood as much as it does the promotional book tour of an Evangelical celebrity. Second, a dialogic approach is not equivalent to marketplace conceptualizations that have been so popular among scholars of American religion (Finke and Starke 1992). This economic metaphor is concerned primarily with identifying which segments of a population affiliate with which religious tradition. The point of overlap is recognizing that a plurality of Christian traditions exist in the same social landscape and their relative fates have something to do with one another. But a properly dialogic understanding is distinguished by being much more concerned with specific communities of practice and the connections that everyday religious subjectivity has with the structuring force of shared institutions. Third, a dialogic approach is not restricted to a discursive analysis. Examining the problems that Christians themselves are preoccupied with certainly includes text and talk, but it also extends to other forms of religious mediation: bodies, senses, materiality, places, and fellow adherents. The problems that Christians themselves are concerned with cannot be reduced to what is talked about or how they talk; it must encompass the lived experience of addressing those problems.

All of us devoted to the study of American Christianity, in particular the cultural complex of Evangelicalism, need this dialogic understanding. This approach pushes the theoretical and question-asking agenda forward in a research tradition traditionally challenged by attempts to settle on categorical definitions. That is, much ink has been spilled on what constitutes "an Evangelical" and how "they" differ from other Christians. Consider an exchange that took place between July and November 2008. It occurred on The Immanent Frame, a "collective blog publishing interdisciplinary perspectives on secularism, religion, and the public sphere" that began in 2007 and is sponsored by the Social Science Research Council. The exchange was called "Evangelicals and Evangelicalisms: How People Understand and Apply a Contested Religious Category." This discussion forum included twelve very astute, very helpful postings by accomplished scholars in anthropology, sociology, history, and theology. The premise of the discussion was twofold: Evangelicalism is an extremely heterogeneous cultural object and there are no silver bullet definitions for distinguishing Evangelicals from other kinds of Christians. Irrespective of this latter starting point (or perhaps because of it), most contributors rehearsed commonly cited definitions or offered their own, more nuanced version of an idea behind a commonly cited definition. Contributors echoed early definitional attempts—for example, Bebbington's (1989) quadrilateral of Biblicism, crucicentrism, conversionism, and activism—and eventually focused on the attractions and limits of three categories: belief, practice, and cultural participation.

A focus on beliefs is probably the most widely used definitional measure. In this logic, to be an Evangelical means you accept certain belief propositions as true. The usual suspects include: the Bible as the final authority, the death of Christ on the cross as penal substitutionary atonement, the virgin birth of Christ, and Christ as both personal and global messiah. Criticisms of belief-centered definitions highlight a number of tensions: privileging official over popular voices; lack of differentiation between belief as propositional assent, as social-psychological-emotive commitment, and as a symbol of group belonging; and the troubling lack of clarity surrounding individual doctrines (for example, what exactly is being claimed when one claims biblical inerrancy?). While it is certain that beliefs matter for Evangelicals, how to understand, measure, and deploy the category of *belief* in a definition remains elusive (cf. Lindquist and Coleman 2008).

Evangelicalism is also said to be defined by a set of everyday and ritual practices. If you experienced a born-again conversion and have a narrative of self-transformation to accompany it, evangelize on a regular basis, are competent in certain speech genres (for example, witnessing), center prayer on a personal relationship with Jesus, and/or mobilize politically for theologically motivated causes, then you might be an Evangelical. Using religious practices as a benchmark also has setbacks: distinguishing shared practice from shared motivation for practice; different meanings assigned to the same practice across individuals and communities; and how to understand divergent practices within the same tradition of community.

A third definitional approach uses participation in the world of Evangelicalism as an index of whether someone is an Evangelical. That is, if you consume knowledge produced by self-consciously Evangelical actors and institutions then your own status as an Evangelical is confirmed. This includes a diverse set of phenomena: congregational membership, denominational affiliation, conference attendance, retail consumption, book readership, periodical subscription, music and radio listening, film watching, and Internet visitation. The trouble with this approach is severalfold: individuals and groups do not participate in these institutions in the same way or for the same reasons; these domains of knowledge production are not a singular entity, and in fact are often at odds with each other; and there is a potentially large gulf that separates knowledge consumed from knowledge internalized as a script for action.

Along with their respective challenges, these definitional orientations share some problems. There is a danger of arbitrariness: why certain markers are labeled as distinctive while others are deemed negotiable or irrelevant. There is an exclusionary danger: unduly separating individuals and groups on the basis of some belief, practice, or affiliation when they are otherwise part of a shared movement. There is an inclusionary danger: unduly casting individuals and groups as culturally similar on the basis of some belief, practice, or affiliation when they are otherwise not part of a shared movement. There is a danger of relying on categories bogged down in other discourses to produce a discrete "Evangelicalism": using the labels "conservative" and "liberal" is the exemplary case. There is a danger of false continuity: treating any belief, practice, or affiliation as an essential, permanent marker of Evangelicalism; one that is stable over time, across contexts, and immune to sociocultural change. Another danger, one highlighted by numerous contributors to the Immanent Frame exchange, is the problem of importing theological assumptions into the analytical arsenal of social science.

A dialogic approach promises a better way forward. Rather than ask, "what is an Evangelical?" might we ask, "what dialogues, contentious and collaborative, unfold among the individuals and institutions that claim a Christian identity?" Rather than ask, "what do Evangelicals believe?" or "what practices define Evangelicalism?" might we ask, "what beliefs and practices are the focus of interest, concern, and argument?" This reorientation immediately responds to two problems of definitional approaches. First, focusing on belief, practice, and cultural participation invites, and at times requires, assumptions of sharedness, unity, cohesion, and continuity. To talk about "what Evangelicals believe" is to talk about a binding element, a mutual ground, a feature in common. A dialogic approach requires only that religious subjects share a dialogue, through which they may agree, disagree, argue vehemently, work cooperatively, or many other variations. Second, definitional approaches, because they seek to pin down Evangelicalism as categorically distinct from other kinds of Christianities, artificially separate a religious field that exists in constant interaction. A dialogic approach seeks to capture multiple voices as they speak to, for, about, and against one another. While we might maintain the language of "Protestant," "Evangelical," "charismatic," "Fundamentalist," and "Pentecostal," might our interest shift from what makes them discrete to what continually enlivens them to be in dialogue with one another?

This book can be read as an ethnography attempting to privilege the dialogic approach. My consultants are very much religious subjects asking and responding to questions of historic interest among multiple varieties of American Christianity. What does it mean to have authentic faith? What does it mean to live in authentic community? What are the proper and most effective uses of religious language? What kind of biblical hermeneutic should be followed? What is the most assured way to feel the presence of God? What forms of worship are theologically sound and personally effective? What kind of relationship should be maintained with past Christianities? What channels of church history should be claimed? What methods of evangelism should be practiced? What does it mean to be a disciple of God? Ultimately, this is what defines Emerging Evangelicalism—the dialogues that are posed, conducted, and deemed significant for everyday life. This dialogic approach is especially congruent with the person-centered ethnography discussed in the Introduction. By focusing on the problems Christians pose and the responses they enact, we are necessarily drawn to the individuals and communities that conduct those dialogues.

Throughout this book we have also illustrated how the dialogues that matter in the Emerging movement must be contextualized within broader cultural conditions. What structures the posing of, and the responding to, questions that communities invest in? We have seen that Emerging Evangelicals are both modern and late modern religious subjects, reproducing dispositions from both eras. Their religious lives, and the dialogues that populate them, cannot be abstracted from these engulfing historical eras. Recall the example of church planting. This aspect of the Emerging movement integrates multiple dialogues of importance in American Christian culture: what should be the institutional shape of our church community? How should we evangelize? To what socio-geographic locations should our ministry efforts be directed? What should the gendered division of labor look like? Yet we cannot fully examine these dialogues apart from the modern and late modern dispositions that animate the actions and decisions of church planters. The shape of Emerging Evangelical subjectivities and institutions owes to the dual influence of modernity and late modernity, just as it does dialogues about theology, worship, and evangelism. This kind of broad contextualizing is a crucial lesson to remember for any dialogic analysis.

Keeping our analytical ears sharp to the dialogues that Evangelicals take seriously is vital as we continue to ask research questions about the ever-evolving cultural life of American Christianity. We cannot be sure what the fate of the "Emerging Church" will be. Based on my three years of fieldwork, I do not expect that label to have significant longevity. Many of my consultants expressed little interest, or outright disregard, for the label itself. Whatever its initial intention, my consultants found it increasingly unhelpful as a way to understand themselves and their desires for religious community. They were much more apt to prefer other self-identifiers: Evangelical, new monastic, Christ-follower, or missional Christian. But labels and dialogues are very much not the same. I wager that the problems Emerging Evangelicals have internalized and introduced into public discourse will powerfully shape American Christian subjectivities and institutions well into the future. I also wager that whatever the extent of that impact, it will only unfold in dynamic relationship to whatever the next movement of cultural critique proves to be. If the version of "authentic faith" that my consultants promote becomes mainstream—say, if FORMED becomes the next *40 Days of Purpose*—I wager it will incite discontents in a future cohort of Evangelicals. It is these dialogues, and those who engage them, that should orient our future efforts to understand the cultures and identities constituting American Christianity.

Appendix

Ethnographic Consultants

The following table introduces the 90 individuals (22 women; 68 men) who were my ethnographic consultants. My fieldwork brought me into contact with many others who were affiliated with, interested in, or critical of Emerging Evangelicalism. This list presents only those with whom I conducted formal ethnographic work. They were selected as consultants based on several criteria: participation in a self-consciously Emerging community; consumption of knowledge produced by Emerging institutions over time; and, as with all ethnography, a willingness to tolerate endless questioning.

TABLE A.1

Name	Sex	Age*	Role**	Denomination	Location
Bill	M	51-55	S. Pastor	United Methodist	Lansing, Michigan
Jess	F	21-25	A. Pastor	United Methodist	Lansing, Michigan
Chad	M	36-40	S. Pastor	Reformed Church of America	Lansing, Michigan
Noah	M	21-25	S. Pastor	Baptist General Conference	Lansing, Michigan
Ben S.	M	21-25	A. Pastor	Southern Baptist Convention	Lansing, Michigan
Dave	M	36-40	A. Pastor	Southern Baptist Convention	Lansing, Michigan
Noel	M	36-40	A. Pastor	Non-Denominational	Lansing, Michigan
Barb	F	51-55	S. Pastor	United Methodist	Lansing, Michigan
Jeremy	M	31-35	S. Pastor	Reformed Church of America	Lansing, Michigan

Name	Sex	Age*	Role**	Denomination	Location
Jack	M	31-35	S. Pastor	Anglican Mission in the Americas	Lansing, Michigan
Chad	M	36-40	Laity	Episcopalian	Grand Rapids, Michigan
Robert	M	41-45	Laity	Non-Denominational	Grand Rapids, Michigan
John	M	46-50	Laity	Non-Denominational	Grand Rapids, Michigan
Glenn	M	36-40	S. Pastor	Southern Baptist Convention	Oxford, Ohio
Cathy	F	36-40	Laity	Southern Baptist Convention	Oxford, Ohio
Jason	M	36-40	Laity	Southern Baptist Convention	Oxford, Ohio
Andrea	F	36-40	Laity	Southern Baptist Convention	Oxford, Ohio
Kim	F	26-30	Laity	Southern Baptist Convention	Oxford, Ohio
Spencer	M	26-30	Laity	Southern Baptist Convention	Oxford, Ohio
Chad	M	26-30	S. Pastor	Southern Baptist Convention	Oxford, Ohio
Bob	M	51-55	S. Pastor	Non-Denominational	Oxford, Ohio
Steve	M	21-25	Laity	Non-Denominational	Oxford, Ohio
Michael	M	31-35	S. Pastor	Non-Denominational	Hamilton, Ohio
Chris	M	36-40	S. Pastor	Baptist General Conference	Cincinnati, Ohio
Niki	F	41-45	Laity	Baptist General Conference	Cincinnati, Ohio
Jamie	F	41-45	Laity	Baptist General Conference	Cincinnati, Ohio
Todd	M	41-45	Laity	Baptist General Conference	Cincinnati, Ohio
Dave	M	26-30	S. Pastor	Southern Baptist Convention	Cincinnati, Ohio

Name	Sex	Age*	Role**	Denomination	Location
Carl	M	41-45	S. Pastor	Non-Denominational	Cincinnati, Ohio
Randall	M	46-50	Laity	Non-Denominational	Cincinnati, Ohio
Adam	M	29-30	S. Pastor	Non-Denominational	Cincinnati, Ohio
Matt	M	41-45	S. Pastor	Vineyard Fellowship	Cincinnati, Ohio
Lilly	F	41-45	S. Pastor	Vineyard Fellowship	Cincinnati, Ohio
Rob	M	41-45	S. Pastor	Vineyard Fellowship	Cincinnati, Ohio
Ed	M	31-35	S. Pastor	Presbyterian Church-USA	Cincinnati, Ohio
Amy	F	31-35	Laity	Presbyterian Church-USA	Cincinnati, Ohio
Kevin	M	39-40	Laity	Vineyard Fellowship	Cincinnati, Ohio
Jeremiah	M	31-35	A. Pastor	Vineyard Fellowship	Cincinnati, Ohio
Aaron	M	31-35	S. Pastor	United Methodist	Cincinnati, Ohio
Becky	F	31-35	Laity	United Methodist	Cincinnati, Ohio
Larry	M	51-55	Laity	Vineyard Fellowship	Cincinnati, Ohio
Josh	M	31-35	S. Pastor	Presbyterian Church of America	Cincinnati, Ohio
Paige	F	26-30	Laity	Presbyterian Church of America	Cincinnati, Ohio
Mike	M	26-30	Laity	Presbyterian Church of America	Cincinnati, Ohio
Becky	F	31-35	Laity	Presbyterian Church of America	Cincinnati, Ohio
Mike	M	31-35	Laity	Presbyterian Church of America	Cincinnati, Ohio
Tom	M	46-50	Laity	Presbyterian Church of America	Cincinnati, Ohio
Melissa	F	46-50	Laity	Presbyterian Church of America	Cincinnati, Ohio
Tim	M	26-30	Laity	Presbyterian Church of America	Cincinnati, Ohio
Claire	F	26-30	Laity	Presbyterian Church of America	Cincinnati, Ohio

Name	Sex	Age*	Role**	Denomination	Location
Matt	M	31-35	Laity	Presbyterian Church of America	Cincinnati, Ohio
Katie	F	26-30	Laity	Presbyterian Church of America	Cincinnati, Ohio
Dave	M	56-60	Laity	Presbyterian Church of America	Cincinnati, Ohio
Meg	F	56-60	Laity	Presbyterian Church of America	Cincinnati, Ohio
Nathan	M	21-25	Laity	Non-Denominational	Cincinnati, Ohio
Jason	M	26-30	S. Pastor	Non-Denominational	Cincinnati, Ohio
Justin	M	26-30	S. Pastor	Non-Denominational	Cincinnati, Ohio
Charlie	M	31-35	Laity	Non-Denominational	Cincinnati, Ohio
Bart	M	41-45	S. Pastor	Non-Denominational	Cincinnati, Ohio
Adam	M	26-30	Laity	Non-Denominational	Cincinnati, Ohio
Aaron	M	31-35	S. Pastor	Vineyard Fellowship	Cincinnati, Ohio
Steve	M	31-35	Laity	Non-Denominational	Cincinnati, Ohio
Candyce	F	26-30	A. Pastor	Vineyard Fellowship	Cincinnati, Ohio
Jeff	M	36-40	A. Pastor	Non-Denominational	Cincinnati, Ohio
Tim	M	31-35	S. Pastor	Non-Denominational	Cincinnati, Ohio
Alan	M	26-30	A. Pastor	Non-Denominational	Cincinnati, Ohio
Chris	M	36-40	S. Pastor	Church of the Nazarene	Cincinnati, Ohio
Michael	M	31-35	S. Pastor	Southern Baptist Convention	Cincinnati, Ohio
Laura	F	31-35	Laity	Southern Baptist Convention	Cincinnati, Ohio
Doug	M	31-35	A. Pastor	Southern Baptist Convention	Cincinnati, Ohio
Ken	M	51-55	S. Pastor	Church of Christ	Cincinnati, Ohio
Ben	M	36-40	Laity	Non-Denominational	Cincinnati, Ohio
Tim	M	41-45	S. Pastor	Vineyard Fellowship	Cincinnati, Ohio
Ford	M	26-30	S. Pastor	Non-Denominational	Cincinnati, Ohio
D.G.	M	31-35	S. Pastor	United Methodist	Cincinnati, Ohio
Kevin	M	26-30	S. Pastor	Non-Denominational	Middletown, Ohio

Name	Sex	Age*	Role**	Denomination	Location
Stephanie	F	26-30	Laity	Non-Denominational	Middletown, Ohio
Bryan	M	26-30	A. Pastor	Non-Denominational	Middletown, Ohio
Jackie	F	26-30	Laity	Non-Denominational	Middletown, Ohio
Emily	F	21-25	Laity	Non-Denominational	Middletown, Ohio
Virgil	M	36-40	Laity	Non-Denominational	Dayton, Ohio
Jaime	F	36-40	Laity	Non-Denominational	Dayton, Ohio
Ryan	M	26-30	S. Pastor	Southern Baptist Convention	Dayton, Ohio
Nick	M	31-35	S. Pastor	Non-Denominational	Columbus, Ohio
Vince	M	21-25	Laity	Non-Denominational	Columbus, Ohio
Aaron	M	31-35	S. Pastor	Southern Baptist Convention	Phoenix, Arizona
Scott	M	41-45	S. Pastor	Presbyterian Church of America	Phoenix, Arizona
Bobby	M	41-45	S. Pastor	Non-Denominational	Phoenix, Arizona
Justin	M	26-30	S. Pastor	Non-Denominational	Phoenix, Arizona
Michael	M	31-35	Laity	Non-Denominational	Raleigh, North Carolina

* This column shows the age range of the consultant on the date of the first interview. All initial interviews occurred between October 2007 and June 2010.

** This column shows the consultant's role in their church community. "S. Pastor" refers to a lead pastor and "A. Pastor" refers to an assistant pastor (for example: worship, discipleship, and youth pastors).

References

PRIMARY REFERENCES

Bell, Rob. 2005. *Velvet Elvis: Repainting the Christian Faith*. Grand Rapids, Mich.: Zondervan.

Bible. 1978. *The Holy Bible: New International Version*. Grand Rapids, Mich.: Zondervan.

Bishop, Mike. 2008. *What Is Church? A Story of Transition*. Harmon Press.

Brueggemann, Walter. 1978. *The Prophetic Imagination*. Minneapolis, Minn.: Fortress.

Campolo, Tony. 1988. *20 Hot Potatoes Christians Are Afraid to Touch*. Nashville, Tenn.: Thomas Nelson.

Claiborne, Shane. 2006. *The Irresistible Revolution: Living as an Ordinary Radical*. Grand Rapids, Mich.: Zondervan.

———. 2008. *Jesus for President: Politics for Ordinary Radicals*. Grand Rapids, Mich.: Zondervan.

Dark, David. 2002. *Everyday Apocalypse: The Sacred Revealed in Radiohead, the Simpsons, and Other Pop Culture Icons*. Grand Rapids, Mich.: Baker Books.

DeYoung, Kevin, and Ted Kluck. 2008. *Why We're Not Emergent (By Two Guys Who Should Be)*. Chicago: Moody.

Frost, Michael, and Alan Hirsch. 2003. *The Shaping of Things to Come: Innovation and Mission for the 21st Century Church*. Peabody, Mass.: Hendrickson Publishers.

Gibbs, Eddie, and Ryan K. Bolger. 2005. *Emerging Churches: Creating Christian Community in Postmodern Cultures*. Grand Rapids, Mich.: Baker Books.

Grenz, Stanley, and John Franke. 2001. *Beyond Foundationalism: Shaping Theology in a Postmodern Context*. Louisville, Ky.: Westminster.

Guder, Darrell L., and Lois Barrett, eds. 1998. *Missional Church: A Vision for the Sending of the Church in North America*. Grand Rapids, Mich.: William B. Eerdmans.

Hansen, Collin. 2008. *Young, Restless, Reformed: A Journalist's Journey with the New Calvinists*. Wheaton, Ill.: Crossways Books.

Hunter, George III. 2000. *The Celtic Way of Evangelism: How Christianity Can Reach the West ... Again*. Nashville, Tenn.: Abingdon.

Jethani, Skye. 2009. *The Divine Commodity: Discovering a Faith beyond Consumer Christianity*. Grand Rapids, Mich.: Zondervan.

Jones, Tony. 2008. *The New Christians: Dispatches from the Emergent Frontier*. San Francisco: Jossey-Bass.

Kimball, Dan. 2003. *The Emerging Church: Vintage Christianity for New Generations*. Grand Rapids, Mich.: Zondervan.

King, Max. 1987. *The Cross and the Parousia of Christ: The Two Dimensions of One Age-Changing Eschaton*. Warren, Oh.: Parkman Road Church of Christ.

Lindbeck, George. 1984. *The Nature of Doctrine: Religion and Theology in a Postliberal Age.* Westminster: John Knox Press.

MacArthur, John. 2007. *The Truth War: Fighting for Certainty in an Age of Deception.* Nashville, Tenn.: Thomas Nelson.

McLaren, Brian. 1998. *The Church on the Other Side: Doing Ministry in the Postmodern Matrix.* Grand Rapids, Mich.: Zondervan.

———. 2001. *A New Kind of Christian: A Tale of Two Friends on a Spiritual Journey.* San Francisco: Jossey-Bass.

———. 2003. *The Story We Find Ourselves In: Further Adventures of a New Kind of Christian.* San Francisco: Jossey-Bass.

McNeal, Reggie. 2003. *The Present Future: Six Tough Questions for the Church.* San Francisco: Jossey-Bass.

Miller, Donald. 2003. *Blue Like Jazz: Nonreligious Thoughts on Christian Spirituality.* Nashville, Tenn.: Thomas Nelson.

Murphy, Nancey. 1996. *Beyond Liberalism and Fundamentalism: How Modern and Postmodern Philosophy Set the Theological Agenda.* Harrisburg, Pa.: Trinity Press International.

Newbigin, Lesslie. 1983. *The Other Side of 1984: Questions for the Churches.* Geneva, Switzerland: World Council of Churches.

———.1986. *Foolishness to the Greeks: The Gospel and Western Culture.* Grand Rapids, Mich.: William B. Eerdmans.

Oden, Thomas C. 1990. *After Modernity . . . What? Agenda for Theology.* Grand Rapids, Mich.: Zondervan.

Pagitt, Doug. 2008. *A Christianity Worth Believing: Hope-Filled, Open-Armed, Alive-and-Well Faith for the Left Out, Left Behind, and Let Down in Us All.* San Francisco: Jossey-Bass.

Rah, Soong-Chan. 2009. *The Next Evangelicalism: Freeing the Church from Western Cultural Captivity.* Downers Grove, Ill.: InterVarsity Press.

Rollins, Peter. 2006. *How (Not) to Speak of God.* London: Paraclete.

Seay, Chris. 2002. *The Gospel according to Tony Soprano: An Unauthorized Look into the Soul of TV's Top Mob Boss and His Family.* New York: Penguin.

Sider, Ron. 1993. *Good News and Good Works: A Theology for the Whole Gospel.* Grand Rapids, Mich.: Baker Books.

Sweet, Leonard. 1999. *SoulTsunami: Sink or Swim in New Millennium Culture.* Grand Rapids, Mich.: Zondervan.

Tomlinson, Dave. 2003. *The Post-Evangelical.* Grand Rapids, Mich.: Zondervan.

Volf, Miroslav. 1996. *Exclusion and Embrace: A Theological Exploration of Identity, Otherness, and Reconciliation.* Nashville, Tenn.: Abingdon.

Wallis, Jim. 1994. *The Soul of Politics: Beyond "Religious Right" and "Secular Left."* New York: New Press.

Warren, Rick. 2003. *The Purpose Driven Life.* Grand Rapids, Mich.: Zondervan.

Webber, Robert. 1999. *Ancient-Future Faith: Rethinking Evangelicalism for a Postmodern World.* Grand Rapids, Mich.: Baker Academic.

Wilkerson, Bruce. 2000. *The Prayer of Jabez.* Sisters, Oreg.: Multnomah Books.

Willard, Dallas. 1998. *The Divine Conspiracy: Rediscovering Our Hidden Life in God.* New York: HarperCollins.

Wright, N.T. 2008. *Surprised by Hope: Rethinking Heaven, the Resurrection, and the Mission of the Church.* New York: HarperCollins.

Allison, Anne. 2006. *Millennial Monsters: Japanese Toys and the Global Imagination*. Berkeley: University of California Press.

Appadurai, Arjun. 1996. "Disjuncture and Difference in the Global Cultural Economy." In *Modernity at Large: Cultural Dimensions of Globalization*, 27–47. Minneapolis: University of Minnesota Press.

Bakhtin, Mikhail. 1934 [1981]. *The Dialogic Imagination: Four Essays*. Austin: University of Texas Press.

Bajc, Vida. 2007. "Christian Pilgrimage Groups in Jerusalem: Framing the Experience through Linear Meta-Narrative." *Journeys* 7 (2): 1–28.

Bajc, Vida, Simon Coleman, and John Eade. 2007. "Introduction: Mobility and Centring in Pilgrimage." *Mobilities* 2 (3): 321–29.

Barbour, John. 1994. *Versions of Deconversion: Autobiography and the Loss of Faith*. Charlottesville: University of Virginia Press.

Bartkowski, John P. 1997. "Debating Patriarchy: Discursive Disputes over Spousal Authority among Evangelical Family Commentators." *Journal for the Social Scientific Study of Religion* 36 (3): 393–410.

Basso, Keith H. 1996. "Wisdom Sits in Places: Notes on a Western Apache Landscape." In *Senses of Place*, edited by Steven Feld and Keith H. Basso, 53–90. Santa Fe, N.Mex.: School of American Research Press.

Baudrillard, Jean. 1981. *Simulacra and Simulation*. Ann Arbor: University of Michigan Press.

Bauman, Richard. 1974. "Speaking in the Light: The Role of the Quaker Minister." In *Explorations in the Ethnography of Speaking*, edited by Richard Bauman and Joel Sherzer, 144–160. Cambridge: Cambridge University Press.

Bebbington, David. 1989. *Evangelicalism in Modern Britain: A History from the 1730s to the 1980s*. London: Routledge.

Behler, Ernst. 1990. *Irony and the Discourse of Modernity*. Seattle: University of Washington Press.

Benson, Peter. 2005. "Rooting Culture: Nostalgia, Urban Revitalization, and the Ambivalence of Community at the Ballpark." *City and Society* 17 (1): 93–125.

Bernard, H. Russell. 2006. *Research Methods in Anthropology: Qualitative and Quantitative Approaches*. 4th ed.. Walnut Creek, Calif.: AltaMira Press.

Bialecki, Jon. 2009. "Disjuncture, Continental Philosophy's New 'Political Paul,' and the Question of Progressive Christianity in a Southern California Third Wave Church." *American Ethnologist* 36 (1): 35–48.

Bialecki, Jon, Naomi Haynes, and Joel Robbins. 2008. "The Anthropology of Christianity." *Religion Compass* 2 (6): 1139–58.

Bielo, James S. 2009. *Words upon the Word: An Ethnography of Evangelical Group Bible Study*. New York: NYU Press.

Boler, Megan. 2006. "*The Daily Show*, Crossfire, and the Will to Truth." *Scan Journal of Media Arts and Culture* 3 (1).

Bourdieu, Pierre. 1977. *Outline of a Theory of Practice*. Cambridge: Cambridge University Press.

Brown-Saracino, Japonica. 2009. *A Neighborhood that Never Changes: Gentrification, Social Preservation, and the Search for Authenticity*. Chicago: University of Chicago Press.

Cannell, Fenella. 2005. "The Christianity of Anthropology." *Journal of the Royal Anthropological Institute* 11(2): 335–56.

———. 2006. "Introduction: The Anthropology of Christianity." In *The Anthropology of Christianity*, edited by Fenella Cannell, 1–50. Durham: Duke University Press.

Cattell, Maria G. and Jacob J. Climo. 2002. "Meaning in Social History and Memory: Anthropological Perspectives." In *Social Memory and History: Anthropological Perspectives*, edited by Jacob J. Climo and Maria G. Cattell, 1–38. Lanham, Md.: AltaMira Press.

Chidester, David, and Edward T. Linenthal. 1995. *American Sacred Space*. Bloomington: Indiana University Press.

Cintron, Ralph. 1997. *Angels' Town: Chero Ways, Gang Life, and the Rhetorics of the Everyday*. Boston: Beacon Press.

Colebrook, Claire. 2004. *Irony*. London: Routledge.

Coleman, Simon. 1996. "Words as Things: Language, Aesthetics, and the Objectification of Protestant Evangelicalism." *Journal of Material Culture* 1: 107–28.

———. 2000. *The Globalisation of Charismatic Christianity: Spreading the Gospel of Prosperity*. Cambridge: Cambridge University Press.

———. 2006. "Materializing the Self: Words and Gifts in the Construction of Charismatic Protestant Identity." In *The Anthropology of Christianity*, edited by Fenella Cannell, 163–84. Durham: Duke University Press.

Coleman, Simon, and John Eade. 2004. *Reframing Pilgrimage: Cultures in Motion*. London: Routledge.

Condry, Ian. 2006. *Hip Hop Japan: Rap and the Paths of Cultural Globalization*. Durham: Duke University Press.

Conkin, Paul K. 1997. *American Originals: Homemade Varieties of Christianity*. Chapel Hill: University of North Carolina Press.

Conn, Harvie M. 1994. *The American City and the Evangelical Church: A Historical Overview*. Grand Rapids, Mich.: Baker Press.

Cusset, Francois. 2008. *French Theory: How Foucault, Derrida, Deleuze, and Co. Transformed the Intellectual Life of the United States*. Minneapolis: University of Minnesota Press.

Doostdar, Alireza. 2004. "'The Vulgar Spirit of Blogging': On Language, Culture, and Power in Persian Weblogestan." *American Anthropologist* 106: 651–662.

Douglas, Mary. 1966. *Purity and Danger*. London: Routledge.

Drane, John. 2006. Editorial: The Emerging Church. *International Journal for the Study of the Christian Church* 6: 3–11.

Dumont, Louis. 1985. "A Modified Vew of Our Origins: The Christian Beginnings of Modern Individualism." In *The Category of the Person: Anthropology, Philosophy, History*, edited by Michael Carrithers, Steven Collins, and Steven Lukes, 93–122. Cambridge: Cambridge University Press.

Durkheim, Emile. 1912 [2001]. *The Elementary Forms of Religious Life*, translated Carol Cosman. Oxford: Oxford University Press.

Eiesland, Nancy L. 2000. *A Particular Place: Urban Restructuring and Religious Ecology in a Southern Exurb*. New Brunswick: Rutgers University Press.

Elisha, Omri. 2008a. "Faith beyond Belief: Evangelical Protestant Conceptions of Faith and the Resonance of Anti-Humanism." *Social Analysis* 52 (1): 56–78.

———. 2008b. "Moral Ambitions of Grace: The Paradox of Compassion and Accountability in Evangelical Faith-Based Activism." *Cultural Anthropology* 23: 154–89.

Engelke, Matthew. 2007. *A Problem of Presence: Beyond Scripture in an African Church.* Berkeley: University of California Press.

———. 2010. "Religion and the Media Turn: A Review Essay." *American Ethnologist* 37 (2): 371–79.

Farnell, Brenda. 2000. "Getting Out of the Habitus: An Alternative Model of Dynamically Embodied Social Action." *Journal of the Royal Anthropological Institute* 6 (3): 397–418.

Feld, Steven, and Keith H. Basso, eds. 1996. *Senses of Place.* Santa Fe, N.Mex.: School of American Research Press.

Feldman, Jackie. 2007. "Constructing a Shared Bible Land: Jewish Israeli Guiding Performances for Protestant Pilgrims." *American Ethnologist* 34 (2): 351–74.

Finke, Roger, and Rodney Starke. 1992. *The Churching of America, 1776–1990: Winners and Losers in Our Religious Economy.* New Brunswick: Rutgers University Press.

Fischer, Michael M. J. 1999. "Emergent Forms of Life: Anthropologies of Late or Postmodernities." *Annual Review of Anthropology* 28: 455–78.

Fisher, Allan. 2003. "Five Surprising Years for Evangelical Christian Publishing: 1998 to 2002." *Publishing Research Quarterly* (Summer): 20–36.

Freeman, Carla. 2007. "The 'Reputation' of Neoliberalism." *American Ethnologist* 34 (2): 252–67.

Flores, Aaron O. 2005. "An Exploration of the Emerging Church in the United States: The Missiological Intent and Potential Implications for the Future." M.A. thesis, Vanguard University. Department of Religion.

Frank, Katherine. 2002. *G-Strings and Sympathy: Strip Club Regulars and Male Desire.* Durham: Duke University Press.

Frykholm, Amy. 2004. *Rapture Culture: Left Behind in Evangelical America.* Oxford: Oxford University Press.

Gallagher, Sally K., and Christian Smith. 1999. "Symbolic Traditionalism and Pragmatic Egalitarianism: Contemporary Evangelicals, Families, and Gender." *Gender and Society* 13 (2): 211–33.

Garreau, Joel. 1992. *Edge City: Life on the New Frontier.* New York: Anchor.

Garriott, William, and Kevin Lewis O'Neill. 2008. "Who Is a Christian? Toward a Dialogic Approach in the Anthropology of Christianity." *Anthropological Theory* 8: 381–98.

Goheen, Michael W. 2000. "'As the Father Has Sent Me, I Am Sending You': J. E. Lesslie Newbigin's Missionary Ecclesiology." Ph.D. dissertation. University of Utrecht, Netherlands.

Gould, Rebecca Kneale. 2005. *At Home in Nature: Modern Homesteading and Spiritual Practice in America.* Berkeley: University of California Press.

Graham, Laura. 2002. "How Should an Indian Speak? Amazonian Indians and the Politics of Language in the Global Public Sphere." In *Indigenous Movements, Self Representation, and the State in Latin America*, edited by Kay B. Warren and Jean E. Jackson, 181–228. Austin: University of Texas Press.

Griffith, R. Marie. 1997. *God's Daughters: Evangelical Women and the Power of Submission.* Berkeley: University of California Press.

Guadeloupe, Francio. 2009. *Chanting Down the New Jerusalem: Calypso, Christianity, and Capitalism in the Caribbean.* Berkeley: University of California Press.

Gundaker, Grey. 2000. "The Bible *as* and *at* a Threshold: Reading, Performance, and Blessed Space." In *African Americans and the Bible: Sacred Texts and Social Textures*, edited by Vincent Wimbush, 754–72. New York: Continuum Press.

Gupta, Akhil, and James Ferguson. 1992. Beyond "Culture": Space, Identity, and the Politics of Difference. *Cultural Anthropology* 7 (1): 6–23.

Gusterman, Hugh and Catherine Besteman, eds. 2010. *The Insecure American: How We Got Here and What We Should Do about It.* Berkeley: University of California Press.

Hall, Charles F. 1997. "The Christian Left: Who Are They and How Are They Different from the Christian Right?" *Review of Religious Research* 39: 27–45.

Hall, David, ed. 1997. *Lived Religion in America: Toward a History of Practice.* Princeton: Princeton University Press.

Halperin, Rhoda. 1998. *Practicing Community: Class, Culture, and Power in an Urban Neighborhood.* Austin: University of Texas Press.

Harding, Susan. 1987. "Convicted by the Holy Spirit: The Rhetoric of Fundamental Baptist Conversion." *American Ethnologist* 14: 167–81.

———. 2000. *The Book of Jerry Falwell: Fundamentalist Language and Politics.* Princeton: Princeton University Press.

———. 2009. "Revolve, the Biblezine: A Transevangelical Text." In *The Social Life of Scriptures: Cross-Cultural Perspectives on Biblicism,* edited by James S. Bielo, 176–93. New Brunswick: Rutgers University Press.

———. 2010. "Get Religion." In *The Insecure American: How We Got Here and What We Should Do about It,* edited by Hugh Gusterson and Catherine Besteman. Berkeley: University of California Press.

Harrold, Philip. 2006. "Deconversion in the Emerging Church." *International Journal for the Study of the Christian Church* 6: 79–90.

Harvey, David. 1989. *The Condition of Postmodernity.* London: Blackwell.

Hempton, David. 2008. *Evangelical Disenchantment: Nine Portraits of Faith and Doubt.* New Haven: Yale University Press.

Ingersoll, Julie. 2003. *Evangelical Christian Women: War Stories in the Gender Battle.* New York: NYU Press.

Jackson, Michael. 1989. *Paths toward a Clearing: Radical Empiricism and Ethnographic Inquiry.* Bloomington: Indiana University Press.

Kaufman, Will. 1997. *The Comedian as Confidence Man: Studies in Irony Fatigue.* Detroit, Mich.: Wayne State University Press.

Keane, Webb. 2006. "Anxious Transcendence." In *The Anthropology of Christianity,* edited by Fenella Cannell, 308–24. Durham: Duke University Press.

———. 2007. *Christian Moderns: Freedom and Fetish in the Mission Encounter.* Berkeley: University of California Press.

Keller, Eva. *The Road to Clarity: Seventh-Day Adventism in Madagascar.* New York: Palgrave Macmillan, 2005.

Ketchell, Aaron. 2007. *Holy Hills of the Ozarks: Religion and Tourism in Branson, Missouri.* Baltimore: Johns Hopkins University Press.

Kirsch, Thomas. 2008. *Spirits and Letters: Reading, Writing, and Charisma in African Christianity.* New York: Berghahn.

Lassiter, Luke Eric. 2004. "Collaborative Ethnography." *AnthroNotes* 25 (1): 1–14.

Lee, Raymond, and Susan E. Ackerman. 2002. *The Challenge of Religion after Modernity: Beyond Disenchantment.* London: Ashgate.

Lee, Shayne, and Phillip Luke Sinitiere. 2009. *Holy Mavericks: Evangelical Innovators and the Spiritual Marketplace.* New York: NYU Press.

Lindholm, Charles. 2008. *Culture and Authenticity*. London: Blackwell.

Lindquist, Galina, and Simon Coleman. 2008. "Against Belief?" *Social Analysis* 52 (1): 1–18.

Low, Setha. 2001. "The Edge and the Center: Gated Communities and the Discourse of Urban Fear." *American Anthropologist* 103 (1): 45–58.

Luhr, Eileen. 2009. *Witnessing Suburbia: Conservatives and Christian Youth Culture*. Berkeley: University of California Press.

Luhrmann, Tanya M. 2004. "Metakinesis: How God Becomes Intimate in Contemporary U.S. Christianity." *American Anthropologist* 106: 518–28.

———. 2010. "The Absorption Hypothesis: Learning to Hear God in Evangelical Christianity." *American Anthropologist* 106b (3): 518–28.

Madsen, Richard, et al. 2002. "Introduction." In *Meaning and Modernity: Religion, Polity, and Self*, edited by Richard Madsen et al. Berkeley: University of California Press.

Mahmood, Saba. 2005. *Politics of Piety: The Islamic Revival and the Feminist Subject*. Princeton: Princeton University Press.

Marcus, George. 1995. "Ethnography in/of the World System: The Emergence of Multi-Sited Ethnography." *Annual Review of Anthropology* 24: 95–117.

Marti, Gerardo. 2005. *A Mosaic of Believers: Diversity and Innovation in a Multi-Ethnic Church*. Bloomington: Indiana University Press.

McDannell, Colleen. 1995. *Material Christianity: Religion and Popular Culture in America*. New Haven: Yale University Press.

McGuire, Meredith B. 2008. *Lived Religion: Faith and Practice in Everyday Life*. Oxford: Oxford University Press.

Meigs, Anna. 1995. "Ritual Language in Everyday Life: The Christian Right." *Journal of the American Academy of Religion* 63: 85-103.

Menand, Louis. 2001. *The Metaphysical Club: A Story of Ideas in America*. New York: Farrar, Strauss, and Giroux.

Meyer, Birgit, and Peter Geschiere. 1999. "Introduction." In *Globalization and Identity: Dialectics of Flow and Closure*, edited by Birgit Meyer and Peter Geschiere, 1–16. London: Blackwell.

Miller, Donald. 1997. *Reinventing American Protestantism: Christianity in the New Millennium*.Berkeley: University of California Press.

Miller, Zane, and Bruce Tucker. 1998. *Changing Plans for America's Inner Cities: Cincinnati's Over-The-Rhine and Twentieth Century Urbanism*. Columbus: Ohio State University Press.

Monahan, Torin. 2008. "Marketing the Beast: *Left Behind* and the Apocalypse Industry." *Media, Culture, and Society* 30 (6): 813–30.

Noll, Mark. 2003. *The Rise of Evangelicalism: The Age of Edwards, Whitefield, and the Wesleys*. Downers Grove, Ill.: InterVarsity Press.

O'Neill, Kevin Lewis. 2010. *City of God: Christian Citizenship in Postwar Guatemala*. Berkeley: University of California Press.

Orsi, Robert. 1997. "Everyday Miracles: The Study of Lived Religion." In *Lived Religion in America: Toward a History of Practice*, edited by David D. Hall, 3-21. Princeton: Princeton University Press.

Ortner, Sherry. 2005. "Subjectivity and Cultural Critique." *Anthropological Theory* 5 (1): 31–52.

Pals, Daniel L. 2006. *Eight Theories of Religion.* New York, Oxford: Oxford University Press.

Parish, Steven. 2009. "Review Essay: Are We Condemned to Authenticity?" *Ethos* 37 (1): 139–48.

Poloma, Margaret, and Ralph Hood, Jr. 2008. *Blood and Fire: Godly Love in a Pentecostal Emerging Church.* New York: NYU Press.

Purdy, Jedediah. 1999. *For Common Things: Irony, Trust, and Commitment in America Today.* New York: Vintage.

Robbins, Joel. 2001. "Secrecy and the Sense of an Ending: Narrative, Time, and Everyday Millenarianism in Papua New Guinea and in Christian Fundamentalism." *Comparative Studies in Society and History* 43 (3): 525–51.

———. 2003. "What Is a Christian? Notes Toward an Anthropology of Christianity." *Religion* 33: 191–99.

———. 2007. "Continuity Thinking and the Problem of Christian Culture." *Current Anthropology* 48: 5–38.

Rodman, Margaret C. 1992. "Empowering Place: Multilocality and Multivocality. *American Anthropologist* 94 (3): 640–56.

Said, Edward W. 1979. "Zionism from the Standpoint of Its Victims." *Social Text* 1: 7–58.

Sargeant, Kimon H. 2000. *Seeker Churches: Promoting Traditional Religion in a Nontraditional Way.* New Brunswick: Rutgers University Press.

Schmidt, Leigh Eric. 2000. *Hearing Things: Religion, Illusion, and the American Enlightenment.* Cambridge: Harvard University Press.

Smith, Kevin. 1996. *Dogma: A Screenplay.* New York: STK.

Smith, Neill. 1996. *The New Urban Frontier: Gentrification and the Revanchist City.* London: Routledge.

Stewart, Kathleen. 1988. "Nostalgia—A Polemic." *Cultural Anthropology* 3 (3): 227–41.

Stock, Brian. 1996. *Augustine the Reader: Meditation, Self-Knowledge, and the Ethics of Interpretation.* Cambridge: Harvard University Press.

Stromberg, Peter. 1993. *Language and Self-Transformation: A Study of the Christian Conversion Narrative.* Cambridge: Cambridge University Press.

Teaford, Jon C. 1986. *The Twentieth Century American City.* Baltimore: Johns Hopkins University Press.

Theusen, Peter. 1999. *In Discordance with the Scriptures: American Protestant Battles over Translating the Bible.* New York, Oxford: Oxford University Press.

Tomlinson, Matt. 2009. *In God's Image: The Metaculture of Fijian Christianity.* Berkeley: University of California Press.

Turner, James. 2003. *Language, Religion, Knowledge: Past and Present.* South Bend, Ind.: University of Notre Dame Press.

Turner, Victor, and Edith Turner. 1978. *Image and Pilgrimage in Christian Culture.* New York: Columbia University Press.

U.S. Census Bureau. 2000.

Wacker, Grant. 2001. *Heaven Below: Early Pentecostals and American Culture.* Cambridge: Harvard University Press.

Warner, R. Stephen. 1979. "Theoretical Barriers to the Understanding of Evangelical Christianity." *Sociological Analysis* 40 (1): 1–9.

Weber, Max. 1904–5 [1930]. *The Protestant Ethic and the Spirit of Capitalism*, translated by Talcott Parsons. London: Urwin Press.

———. 1922 [1991]. *The Sociology of Religion*. Translated by Ephraim Fischoff. Boston: Beacon Press.

Wilk, Richard, ed. 2006. *Fast Food/Slow Food: The Cultural Economy of the Global Food System*. Lanham, Md.: AltaMira Press.

Woolsey, Matt. 2008. "America's Fastest-Dying Towns." *Forbes Magazine*.

Index

Acts 29, 12, 26, 135–36, 144–48, 157–59, 166–75, 183–87. *See also* Church planting; Missional

American Evangelicals: definitions of, 7, 200–202; history of, 7, 198; and mega-churches, 8, 34, 53, 103, 122, 127, 129–30, 150, 196; and politics, 8, 15, 99, 105, 126, 140, 142–44, 150; and reading, 9, 43, 60, 121, 201; and suburbia, 7, 34, 36, 38, 105, 122–26, 129–30, 145–46, 168–69, 186, 196; and worship, 14, 40, 70–71, 122–23

Ancient-Future, 14–15, 41–42, 70–71, 94–97, 99, 118, 131. *See also* Kimball, Dan; New Monasticism; Webber, Robert

Anglican Church, 11, 23, 60, 65

Anthropology of Christianity: and cultural critique, 197–203; and dialogism, 7, 152–53, 198; and mediation, 51, 74–75; and modernity, 19–21; and temporality, 154–56

Authenticity: and cultural critique, 197–203; and irony, 50–51;and memory, 96, 117, 182; and modernity, 17–19, 95

Bell, Rob, 9, 22

Bialecki, Jon, 19–20, 100, 139–40, 143, 148, 151–52

Biblical hermeneutics, 7, 10, 13, 16, 35, 37, 41, 57, 61–62, 65, 81–82, 95, 111, 125, 141, 151, 172, 197, 202. See also *Lectiodivina*

Blogging, 25, 41, 54–55, 60, 66, 108–9, 112–13, 120, 200

Christian Community Development Asso-ciation, 133–36

Christianity Today, 47, 70, 120

Church planting, 12, 23, 25, 32, 34, 37, 58, 98, 100, 127–37, 145–48, 150, 157–60, 173–75, 178–80, 192–94, 202–3. *See also* Acts 29

Cincinnati, 22, 37–38, 48, 62, 76, 109, 118, 125–32, 152, 162, 169–72, 175, 178–80, 187–91, 193–97. *See also* Urban neighborhoods

Claiborne, Shane, 100, 102–3, 115–16

Coleman, Simon, 51, 75, 124, 192–93, 200

Culture critique, 5–8, 10, 12–13, 16, 21, 29, 31, 35, 46, 50, 52–55, 65–66, 100, 103–5, 108–9, 114, 116–19, 124, 135, 143, 160, 167–68, 171, 176, 181, 197–203

Deconversion: and authenticity, 30–31, 44–45; and cultural critique, 29–31, 198; and irony, 50, 62; and modernity, 45–46; as narrative, 29–31, 81, 100, 124, 143, 150, 196

Discipleship, 37–38, 52, 195–97, 199

Discourse of measurement, 160–64

Driscoll, Mark, 9, 130

Elisha, Omri, 95, 122, 130, 169

Emergent Village, 8, 26, 55, 68, 105, 151

Emerging Church: and Calvinism, 9, 130, 158, 185; demographics of, 5, 25–26; ecclesiological lineage of, 12–14; and ecumenism, 8, 40, 121, 133; and entre-preneurialism, 39, 164–67; and gender, 9, 67, 158, 165, 172–75;history of, 8–16; knowledge production in, 5–6, 22, 102–3, 138, 149, 151, 199–201; as label, 5, 203; liturgical lineage of, 14–15; and Mainline Protestants, 4, 62–65;

Race, 14, 127–37, 145–48, 155, 162, 167, 169–72, 179, 183–92
Reformed Church of America, 23, 58
Robbins, Joel, 19, 140–42

Secularity, 19, 120, 163, 172, 183, 200
Sense of place, 5, 19, 24, 111, 113, 120, 132, 163, 179–82, 192–94
Social class, 1, 5, 14, 33, 43, 58, 106, 115–16, 118, 125–26, 133–37, 145–48, 157, 162–63, 167, 169–72, 178–80, 183–92. *See also* Gentrification
Southern Baptists, 11–12, 23, 31–32, 36, 53, 100, 105, 135–36, 162, 165, 170
St. Augustine, 30, 131

Temporality, 100, 140–41, 153–56. *See also* Eschatology; Kingdom theology

United Methodist, 3, 21, 23, 35, 94, 115
Urban neighborhoods, 1–2, 62, 76, 109, 118, 125–32, 152, 169–72, 178–80, 183–91, 193–97. *See also* Cincinnati; Gentrification

Vineyard Fellowship, 2, 13, 23, 38–40, 79, 109, 127, 139–40, 144, 148, 150, 165, 195

Warren, Rick, 7, 53, 99, 196
Webber, Robert, 14–15, 58, 71
Weber, Max, 11, 19, 101, 108
Willard, Dallas, 10, 43, 196

About the Author

JAMES S. BIELO is Visiting Assistant Professor in Anthropology at Miami University. He is the author of *Words upon the Word: An Ethnography of Evangelical Group Bible Study* (NYU Press, 2009) and editor of *The Social Life of Scriptures: Cross-Cultural Perspectives on Biblicism* (2009).